STEALTH CONFLICTS

'Most people are mirrors, reflecting the moods and emotions of the times; few are windows, bringing light to bear on the dark corners where troubles fester.'

Sydney J. Harris

Stealth Conflicts
How the World's Worst Violence Is Ignored

VIRGIL HAWKINS
Osaka University, Japan

ASHGATE

Published by
Ashgate Publishing Limited
Gower House
Croft Road
Aldershot
Hampshire GU11 3HR
England

Ashgate Publishing Company
Suite 420
101 Cherry Street
Burlington, VT 05401-4405
USA

www.ashgate.com

British Library Cataloguing in Publication Data
Hawkins, Virgil
   Stealth conflicts : how the world's worst violence is
   ignored
   1. Violence 2. War 3. World politics 4. International
   relations
   I. Title
   303.6'09

Library of Congress Cataloging-in-Publication Data
Hawkins, Virgil.
  Stealth conflicts : how the world's worst violence is ignored / by Virgil Hawkins.
    p. cm.
  Includes bibliographical references and index.
  ISBN 978-0-7546-7506-8
  1. Violence--History--20th century. 2. International relations. 3. Security, International. 4. World politics--1989- 5. Conflict management. I. Title.

JC328.6.H39 2008
303.6--dc22

2008019103

ISBN: 978-0-7546-7506-8

Mixed Sources
Product group from well-managed forests and other controlled sources
www.fsc.org Cert no. SA-COC-1565
© 1996 Forest Stewardship Council
FSC

Printed and bound in Great Britain by
MPG Books Ltd, Bodmin, Cornwall.

Contents

List of Figures

List of Tables

List of Abbreviations

ABC	Australian Broadcasting Corporation
AFP	Agence France-Presse
AP	Associated Press
AU	African Union
BBC	British Broadcasting Corporation
CAP	Consolidated Appeal Process
CNN	Cable News Network
DPRK	Democratic People's Republic of Korea
DRC	Democratic Republic of Congo
ECOWAS	Economic Community of Western African States
EU	European Union
FTS	Financial Tracking System
ICC	International Criminal Court
ICJ	International Court of Justice
IISS	International Institute for Strategic Studies
IRC	International Rescue Committee
LRA	Lord's Resistance Army
MLC	Movement for the Liberation of Congo
MONUC	UN Organization Mission in the Democratic Republic of the Congo
MSF	*Médecins Sans Frontières*
NATO	North Atlantic Treaty Organization
NGO	Non-Governmental Organization
OAU	Organization of African Unity
OCHA	Office for the Coordination of Humanitarian Affairs
PRIO	International Peace Research Institute, Oslo
SIPRI	Stockholm International Peace Research Institute
UCDP	Uppsala Conflict Data Project
UK	United Kingdom
UN	United Nations
UNHCR	United Nations High Commissioner for Refugees
UNITA	National Union for the Total Independence of Angola
USA	United States of America
WFP	World Food Programme

Acknowledgements

The author would like to thank Shunsuke Suzuki, AMDA MINDS and all the staff at AMDA Zambia for generously allowing him to shift from a full-time position to a lengthy part-time position, giving him the time and environment needed to draft this book. He would also like to express his gratitude to the representatives from the policymaking, media and academic arenas who agreed to be interviewed, assisting the author's attempts to gain insights into the agenda-setting process, but who remain anonymous.

Thanks go to Kirstin Howgate, Margaret Younger, Jude Chillman, Nikki Dines and Alison Oughton at Ashgate for their assistance in the preparation of the manuscript and the production process of this book. The author would also like to convey his profound appreciation to Michelle Hawkins for her tireless work in proof-reading the final manuscript and enhancing its clarity. Any errors that remain in the text are, of course, entirely the author's own. Special thanks go to Yasmin Hawkins and Thomas Mabwe for conducting surveys, and to Reiko Okumura for assistance in compiling data. Last but not least, the author would like to thank Kaoru for her constant support, without which this book would not have been possible.

Introduction

In January 2008, it became known that 5.4 million people had died because of conflict in the Democratic Republic of Congo (DRC), the vast majority from preventable disease and starvation (IRC 2008). Not only is it by far the deadliest conflict in the world today, it is the deadliest of the past half-century. It began in August 1998, in the form of a Rwandan-led invasion (joined by Uganda, and, to a lesser extent, Burundi), ostensibly in support of a number of local rebellions. It was a lightning strike consisting of an eastern front beginning from the areas bordering the invading states, and a western front that commenced with the hijacking of civilian planes in the east, which were used to ferry hundreds of soldiers to a military base west of Kinshasa, who then joined with disgruntled forces there to occupy the Inga Dam and move on the capital. Five African countries came to the aid of the DRC government, and a combination of Angolan, Zimbabwean and DRC troops were able to stop the advance on the capital and shut down the western front. The eastern advance was eventually halted as well, resulting in a stalemate that left the country (the size of Western Europe) effectively cut in half. Although foreign troops had withdrawn by 2003, and the conflict has largely subsided, violence has continued from overlapping local and national conflicts (that accompanied the international conflict), insecurity and human rights abuse are rife in parts of the country, and the abysmal humanitarian conditions resulting from the conflict continue to cause levels of death and suffering unparalleled anywhere else in the world.

The announcement of such a high death toll should not have come as a surprise. It was already known in May 2000 that the conflict in the DRC was the deadliest in the world when the International Rescue Committee (IRC) announced the results of its first mortality survey in that country, revealing a death toll of 1.7 million people. And the same organization continued to provide updates on the growing death toll through its surveys: 2.5 million in 2001, 3.3 million in 2003, and 3.8 million in 2004. It was also known that, even as the fighting died down, the failure to address the needs of the displaced and otherwise affected, and the damage to life-sustaining social structures and services, meant that the death toll would continue to rise: far beyond the toll caused by the bullets and bombs.

What should have come as a surprise was the resounding silence with which the revelations of the conflict's unparalleled scale were met: from policymakers, the media, the public and academia alike. It seemed that no matter how large it was, or how high the death toll became, the conflict simply could not elicit a serious response from the world outside the region. Policy interest has been scant, and media corporations appear to have cast a virtual news blackout over the region. Non-Governmental Organizations (NGOs) have not flocked to the region en masse, and there have been no major star-studded civil society movements to 'save' the DRC.

In fact, in most of the world outside the region, one could even be forgiven for not knowing that such a conflict ever existed.

And the DRC is hardly alone in this regard. Twelve of the world's fifteen deadliest conflicts, and almost 90 percent of the world's conflict-related deaths since the end of the Cold War, have occurred in Africa. But the allocation of attentional and material resources in response to most of these conflicts by a wide variety of actors in a position to respond has been minimal: certainly not remotely commensurate with the needs in most cases. It seems that international consciousness, recognition, outrage, and action coming from outside the continent rarely extend far beyond the Suez Canal. Far from dominating individual and institutional consciousness, from the perspective of policy, media, public and academic agendas outside the continent, Africa seems hardly to exist.

How is it possible that in this day and age, a conflict of the magnitude of that in the DRC (or of the magnitude of Angola, or Burundi, for that matter) can simply be 'missed'? And this considered, how can one explain the overwhelming, emotive and almost exclusive response by policymakers, the media, the public and academia alike, to conflict resulting in the deaths of roughly 2,000 people in Kosovo in 1998–99, from the perspectives of 'moral imperative' and 'humanitarianism' (see Associated Press 1999a; and *Independent* 1998)? This was happening at a time when not only was the massive nine-nation conflict in full swing in the DRC, but also when rebels in Sierra Leone were succeeding in a brutal campaign to take the capital, Freetown, arbitrarily killing and mutilating their victims; when rebels in Angola were launching another brutal campaign that included the downing of civilian aircraft; and when Ethiopia and Eritrea were squaring off in devastating nation-on-nation conflict over a border dispute, among other conflicts. In 1999, Kosovo received more attention and aid money than all of Africa's humanitarian emergencies combined. And how can one explain the fact that post-election violence in East Timor (with a death toll of roughly 1,000) sparked as much as ten times more aid than did the DRC in 1999?

How is it that newspaper articles, academic papers and foreign policy statements on the Israel-Palestine conflict (roughly 5,000 deaths) are consistently (almost obsessively) churned out throughout the world on a daily basis, full of lengthy details and insights on the complex political intricacies of the situation, when infinitely larger conflicts in Africa, on the rare occasion that they are discussed at all, are framed only in overly simplistic humanitarian formats, and are treated as having little or no political value? Some major Western news corporations have devoted 50 times more coverage to Israel-Palestine than they have to the DRC. It is not at all rare for major Western academic journals that examine international security issues to publish more articles focusing on Israel-Palestine in recent years than they have on all of Africa's conflicts combined. And how is it that there is so much attention to and discussion of terrorist attacks on trains in Spain, and buses in the UK, but a terrorist attack by rebels on a train in Angola in 2001, resulting in more than 300 deaths, barely rates a mention? Why does there appear to be almost an obsession with global terrorism (most notably in the West), but virtually no awareness of global warlordism? Levels of attention and response to conflict in the world seem to defy any semblance of proportionality.

Evidence points to the marginalization of most of the world's deadliest conflicts, particularly those in Africa. It is almost as if the actors in a position to respond have by and large tacitly agreed on some form of global-level triage: they have somehow all arrived at the fatalistic and highly simplistic conclusion that Africa's problems are too massive and intractable for the continent as a whole to be 'saved', and that attention and energies are therefore best devoted elsewhere. It would be easy to jump to the conclusion that Africa's conflicts are ignored because the continent does not have a great deal of national interest value for the West: perhaps primarily because it is not as oil-soaked as the Middle East, and because the conflicts predominantly affect poor black people in a rich and white-dominated world. While there is certainly a great deal of truth in these generalizations, they are somewhat simplistic and fail to properly explain the response of the outside world to conflict in Africa. The continent is in fact a veritable storehouse of minerals and other natural resources, including large quantities of oil, upon which the outside world is increasingly coming to rely. Furthermore, Africa's conflicts are not completely ignored across the board. There are large discrepancies in the levels of outside attention allocated to the various African conflicts, and again, scale and severity do not appear to be major indicators of the response. So to simply leave explanation at this point leaves too many questions unanswered.

Why, for example, was the humanitarian tragedy caused by conflict and famine in Somalia chosen for intervention in the early 1990s when a similar situation in southern Sudan was not? Why did large-scale massacres in Rwanda attract some measure of (albeit belated) outside attention, indignation and a great deal of guilt in 1994 and beyond, whereas similar massacres in neighbouring Burundi in 1993, leaving more than 200,000 dead, had failed to attract any outside attention or residual guilt? Why, after eight years of relative silence on the problems of violence in Africa, did the outside world suddenly begin to collectively suffer the pangs of moral outrage over the conflict in Darfur, at a time when death toll estimates from conflict in the DRC were almost 80 times greater? And why have so many in the West apparently been so incensed with the repression and political instability in Zimbabwe? At roughly the same time as government reaction to opposition activity in Zimbabwe in March 2007 left one dead and a number of opposition leaders beaten and arrested, similar government reaction to opposition activity in Guinea left 130 people dead (as security forces opened fire indiscriminately on protestors) and civil society leaders imprisoned (see Amnesty International 2007); and clashes between government troops and forces loyal to the opposition leader in the DRC left at least 400, possibly 600 people dead. And yet it is Zimbabwe alone that has been the target of outrage and indignation in the outside world. The situation in Guinea is, to all intents and purposes, as good as unknown. Why is it that names like Mugabe, and places like Darfur, are so commonly known in the West, when names like Conté and Kabila, and places like Kivu and Ituri are not?

Our collective perception of the state of conflict in the world can perhaps be likened to a reflection in a distorted mirror that makes certain parts of its subjects appear much larger than they actually are, and others much smaller. That is, while certain (often relatively minor) conflicts are disproportionately prominent in the sphere of individual and institutional consciousness around the world, the vast majority of others (including the most major conflicts) are given disproportionately low levels of attention. Far from being a major determinant of attention, the absolute scale of conflict can rarely be seen as playing any significant role at all in determining the levels of response of any of the actors in question. The responses by these various actors also appear to be highly assimilated, reflecting very similar concerns and priorities. While there may be a host of varying viewpoints and opinions from different actors on what a particular conflict is about and what should be done in response to it, the object of the attention of all the actors is generally the same: they are responding to one and the same conflict and are barely responding to any of the others.

The failure to take conflict scale into account, combined with the assimilation of agendas, in many cases reaches the point where the resulting focus of these actors brings into question their adherence to their own professed objectives, interests and concerns, as well as their roles in society. Interestingly, words and actions (and calls to action) in response to conflicts are so frequently couched in humanitarian terms by a wide variety of actors, all emphasizing the need to save human lives and prevent human suffering. But such 'humanitarian' principles ring quite hollow when one considers how highly selectively and disproportionately they are applied. It is understandable, and largely unavoidable, that, if left to their own devices, national governments will respond to conflict in accordance with narrowly defined political and national interests (humanitarian rhetoric notwithstanding), largely ignoring the world's deadliest conflicts if they do not particularly affect these interests, or if it suits their interests to do so. It is less understandable that the media, the general public, NGOs and academia end up with similar agendas and priorities, particularly when many of these actors see their roles in society as watchdogs of (or counterbalances to) policymakers, as independent agents of humanitarianism, or as the keepers of objective reality.

Such assimilation also seems odd in the context of vibrantly diverse 'free' democracies in which virtually unlimited amounts of information flow unhindered throughout all levels of society. Media corporations, the public, and academia in developed countries are independent entities which essentially have the freedom and the power to discuss, investigate, research, announce and print virtually anything about anything. The media is free to (and frequently does) question, disagree with, and criticize the government. Furthermore, advances in communication technology have provided us with the unprecedented ability to gather, process and disseminate news on events from any part of the globe to any other part of the globe.

The members of the public at large are exposed to what both the government and the media have to say, and, thanks to the Internet, are now able to independently access a seemingly infinite amount of information from and about any part of the world from the comfort of their homes. This can increasingly be done even without using the formal mass media corporations as intermediaries. The more active members of the public are able to investigate, speak out about, fundraise for, and even become directly involved in, alleviating human suffering resulting from conflict in foreign countries, through forming or joining aid, advocacy, or other NGOs. Researchers and academics generally have the freedom to choose their research topics and focus (in terms of geographical region), and have access to funding for conducting research, both at their universities or think tanks, and in the field. As with the media and the general public, the ability of academics and researchers to examine and analyze distant conflict has also been greatly enhanced by advances in communication technology (most notably the Internet).

But 'freedom' is an all-too-convenient term that is usually used to describe the absence of intimidation and legal constraints that prevent speech, observation, research, movement and association. Governmental censorship, arrest, and intimidation are by no means the only barriers to the freedom to discuss, research, publish, and take action on matters of foreign affairs. Numerous other (often invisible) barriers prevent, inhibit and discourage attention from being given to certain conflicts, while many external influences encourage attention to be given to other conflicts. The large number of foreign conflicts makes the setting of priorities for attention, at both an individual and institutional level, an inevitable process of selection and elimination.

In this process of determining responses to foreign conflict, internal interests, priorities and dynamics are certainly major considerations, but actors are also susceptible to external influences. This susceptibility is typically inversely proportional to the power those same actors wield, although the level of importance that an actor attaches to a particular conflict also affects the level of influence and susceptibility to influence. Once an issue appears to be important for one powerful actor, it often becomes important for some or all of the others, and its perceived importance snowballs. Such a bandwagon effect plays a major role in bringing the agendas of diverse actors together. Within national boundaries, so too does the socially constructed and highly pervasive ideology of nationalism, in which individuals and institutions are raised and constantly reminded to see foreign events in terms of how they affect their own nation. Finally, the increasing globalization of power and information through influential governments, media corporations and other actors means that the projection of influence is all the more powerful, such that what is seen as being important to a country, institution or individual becomes (as if by default) important for other countries, institutions or individuals on the other side of the globe.

Hence, the priorities on the agendas of the various actors seem to merge, and consciousness appears to be increasingly assimilated and unified in terms of the conflicts that are selected for consideration as being important, even though the individual perspectives and opinions regarding those particular conflicts may be highly divergent. Understanding the process by which conflicts are 'chosen' for highly concentrated levels of attention is useful not simply for the sake of understanding these conflicts and how we respond to them, but perhaps more importantly because it helps us understand how and why the vast majority of other conflicts are not given the attention they deserve – to the point that, in many cases, most major conflicts are almost entirely hidden from view. Consciousness of and attention to conflicts ranges from obsessive to virtually nonexistent, with a yawning gap between the two. And while some conflicts may occasionally find themselves to be the temporary object of focus (flash-in-the-pan style), and others may be focused on more consistently, the majority (including the largest and deadliest) belong to the 'virtually nonexistent' category of attention levels. These are 'stealth conflicts': those that remain 'off the radar' of the collective consciousness of those actors in a position to respond.

That certain actors focus disproportionately on certain conflicts is not necessarily a major problem: selectivity in responding to conflict is inevitable, as is prioritization based on the interests of each actor. But when all of the actors (including those that are supposedly charged with the task of checking and balancing other actors) develop and follow similar priorities in their selection of which conflicts are to be considered important, not only does a major problem arise, but, because there is almost no one left to point it out, the problem itself goes largely unnoticed. The higher the collective level of importance attached to a particular conflict, the greater the frenzy of attention and the degree to which it is accentuated by the bandwagon effect. The more disproportionate this becomes (in relation to other conflicts), the more the opportunities for attention to other conflicts are eliminated. Deprived of vital attention, these 'other' conflicts (regardless of their scale) carry on, often largely unchecked, and ironically, it is because they are unchecked that the death tolls of such conflicts continue to rise, usually far exceeding those of conflicts that do manage to attract attention. Not only are they absent from the collective international consciousness of today, they will also be absent from the history books of tomorrow. Such is the plight of stealth conflicts.

The purpose of this book is to reveal how skewed and assimilated is the collective response to foreign conflict by major actors in the world (a situation that results in many of the world's deadliest conflicts being largely ignored) and to analyze why this is so. The book is divided into seven main chapters. The first begins by putting into perspective the state of conflict in the world. Focusing primarily on the death toll as the most representative indicator of scale, it looks at the relative scale of conflicts as they have occurred throughout the world since the end of the Cold War, and examines some trends in conflict throughout the world. The second chapter attempts to provide an overview of the mechanics of individual and institutional consciousness among those in a position to respond to foreign conflicts, presenting a simple agenda-setting model of how these actors interact in determining their response (or lack thereof). This leads to the explanation and development of the concept of stealth conflicts.

The following four chapters each deal with one of the actors in this agenda-setting process: policymakers, the media, the public (including NGOs, interest groups and corporations) and academia. Each quantitatively and qualitatively examines the responses of these actors to foreign conflicts, and the mechanics of their agenda-setting process in this regard, including their internal dynamics and how they are influenced by the other actors. The final chapter brings these arguments together. All conflicts, together with the factors that lead external actors to make choices in how they respond to them, are complex and unique. As such, fixed formulas designed to predict which conflicts will be chosen for attention, and which will not, are unlikely to be universally viable. Even so, it is possible to narrow down many of the key factors that determine the level of attention a conflict receives from external actors, and to gain an overview of how these factors come together in making such determinations, thereby somehow systematizing the concept of stealth conflicts. This is the purpose of the final chapter of the book.

Chapter 1

The State of World Conflict

The key premise of this book is that our perception of the state of conflict in the world is distorted, such that while we are overly focused on certain conflicts (which are very often comparatively minor in scale), the majority of major conflicts are almost entirely hidden from our view. Before we can even begin to arrive at such a conclusion, however, we need an objective starting point, some kind of a yardstick, against which we can compare our perceptions, and thereby observe how far removed our image of the state of world conflict is from the reality. With a view to doing so, this chapter first discusses the issues surrounding the objective measurement of conflict scale. Using the death toll as the key indicator, it goes on to compare the scale of the world's conflicts that have occurred since the end of the Cold War, providing summaries of these conflicts in order of scale. Finally, it looks at some general trends in the scale and nature of conflict: where in the world conflict is concentrated, and the characteristics that conflicts appear to have in common.

Measuring the State of Conflict in the World

The absolute scale of a conflict is probably the most appropriate method of objectively measuring and comparing the seriousness of conflicts. Absolute scale may include the death toll, the number of people displaced, the level of humanitarian suffering or need, and the spread (or threat thereof) to the surrounding countries or territories (see Hawkins 2004, 183–216). But among these, the loss of human life, the death toll, irreversible – unlike the other three factors – is probably the most representative of the scale of conflict. It will be used in this study as the yardstick to help us to see a clearer picture of the state of conflict in the world.

Of course, measuring the death tolls of the world's conflicts is more easily said than done. There are huge obstacles both in maintaining objectivity and in physically measuring the death toll of any conflict. In fact, before the counting stage can even be reached, there may be some disagreement over whether an 'armed conflict' actually exists or not, depending on which criteria are used. At one extreme, relatively minor political violence in a country may be considered by some as an 'official' conflict and not by others. The National Defense Council Foundation (2002), for example, in its World Conflict Report counted violent protests, organized crime, the murder of a foreign diplomat, and drug-related violence as factors constituting 'conflict' in countries such as Bolivia, Venezuela, Cambodia and Jordan. At the other extreme, what appears to be a large-scale conflict resulting in massive loss of life may be excluded from consideration as a conflict because it does not meet a set of predetermined criteria. The influential Uppsala Conflict Data Project (UCDP), for example, excluded the DRC from its 2002 list of world conflicts because it recorded no fighting involving any government party: one of its criteria for the existence of a conflict is the involvement of a government party (Eriksson, Wallensteen and Sollenberg 2003, 595). This was despite the fact that fighting among non-government parties (and most likely with government involvement in some form) continued throughout that year, resulting in hundreds of thousands of deaths. Thus, how one defines the term 'conflict' can make the difference in whether a conflict 'exists' or not.

Death Toll Count Methodologies

In terms of measuring the actual death toll, the first problem one faces is which deaths should be counted? Should the death count be restricted to those killed by actual violence (bullets and bombs), or should it include those who were the indirect victims, such as those who died of disease or hunger directly resulting from people fleeing their homes and sources of livelihood into inhospitable environments; the destruction of infrastructure (including electricity grids and water purification plants); and the breakdown of agriculture, public services (most notably health) and supply lines? Although many studies may exclude nonviolent deaths from consideration, the destructive effect of conflict on social function (particularly in terms of health and food security) is undeniable. Studies reveal massive differences in the incidence of communicable diseases in conflict and non-conflict areas, as well as major improvements in this regard after the violence has ceased (see IRC 2003). In Angola, conflict was estimated by the Carnegie Commission on Preventing Deadly Conflict (1997, 11–2) to have resulted in the abandonment of 80 percent of arable land. In reality, the number of nonviolent deaths attributable to the presence of conflict almost invariably exceeds the number of violent deaths.

Conflicts in which violent deaths are greater than nonviolent deaths are exceptions, and are usually characterized by short-term violence (albeit at high levels), followed by concentrated humanitarian aid. It has been reported, for example, that violent deaths accounted for up to 100 percent of deaths in Kosovo and 85 percent during the initial invasion of Iraq. The more common situation involves protracted conflicts, in which targeting of the general population (and their livelihoods) is pronounced, and very low levels of attention and humanitarian aid are received. In sub-Saharan Africa, for example, violent deaths account for a median of just 23 percent of conflict-related deaths (Small Arms Survey 2005). In extreme cases, the nonviolent conflict-related deaths have been estimated to comprise as much as 94 percent (DRC), 97 percent (Sudan), and 98 percent (Ethiopia) of the total conflict-related deaths (Human Security Report 2005, 128). Numerical differences in estimated death tolls can thus be great, depending on the inclusion or exclusion of such indirect deaths.

Even if these issues are settled, the most critical and probably the most difficult issues still remain: establishing and maintaining acceptable levels of objectivity and accuracy in a death count. There is no organization or international agency charged with independently counting or verifying the deaths attributed to each of the world's conflicts, and even if there were, the logistical costs and risks of such an exercise would be immense. In many cases, attempts to count the dead are simply not made.

If they are, those recording the count are forced to rely on incomplete and often highly unreliable figures. Parties to the conflict and other sources on the ground are almost invariably highly biased, and independent verification is usually highly problematic. The parties to any conflict have a vested interest in downplaying their own casualties, and perhaps in exaggerating the enemy casualties, for the purposes of maintaining high morale at home and damaging enemy morale. Where parties to a conflict profess to be following 'humanitarian' motives, and thereby aim to avoid the label of aggressor, they will also attempt to hide and/or downplay the casualties of their enemy and of civilians as well. Even supposedly neutral NGOs and other humanitarian agencies are likely to overestimate the number of deaths to attract attention and indignation, which will in turn boost the funds available for their activities.

Many organizations that do attempt to count the number of deaths from the world's conflicts use report-based methodologies, in which deaths reported in media sources and some primary sources are recorded. The issue of the questionable accuracy of reports aside, such a method can result in a highly distorted picture of the state of conflict, in which high-profile conflicts appear comparatively larger and low-profile conflicts much smaller than they really are. While high-profile conflicts are closely watched by a wide variety of media sources, and deaths are very likely to be reported and recorded, low-profile conflicts are usually beyond the reach of the media, and the majority of deaths are unlikely to be counted or reported at all. Furthermore, the report-based method ignores nonviolent conflict-related deaths, which, as noted above, are likely to comprise the vast majority of deaths in low-profile conflicts where media and humanitarian attention is scant. In short, death tolls from ignored conflicts are likely to be greatly underreported and also to be made up of a much larger proportion of nonviolent conflict-related deaths when compared to high-profile conflicts (see Leitenberg 2006, 4–6).

Epidemiological surveys (which attempt to calculate crude mortality rates and compare them to pre-conflict levels or other regional data) and in-depth historical investigations (which rely on a wide variety of data including reports, interviews and data from exhumations) are methods that are able to capture nonviolent conflict-related deaths and provide a much clearer picture of the state and scale of conflict and its effects than report-based methodologies. The IRC (see 2000; 2008), for example, used household-based cluster sampling surveys in the DRC to calculate the crude mortality and under-five mortality rates, then compared them to pre-war levels and other regional data on mortality rates, calculating the approximate excess deaths thought to have been caused by the conflict there.

Unfortunately, such methodologies are costly, they are generally restricted in terms of feasibility, and have been applied to very few conflicts. Studies that attempt to compile global data and present and analyze trends on world conflict on an annual basis limit themselves to report-based methodologies (despite the highly distorted picture it provides) for these reasons. The Human Security Report (2005, 72), for example, while acknowledging that 'report-based methodologies under-count battle-related deaths', chooses to use this method to enable it to provide 'timely global and regional death toll data'. The differences in the results, however, are stark. In 2001, the UCDP dataset estimated 200 battle deaths in the DRC (although it admitted that the reliability of the data was low because of sporadic information), while epidemiological surveys put the total of battle deaths at 88,000, and the indirect deaths from conflict at 849,000 – a massive difference (Small Arms Survey 2005, 246).

Accepting and Comprehending Death Toll Figures

Comprehensive academic studies and global conflict data sets aside, the death tolls that are generally 'accepted' or 'recognized', and that therefore remain recorded in history, are usually not the result of meticulous studies (report-based or epidemiological) and are therefore highly dubious. The figures that remain and the manner in which they have been arrived at can tell us, however, a lot about the level of importance attached to the conflicts by key actors responding to conflicts. Deaths from conflicts that are treated with great importance and where logistical challenges are not major barriers, such as in Northern Ireland, Israel-Palestine, and Iraq (although in this case usually only on the side of the occupation troops), for example, are counted in real time to the final digit, and round figures (such as 1,000 or 2,000) are treated as grim milestones. Such cases, however, are very rare exceptions. Death tolls from African conflicts, on the other hand, are likely to be rounded off to the nearest 100,000, or in some cases, even the nearest million (if they are counted at all), and even then, the manner in which the figures were arrived at can rarely be justified.

Quite often, the 'accepted' figures may simply be those that have been somewhat arbitrarily decided upon by those with the loudest voice, and/or accepted simply by virtue of sheer repetition. A figure included in a statement from a high-level official in a powerful government, or from an influential humanitarian agency on the ground, may be enough for it to be picked up by the media and spread before finally settling and taking root in the consciousness of the various actors (and recorded history) as the generally accepted death toll for a particular conflict. Once they have taken root, revisions or corrections are not easily made. Generally accepted death tolls for the Rwandan genocide (800,000) or for the conflict in Bosnia (200,000), for example, have since been challenged by certain researchers as being impossibly high, particularly in the case of Bosnia (National Research Council 2001, 42, 46; Small Arms Survey 2005, 234), but with little apparent impact on how the figures are used by the media and academics. Similarly, the figure of 2 million often cited as representing the final count of deaths from the conflict in southern Sudan until its official end in January 2005 has remained static since 1999 (Associated Press 1999b; 2008), despite the continuation of relatively heavy fighting until at least 2003, and of a precarious humanitarian situation associated with the conflict.

Such difficulties, however, should not discourage us from using death tolls (even at varying degrees of reliability and accuracy) as the measure of the scale of conflicts. Many studies simply exclude from consideration conflicts for which sufficiently reliable information cannot be obtained. If such conflicts include those that are in reality among the deadliest, the omissions can have the effect of massively distorting the results of the analyses (and subsequently our perception) of the state of world conflict. Even if it be deemed a necessary choice in terms of academic respectability, excluding such conflicts from consideration is in effect treating them as if they do not exist, which can hardly allow a viable analysis of conflict trends. If, for lack of accurate data, we do round off the number of deaths of a particular conflict to the nearest 100,000 (however insensitive a leap that may appear), there are few enough conflicts with death tolls above 100,000 that we can still get an idea of the scale of that conflict that is good enough for effective comparison with the others. And if we discover, as we will, that the gap between the larger and smaller conflicts is so great that errors of 100,000 deaths, or even 500,000, in some cases, will not make a considerable difference in terms of evaluating or ranking their relative scale, then the need to have highly accurate and precise death toll figures will seem less important.

Even assuming that we are able to gather and process data on the number of conflict-related deaths, perhaps the final irony is that the higher the numbers are, the more our ability to conceptualize their meaning or magnitude fails us. Stanley Cohen (2001, 189) points to 'an invisible threshold at which statistics (and how they are represented) result not in numbness, but in a strange moral dysfunction'. He raises the hypothetical example of statistics announced on the number of refugees in the world being adjusted from 18 million to 16 million following more reliable estimates becoming available, noting that 'this will not change our emotional or moral reaction at all. A terrifying thought: are we all such amoral brutes, so pseudo-stupid, that those million or two human lives don't matter a toss?' (190). Though it may be a small consolation against such a hopeless aspect of the human condition, perhaps a more visual representation of numbers in the form of a graph can help us at least to somehow better conceptualize and grasp the relative scale of conflict. Another terrifying thought, though, is that even if we attempt to draft a standard bar graph comparing the scale of the world's conflicts, the gap between the large and the small is so great, that both simply cannot be visibly accommodated on the page of a book.

By way of a solution, the graph shown here is created roughly to scale using square area in the form of circles (instead of a one-dimensional height scale) to represent the numbers of conflict-related deaths from the post-Cold War world. This allows us to visually compare, for example, the scale of the conflict in the DRC, with a death toll of roughly 5.4 million, with that in Israel-Palestine, with a death toll of roughly 5,000. The contrast is quite shocking, even if we are not really sure whether one or more million of those Congolese are alive or dead, and even if we do have trouble conceptualizing the magnitude of the loss of 5 million human lives. While a number of various sources have been consulted and compared in an attempt to be as accurate as possible,[1] the graphs do not attempt to provide exact or finalized figures for each (in light of the above discussion). Instead, conflicts are grouped together

---

1   Sources consulted include studies by the Stockholm International Peace Research Institute (SIPRI), the International Institute for Strategic Studies (IISS), Project Ploughshares, the Human Security Report, Small Arms Survey, the Interdisciplinary Research Programme on Root Causes of Human Rights Violations (PIOOM), the International Peace Research Institute, Oslo (PRIO), the IRC, Humanitarian Law Project/ International Educational Development and Parliamentary Human Rights Group (UK), as well as the news media including international press agency reports, and other miscellaneous sources such as encyclopaedias and reference periodicals.

according to their approximate death tolls, enabling ease of comparison based on rough scale, and providing a clear and objective (although highly simplified) picture of the state of conflict in the world. It should be noted that in many of the estimations, nonviolent conflict-related deaths may be somewhat underestimated (and in some cases, unable to be included), which may affect the perception of scale. The scale of conflicts in Zaire, Liberia, Sierra Leone, Uganda and Afghanistan, for example, may well be considerably larger than is portrayed here.

Summary of Recent Conflicts

The following is a brief summary of major conflicts in the post-Cold War world arranged according to rough categories of scale. Although some of these conflicts began well before the end of the Cold War, only post-Cold War death tolls are used here.[2]

5,400,000 Deaths (DRC)

The scale of the conflict in the DRC utterly dwarfs any other in the post-Cold War world. The vast majority of deaths (94 percent) are thought to have been nonviolent. The DRC's conflict is extremely complex, and describing the conflict in a singular sense may be somewhat misleading. It is in fact an intertwined convergence of several conflicts (at local, national and international levels) which are focused primarily on the eastern half of the country. It is closely related to the aftermath of the Rwandan genocide and to the subsequent conflict in the DRC under its former name of Zaire (see below). The trigger to this phase of the conflict was the invasion of the DRC by Rwanda and Uganda (and to a lesser extent, Burundi) in support of various local rebel movements (initially the Congolese Rally for Democracy, RCD, and the Movement for the Liberation of Congo, MLC) in 1998, ostensibly to root out rebel movements from their own countries operating from the DRC, including those held responsible for the Rwandan genocide. The invasion was countered by armed intervention in support of the DRC government by Angola, Zimbabwe and Namibia (and to a lesser extent, Sudan and Chad). The scale and involvement of so many foreign military forces earned it the title of the First African World War. A stalemate ensued, and although various agreements eventually saw the withdrawal of the foreign troops (the last Ugandan troops leaving in 2003), the deployment of a relatively small number of United Nations (UN) peacekeepers, and the establishment of a transitional government, conflict and instability continued, involving local warlords, militias (including proxies of the departed foreign forces) and factions of the national armed forces. Elections in 2006 appeared to strengthen the peace process, but to a degree, fighting continues in the east.

---

2   The percentages of nonviolent deaths are taken from the Human Security Report 2005 and Small Arms Survey 2005. Certain conflicts that caused a significant number of deaths beyond the Cold War period are excluded from these summaries because they were winding down together with the Cold War. These include Ethiopia (1974–92), Mozambique (1976–92) and Cambodia (1970–93).

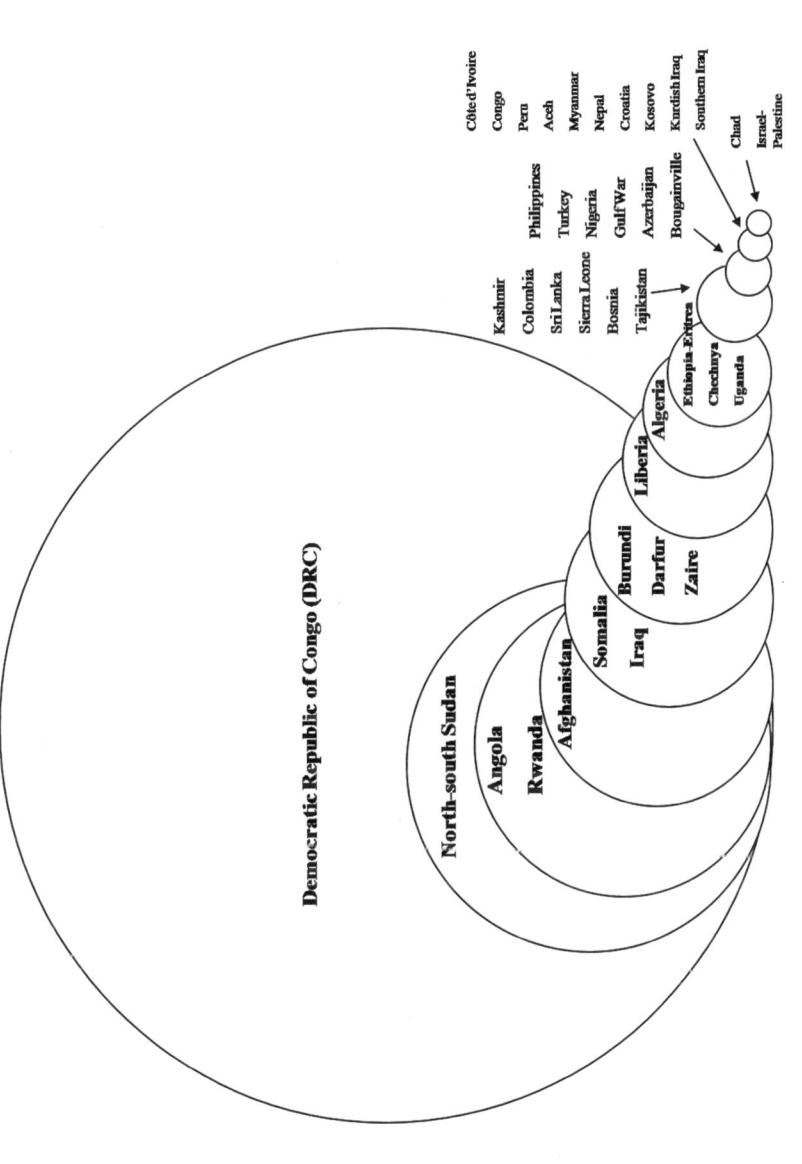

Figure 1.1   Post-Cold War conflict death tolls in proportion

1,200,000 Deaths (Southern Sudan)

Conflict in southern Sudan is thought to have been responsible for approximately 2,000,000 deaths between 1983 and 2005, when a comprehensive peace agreement came into effect. The vast majority of deaths (as many as 97 percent) are thought to have been nonviolent and largely related to famine, caused and/or exacerbated by the displacement of large proportions of the population (as many as 4,000,000 people are thought to have been internally displaced) and the interruption of agriculture. These aspects of the conflict prompted the formation in 1988 of Operation Lifeline Sudan (OLS), a large-scale humanitarian aid operation conducted by UN agencies and numerous NGOs. Conflict was originally related to attempts by the largely African and Christian or animist south to attain independence or at least autonomy from the largely Arab and Muslim north (under British-Egyptian colonial rule the two had been forcibly separated by law and the south left largely undeveloped). Splits and then fighting among the various factions of the southern rebel movement, the Sudan People's Liberation Army (SPLA), also came to be a major source of conflict. The control and exploitation of oil fields was another major factor in the continuation of the conflict. Peace talks gathered momentum in 2003 and 2004, and a comprehensive power-sharing agreement, including autonomy for the south to be followed by a referendum on independence, was reached in 2005.

800,000 Deaths (Angola and Rwanda)

Conflict in Angola, pitting the government primarily against the rebel group National Union for the Total Independence of Angola (UNITA), continued from the time of independence from Portugal in 1975 to 2002, and is thought to have caused approximately 1,500,000 deaths (89 percent of which were nonviolent) during that time. The end of the Cold War saw the withdrawal of foreign support for the conflict (Soviet and Cuban support for the government and US and South African support for the rebels), a respite from the violence, and elections held, but UNITA was unwilling to accept defeat at the polls and the conflict resumed. Government control of the country's oil extraction and rebel control of diamond extraction were key factors in allowing the conflict to continue beyond the support of the parties' respective Cold War patrons. Further peace attempts in 1994 and 1997 failed to hold. Attempts by the government to defeat UNITA were also the rationale behind extensive military interventions by Angola to topple governments in both the Republic of the Congo and Zaire (then later in support of the new government in the renamed DRC). After UNITA leader Jonas Savimbi was shot dead in 2002, however, a ceasefire was reached and UNITA disbanded its military wing. Despite the peace, however, the country is littered with landmines and the humanitarian situation of the former rebel-held areas remains highly precarious.

Conflict began in Rwanda in 1990 between the Hutu-dominated government and a Tutsi-dominated rebel group, the Rwandese Patriotic Front (RPF), when the RPF invaded Rwanda from its bases in Uganda. Conflict was linked largely to grievances over the sharing of power and resources in a country with limited land for its population, and strongly entrenched ethnic identities. Although a peace and power-sharing agreement was reached in 1992 and a small peacekeeping group was deployed, fighting continued. In April 1994, President Juvénal Habyarimana was assassinated (together with his Burundian counterpart) as his plane landed in Kigali. This triggered the genocide of the Rwandan Tutsis and moderate Hutus, led and carried out by the military and by informal militia groups known as the Interahamwe. Instead of bolstering the peacekeeping force, the UN Security Council members voted to have most of the force withdrawn. Massacres are thought to have resulted in the deaths of as many as 800,000 people in just 3 months. A small French peace enforcement force was eventually deployed, but its neutrality was questionable and its effect limited. The RPF advanced on the capital, taking power and ending the war. As many as 2,000,000 Hutus fled to the DRC (then Zaire) fearing reprisals, and although many later returned, the Interahamwe militias remained. Their presence ultimately became one of the key factors triggering the invasions by Rwanda and Uganda of Zaire/DRC and the prolonged conflict that followed.

500,000 Deaths (Afghanistan)

In Afghanistan, the withdrawal of Soviet troops in 1989 was followed by the installation of an interim government, but this was militarily opposed by Mujahideen rebel groups, who captured Kabul in 1992. These groups soon split over control of the city, and fighting continued throughout the country. A new radical Islamic group (the Taliban) emerged, taking control of Kabul in 1996 and most of the country by 1998. In 2001, a US-led coalition invaded Afghanistan in support of an alliance of Mujahideen groups opposing the Taliban (the Northern Alliance), in a bid to root out the al-Qaeda leadership (harboured by the Taliban in Afghanistan), which was suspected to have been responsible for terrorist attacks on the USA. The Taliban were overthrown and a new government was installed, but fighting continued, particularly in the south, between US/government troops and Taliban and al-Qaeda remnants, as did some factional fighting among warlord groups. The death toll of 500,000 may well be underestimated, particularly given that the number of deaths (particularly nonviolent) from fighting among warlord groups in the 1990s is largely unknown. It is estimated that more than 20,000 people were killed during the initial US-led invasion in 2001.

400,000 Deaths (Somalia, Iraq)

Serious conflict began in Somalia in 1988, and following the deposing of President Mohammed Siad Barre in 1991, primarily clan-based conflict among numerous armed factions took over much of the country, particularly in the south. Combined with extensive famine, it is estimated that the conflict cost the lives of approximately 400,000 (as many as 80 percent nonviolent). A small-scale UN peacekeeping force, followed by a US-led force and another UN force, attempted to intervene, but they increasingly became embroiled in clashes with militia (particularly after mounting aggressive disarmament raids) and all operations had withdrawn by 1995, leaving the situation largely as they had found it. Some regions of Somalia (Somaliland and Puntland) have declared their independence and have successfully achieved a large measure of self-governance (although none has been internationally recognized). A transitional parliament was agreed upon and a president elected in 2004. The weak government was not able to control the country, however, and a group known as the Council of Islamic Courts gained in momentum and took over much of the country, briefly achieving a measure of relative stability. They were repulsed in late 2006 by a combined intervention force of Ethiopian and Somali troops under the transitional government that took over the capital. Resistance to these forces led to heavy fighting and the deployment of a small peacekeeping force.

The USA and UK (and to a lesser extent Australia) invaded and occupied Iraq in 2003 on the pretext that Iraq was not cooperating with ongoing UN weapons inspections imposed after the Gulf War and still retained possession of banned weapons (including nuclear and other weapons of mass destruction). A ground invasion followed a large-scale bombing campaign, and the regime of Saddam Hussein fell after approximately two-and-a-half months of fighting. No evidence of weapons of mass destruction was found. The occupying powers disbanded the army and took steps towards developing a new interim authority, including the establishment of the Governing Council, but retained overall authority. Armed resistance to the occupation and to the new interim governing bodies, as well as bloody interfactional fighting, continued. Attacks on UN and other humanitarian agencies also persisted, seeing their effective withdrawal from the country. Elections were held and a new constitution was agreed upon in 2005, but foreign troops remained in the country, and the insurgency and interfactional fighting have continued. Studies of death tolls from the conflict since the invasion have produced results of between 150,000 and 650,000, with the majority from violent deaths.

300,000 Deaths (Burundi, Darfur, Zaire)

The assassination of Burundi's first democratically elected president (of Hutu origin) in 1993, allegedly by Tutsi army officers, plunged that country into conflict, resulting in large-scale massacres of Tutsis and retaliatory massacres of Hutus, followed by long-term insurgency causing the deaths of at least 300,000 people (80 percent or more nonviolent). As with Rwanda, conflict is linked largely to grievances over the sharing of power and resources in a country with limited land for its population and strongly entrenched ethnic identities. Various attempts at peace failed, with the leader of one coalition government killed together with his Rwandan counterpart as his plane landed in Kigali, and a UN-brokered government of unity overthrown by a military coup in 1996. The Burundian pursuit of rebel groups, namely the Forces for the Defence of Democracy (FDD) and the Forces of National Liberation (FNL), led to that country's involvement in the conflicts in Zaire/DRC. In 2000 a peace deal was signed with all rebel groups except the FDD and FNL, but peace agreements were later signed with these as well: the FDD in 2003 and the FNL in 2005. Presidential elections were held but instability continues to some degree.

Conflict in the Darfur region of Sudan broke out in early 2003, pitting the government-backed Janjaweed militia against two main rebel groups: the Sudan Liberation Movement (SLM) and the Justice and Equality Movement (JEM). The death toll is estimated at between 200,000 and 400,000 (as much as 83 percent nonviolent), and there has also been widespread displacement of the population. With the former group often identified as being of indigenous Arab ethnicity, and the latter of African ethnicity, ethnicity is seen as playing a role in the conflict, but probably more significantly, it is linked to perceived political marginalization, and access to fertile land, water and other resources, between the largely nomadic population and the sedentary population, a problem which has been exacerbated by drought and desertification. Other contributing factors include the Sudanese government's arming of the Janjaweed militias in the 1980s as part of its strategy to contain the SPLA active in southern Sudan, and resentment towards power-sharing arrangements giving southern Sudan greater access to the country's power and wealth. Ceasefires and peace deals in Darfur saw the deployment of a small number of African Union (AU) forces (followed by UN forces), but these have not led to any conclusive settlement. The conflict has also been seen as a contributing factor in the destabilization of neighbouring Chad and the Central African Republic.

Following the Rwandan genocide, large numbers of Hutus fearing reprisals fled to Zaire, taking refuge in camps established there. Those who had organized and carried out the massacres, however, continued to regroup and organize attacks on Rwanda using the refugee camps as bases. To counter this, Rwandan troops entered Zaire in 1996 and attacked these camps. While most of the refugees fled back to Rwanda, the militia groups fled deeper into Zaire. In the pursuit, at least 200,000 people are believed to have been killed. Rwandan and Ugandan troops allied with a coalition of local rebel groups and, finding little government resistance, marched on Kinshasa, toppling the regime of President Mobutu Sese Seko in 1997, and installing as president the rebel Laurent Kabila, who went on to change the name of the country to the Democratic Republic of the Congo. Divisions between Kabila and his backers in Rwanda and Uganda developed soon after, and this was to lead to the second invasion of the country little more than one year later.

200,000 Deaths (Liberia)

Internal conflict began in Liberia in 1989, and in 1990 President Samuel Doe was ousted and killed. Fighting continued among various warlord factions, with the National Patriotic Front of Liberia (NPFL), led by Charles Taylor, emerging the strongest. The Economic Community of Western African States (ECOWAS) organized a military observer group (ECOMOG) to intervene in August 1990. Although the force had been deployed as a peacekeeping mission to disarm the factions and form an interim government pending elections, it soon came under fire and responded, becoming a party to the conflict. The warlords were able to sustain their military power largely through the exploitation of timber and diamonds (much of which was brought through neighbouring Sierra Leone). The fighting continued until 1996, and elections officially brought Charles Taylor to power in 1997. At least 200,000 people are thought to have died (84 percent nonviolently) over the course of this phase, and the conflict is closely linked to that in Sierra Leone and Guinea. Fresh fighting began in 2000 with the emergence of a new rebellion. The rebellion closed in on the capital, leading to the exit of Taylor from power in 2003. Elections were held and stability was restored to the country.

150,000 Deaths (Algeria)

Algeria's military-backed regime cancelled elections held in 1991 in a move aimed at preventing certain victory by the Islamic Salvation Front (FIS), sparking armed conflict in that country between the government (together with pro-government militia groups) and various rebel groups including the FIS and the Armed Islamic Group (GIA). Fighting was marked by numerous incidences of massacres and arbitrary killings of civilians by both sides. Between 100,000 and 150,000 are thought to have been killed. A new constitution in 1996 banned religion-based political parties. Although reconciliatory approaches (including amnesties for rebels) were introduced by President Abdelaziz Bouteflika and fighting subsided to some extent, the conflict continued, with the government aligning itself with popular support for strong 'anti-terrorism' policies.

100,000 Deaths (Ethiopia-Eritrea, Chechnya and Uganda)

In Ethiopia and Eritrea, disputes over the demarcation of the border and tensions over trade and foreign policy degenerated into open warfare between the two countries in 1998. The USA brokered a moratorium on air strikes and various peace initiatives were introduced by the Organization of African Unity (OAU) and other individual African countries, but following lengthy stalemates, fighting (marked by trench warfare and artillery exchanges) continued. An Ethiopian offensive deep into Eritrea in 2001 led Eritrea to accept OAU conditions for peace, and fighting came to an end. Between 70,000 and 120,000 are thought to have been killed in the fighting. UN peacekeepers were deployed to the border region and the border was demarcated, but acceptance of the demarcation is shaky and tensions continue.

A republic of Russia, Chechnya declared independence in 1991, but this was not recognized by Russia, which sent in troops in 1994 to reintegrate Chechnya into Russia. Russian defeats led to a peace agreement and troop withdrawal in 1996. Chechen attacks on neighbouring Dagestan, and terrorist bombings in Moscow allegedly linked to Chechen separatists, saw Russian troops re-enter Chechnya in 1999, marking the beginning of the second phase of the conflict. Although Russian troops gained control over most of Chechnya and a government friendly to Moscow was installed in Chechnya, separatist activity continued to a degree. In both phases of the conflict, the total death toll is estimated at approximately 100,000, but may be as high as 150,000.

Conflict in Uganda since 1987 has pitted the government forces against the northern rebel group, the Lord's Resistance Army (LRA), in fighting that is largely related to perceived political marginalization of the northern Acholi and Lango ethnic groups. A rebel group linked to remnants of the Idi Amin regime is also active. The conflict has been marked by brutal methods by the LRA, including the systematic abduction of large numbers of children in their areas of operation, for use in combat and support roles. Despite the issuing of an arrest warrant by the International Criminal Court for LRA leader Joseph Kony, offers of amnesty by the government have been made, and a series of peace talks held in Sudan aimed at ending the conflict. The death toll is unclear, but may be higher than 100,000 since 1987.

50,000 Deaths (Kashmir, Colombia, Sri Lanka, Sierra Leone, Bosnia-Herzegovina and Tajikistan)

The partitioning of Kashmir between India and Pakistan has been the source of conflict between the two countries since 1947. An uprising in 1989 by the Jammu and Kashmir Liberation Front, together with numerous other rebel groups, led to the current conflict, with groups fighting against the Indian government for either independence for Kashmir, or integration with Pakistan. A number of peace initiatives and ceasefires have failed to hold, and India came close to open war with Pakistan in 2002 over the issue of militants infiltrating India from Pakistan. Death toll estimates range from less than 50,000 to more than 100,000 during this period of conflict.

Conflict in Colombia began in 1964, and was largely related to an ideological struggle (linked to Fidel Castro's victory in Cuba) between liberal and conservative sectors of society. It pitted the government and right-wing paramilitaries under its control against a number of rebel groups including the Armed Revolutionary Forces of Colombia (FARC) and the National Liberation Army, Guevarist (ELN). Since the 1970s the conflict has become more related to the production of and trade in illicit drugs. It is marked not only by the drug trade, but also by massacres, assassinations, kidnapping and racketeering by both sides. The paramilitary forces have since become largely autonomous from the government, and were banned in 2002. Numerous peace initiatives have failed, and the government, with large military backing from the USA, is attempting a strong military solution. Deaths since 1964 are thought to exceed 200,000, but difficulties in distinguishing death from criminal activity (largely drug related) from conflict-related death, make estimates unclear.

In Sri Lanka, government policies perceived as pro-Sinhalese by the minority Tamils led to the outbreak of conflict in 1983, which saw the Liberation Tigers of Tamil Eelam (LTTE) fighting for an independent state in the north of the country. The Muslim minority were also involved in the fighting to some extent, and India unsuccessfully attempted intervention from 1987 to 1990. Fighting primarily focused on the Jaffna Peninsular continued through the 1990s. Norwegian mediation and the LTTE's acceptance of autonomy under a federal system, rather than independence, led to peace talks and a ceasefire in 2001. The ceasefire broke down and some violence resumed in 2006. As many as 100,000 people are thought to have been killed since 1983.

Conflict in Sierra Leone began in 1991, pitting the government and a pro-government militia, the Kamajors, against the newly emerged rebel group, the Revolutionary United Front (RUF). Fighting was largely concentrated around control of diamond extraction in the country. A military coup in 1997 sparked the entry of a Nigerian-led ECOWAS force, which finally succeeded in reinstating the government in 1998, but the withdrawal of these forces allowed a rebel counterattack to retake Freetown. Rebel attacks were particularly brutal, leaving thousands deliberately mutilated. ECOWAS forces repulsed the attack and UN peacekeepers were deployed, and with some assistance from UK forces, peace was eventually restored. Elections were held in 2002. Although the death toll estimates are approximately 50,000, the actual death toll is almost certainly far greater than this figure.

Conflict broke out in Bosnia-Herzegovina following a referendum endorsing independence from Yugoslavia in 1992 (boycotted by the Bosnian Serbs). It was fought primarily along ethnic lines among Serbs, Bosnian Muslims and Croats, who had been largely integrated until that time. The conflict was marked by major offensives that involved expelling populations of other ethnic groups, with the aim of expanding and linking territory held by friendly ethnic groups. Peacekeeping and peace enforcement forces were deployed from 1992, but conflict and disagreements over power sharing continued, and a comprehensive peace agreement was not reached until 1995. Although early (and largely unfounded) estimates put the death toll at 200,000 or more, the actual death toll was probably closer to 60,000.

Tajikistan's conflict began in 1992 soon after the declaration of independence from the collapsing Soviet Union, with fighting largely along clan lines. The clans dominating the government under Soviet rule succeeded in taking power, following intervention by Russia and Uzbekistan in the same year. A primarily Russian peacekeeping force under the Commonwealth of Independent States (CIS) was deployed in 1993. A ceasefire with the opposition was reached in 1997 and although elections were held in the same year, a solid political resolution is yet to be reached. The death toll is estimated at over 50,000.

20,000 Deaths (Philippines, Turkey, Nigeria, the Gulf War, Azerbaijan and Bougainville)

Fighting on the Philippine island of Mindanao began in 1971, with the rebel group Moro National Liberation Front (MNLF) fighting for an independent Muslim Mindanao. The roots of the fighting can be traced to large resettlement plans under US colonization, which resulted in a Christian majority in Mindanao. Peace negotiations led to autonomy for four provinces in 1990 and a peace agreement with the MNLF in 1996, but fighting continued between the government (with increasing US support) and various splinter groups, including the Mindanao Islamic Liberation Front (MILF) and the Abu Sayyaf Group (ASG). The death toll since 1971 is thought to be 100,000 or more.

In Turkey, conflict broke out in 1984 with the rebel Kurdish Workers Party (PKK) fighting against the government (and pro-government Kurdish paramilitaries) for independence or autonomy for the Kurds in the southeast of the country. It is linked to government policies aimed at eliminating Kurdish identity through bans on language, culture and media broadcasts. Large numbers of people in pro-PKK areas were displaced, and Turkey has occupied land in northern Iraq in pursuit of rebel forces based there. The capture of PKK leader Abdullah Ocalan led to a decline in fighting, and Turkey began to lift some of its restrictions on Kurdish rights and freedoms. More than 40,000 are thought to have been killed since the fighting began.

In Nigeria, a number of conflicts are ongoing in different parts of the country for a variety of reasons. One of the more prominent is in the Niger Delta region, being fought over what is perceived as lack of access to the benefits from oil production by the local impoverished community (as well as access to land, and environmental degradation caused by the oil extraction). Attacks are increasingly targeted against government and oil installations. Another type of conflict is linked to ethnic and religious intercommunal identities, and has been seen in various parts of the country, most notably in the north. Attempts to address the root causes and stem the violence in both types of conflict have so far met with limited success, and the Niger Delta conflict appears to be escalating. The death toll from these conflicts combined may be 50,000 or more.

In the Persian Gulf region, Iraq invaded and quickly gained control over neighbouring Kuwait in 1990, claiming historical sovereignty over Kuwait, and citing the theft of Iraqi oil from a shared oilfield, among other reasons, as justification for the invasion. Iraq announced soon after that it had annexed Kuwait, and refused to bow to demands by the UN Security Council to withdraw. A Security Council deadline passed, and a US-led coalition of troops initiated a series of air strikes against Iraq before launching a ground offensive, quickly repelling Iraqi troops from Kuwait. Iraq launched scud missile strikes against Israel and Saudi Arabia in a bid to broaden the conflict into an Arab-Israeli war, but this did not happen, and the Iraqi forces were largely destroyed. Some estimates put the death toll from this conflict at 30,000.

Conflict in Azerbaijan began together with independence in 1991, between the government and Armenian forces in the disputed enclave of Nagorno-Karabakh, which has a majority Armenian population. Conflict continued in 1992, with offensives by Armenian forces leading to the establishment of a land corridor between Armenia and the enclave. Further offensives and counteroffensives continued in 1993, despite Russian and US pressure, and a number of ceasefires. Although military conflict was brought to an end in 1994, political stalemate over the future of the enclave continued. The death toll from this conflict is estimated at 22,000.

Conflict began in Bougainville, Papua New Guinea, in 1988, primarily over the issue of compensation for landowners for damages caused by large-scale copper mining operations on the island. Major conflict between government forces and rebels continued into the 1990s, with the government using private security forces and the rebels accusing mining giant Rio Tinto of using the government forces as their own private army. A permanent ceasefire agreement was reached in 1998, and an agreement on autonomy for Bougainville was later made. The death toll from this conflict is estimated at around 20,000, more than half thought to be the result of the economic blockade of the island by the central government.

10,000 Deaths (Côte d'Ivoire, Congo, Peru, Aceh, Myanmar, Nepal, Croatia, Kosovo, Kurdish Iraq and Southern Iraq)

A failed coup attempt in 2002 led to the outbreak of conflict in traditionally stable Côte d'Ivoire, fuelled by perceived inequalities in power distribution between the north and south, and by large-scale immigration from neighbouring countries. Rebels seized the northern part of the country, with the government remaining in control of the south. A French-brokered peace agreement in 2003 broke down, but peacekeepers have been deployed in a buffer zone and violence has largely been contained. A power-sharing deal was reached in 2007, giving the position of prime minister to the rebel leader. In the Republic of Congo, fighting primarily among militia groups loyal to three rival presidential candidates had been ongoing since 1992, but became its most intense when rebels backed by Angolan troops succeeded in overthrowing the democratically elected government in 1997. A ceasefire between the parties was reached in 2000.

In South America, long-running conflict in Peru, pitting the government against a rebel group known as Shining Path (and a smaller group, the Tupac Amaru Revolutionary Movement, MRTA) continued and threatened to escalate towards the end of the Cold War. Violence largely declined in 1992, however, with the capture of the Shining Path leader, but continued on a small scale up until 2000.

A number of conflicts in Asia also caused the deaths of approximately 10,000 people. In Aceh, Indonesia, a secessionist movement began intensifying its military campaign in 1988, and again to a greater degree in 1999 as East Timor headed towards independence. Government counteroffensives against the Free Aceh Movement (GAM) saw heavy fighting in 2002 and 2003. The 2004 Indian Ocean Tsunami, which caused extensive damage in Aceh, appeared to serve as a catalyst for peace in the province. In Myanmar, a series of ceasefire agreements served to halt a number of long-running conflicts between the military government and rebel groups (mostly ethnically identified) in the late 1980s, but some such conflicts continue, particularly along the country's borders. The death tolls from these conflicts are unclear. Large-scale fighting began in Nepal in 1996 between the government and Maoist rebels aiming at establishing a republican state. Fighting further escalated following the massacre of the royal family in 2001, and the King went on to dismiss the government and assume executive powers. A peace deal was signed in 2006 and the rebels agreed to join an interim government.

In Europe, conflict in Croatia preceded and overlapped that in Bosnia-Herzegovina, as Croatia declared independence from Yugoslavia in 1991 and its militias clashed with Serbian-dominated federal troops and Serb irregular forces. After a major Croat offensive expelling large numbers of Serb civilians, a peace agreement was reached in 1995. In Kosovo, clashes between the Yugoslav government and rebels seeking autonomy for the province intensified in 1998. Peace talks in early 1999 failed, and the North Atlantic Treaty Organization (NATO) intervened in the conflict, initiating a two-and-a-half-month bombing campaign against Yugoslavia. The government agreed to a military withdrawal from the province, and the UN temporarily took over its administration.

In northern Iraq in 1991, following the Gulf War, Kurds rebelled against the government, taking control of most of Iraqi Kurdistan. The Iraq government counterattacked, but its troops were forced out of the region by NATO, and by the announcement and enforcing of a no-fly zone by NATO. Factional fighting within Iraqi Kurdistan continued after the withdrawal of Iraqi forces. In southern Iraq, Shia Muslim groups also revolted after the Gulf War, and were suppressed by government forces. As in the north, Western forces declared a no-fly zone in the region. In both of these conflicts, the dynamics of the conflict changed dramatically after the US-led invasion of Iraq in 2003. The death tolls for these conflicts are unclear, with estimates ranging from thousands up to as high as 100,000.

Other Conflicts

The world has seen numerous other conflicts on a smaller scale since the end of the Cold War. In Africa there have been conflicts with death tolls probably less than 10,000 in countries such as Senegal, Guinea, Guinea Bissau, Chad, Mali, Niger and the Central African Republic. In the Americas, conflict was seen in Haiti and Mexico. Asia has hosted a large number of relatively small-scale conflicts, including those in Andrha Pradesh, Gujarat and the northeast regions of India, East Timor, Irian Jaya, Kalimantan, Molucca Islands, and Sulawesi in Indonesia, and in the Philippines (a communist insurgency). Conflict has also been seen in Georgia, Moldova, Northern Ireland and the Basque region of Spain in Europe, as well as in Israel-Palestine, Israel and Lebanon and Yemen in the Middle East.

Conflict Trends

This section examines some key trends in recent conflicts throughout the world, concentrating on both their scale and nature. In terms of scale, it will look at where (geographically) large-scale conflict has been concentrated. In terms of nature, it will look at how conflict has changed since the end of the Cold War, while also addressing some popular misconceptions. It does not attempt to present an analysis of chronological trends in the number of conflicts in the world or in the scale of conflict. There simply does not exist the data (encompassing all conflict-related deaths) that can allow, to a reliable degree, annual analyses of how the level of conflict in the world, and that in each particular region, has changed. Studies presenting annual trends in scale can be highly misleading, and such an approach is not necessary for the purposes of this study. The purpose here is simply to identify and compare the overall aggregate scale of recent (post-Cold War) conflicts based on their total death tolls (according to 'best' estimates) over the course of each conflict. This is important to enable a comparison between conflict scale and conflict response. Similarly, while a detailed examination of the causes of conflict is beyond the scope of this study, it is important to look at some trends in how conflicts are being waged, because to a certain degree their nature affects external consciousness regarding conflict.

Death Toll Trends

Studies examining conflict trends in the world tend to base their assessments largely on the number of conflicts. The trends revealed by these studies can be misleading, considering that a conflict with little more than 25 battle deaths in a year is counted as having the same value as a conflict that is thousands of times more deadly.[3] In a similar vein, the process of distinguishing between singular and multiple conflicts when counting can also make a considerable difference in how conflict trends are

---

3   The UCDP dataset's threshold for the existence of conflict is a minimum of 25 battle deaths in a year. It should be noted, however, that while the UCDP measures conflict trends by counting conflicts, in parts of its analysis it also divides conflicts into the two categories of 'minor' and 'war' (see Harbom and Wallensteen 2007).

viewed. The UCDP datasets, for example, counted six separate conflicts occurring in India in 2004 (Harbom and Wallensteen 2005, 632), but the overlapping local, national and international conflicts in the DRC were counted as a single conflict before being removed from the list in 2002 (Eriksson, Wallensteen and Sollenberg 2003). While this may be a valid categorization, making comparisons based on counts of conflicts in this way can create the impression that there is 'more' conflict in one area than there is in another, where an examination of conflict scale (based on death tolls) provides a completely different picture. This is particularly pertinent considering that the death toll in the DRC is many times greater than that for all of the conflicts in India combined. By counting conflicts, such datasets give the impression that conflict in the world was sharply decreasing in the late 1990s and early 2000s, but this was precisely the time when the conflict in the DRC was causing almost as many conflict-related deaths as all other conflicts in the world combined since the end of the Cold War.

This brings us back to the issue of which conflict-related deaths should be counted. Most studies limit their counts to battle deaths, in effect ignoring the critical social function of modern conflict and consequently the vast majority of conflict-related deaths. The conclusions of conflict trend analyses that combine counts of the number of conflicts and the number of battle deaths can be highly misleading: most notably the notions that there has been a 'dramatic' decline in conflict and that it has become less deadly (Human Security Report 2005). It is certainly true that battle deaths resulting from conflict have decreased compared to those in the Cold War period, and that such direct deaths from conflicts today are far fewer than those resulting from major past conflicts such as the Korean War, Vietnam War or Iran-Iraq War, which involved superpowers and/or superpower support, and thus the deployment of much more destructive methods of violence (Lacina, Gleditsch and Russett 2006). But battle deaths in modern conflict usually account for but a small proportion of conflict-related deaths, and as such, it hardly seems viable to use such deaths alone as the key criteria for measuring trends in conflict.

As already seen, for the majority of major conflicts, nonviolent deaths dominate the death toll – sometimes exceeding 95 percent. Clearly, the consequences of violence are far more damaging than the actual acts of violence themselves in most conflicts. This situation is a reflection of both the nature of conflict and the response (or lack thereof) of the outside world to conflict. The former issue will be discussed below, and the latter in the following chapters. In any case, response to conflict involves far more than simply stopping people from being hit by bullets; it most certainly includes the use of emergency humanitarian aid and rehabilitation of critical health services and supply lines. Thus, for the purposes of this study, the most important trends that need to be examined are those that tell us where conflict is deadliest and how comparatively deadly conflicts are, and must include both the violent and nonviolent causes of death wherever possible.

Looking at such death tolls immediately reveals a number of obvious trends. First of all, the conflict in the DRC is by far the deadliest conflict in the world in recent years. In fact, it is possibly the deadliest conflict in the world since World War II. It rivals the Korean War (between 4.5 million and 7 million deaths), eclipses the Vietnam War (3 million deaths) and the Biafra War (2 to 3 million deaths), and is the deadliest conflict in recorded African history. Its death toll is more than four times that of the second most deadly conflict in the post-Cold War era. Secondly, if we look at the death tolls from the interconnected web of conflicts in the Great Lakes region of Africa (in the DRC, including in its previous phase of conflict as Zaire (1996–97), in Rwanda, Burundi and Uganda) the combined total is almost 7 million, which, at 60 percent of the world total, is considerably greater than the death tolls of all the world's other conflicts combined. This number excludes deaths from the conflict in southern Sudan, although parts of this conflict can also be considered as belonging to the Great Lakes region, and it was certainly connected to conflict in Uganda and the DRC. Thirdly, if we expand this analysis to a continental level, the trends are also clear. Africa has been host to the vast majority (88 percent) of conflict-related deaths. Only two non-African conflicts, those of Afghanistan and Iraq, can be found among the world's ten deadliest conflicts. The region that was host to the second most deadly level of conflict-related deaths was Asia (largely due to Afghanistan), which is hardly comparable at 6 percent.

Conflict and the End of the Cold War

In terms of the nature of conflict, changes in global political and economic structures that accompanied the end of the Cold War have led to changes in how conflict is waged in many parts of the world. In the Cold War environment, many regimes in developing countries with little real internal legitimacy were able to maintain their hold on power through the support of their superpower and former colonial patrons. While they faced challenges from rebel or secession movements (usually backed by the rival superpower), or even from local strongmen or warlords, their access to external loans, grants, arms and legitimacy helped many to maintain and consolidate

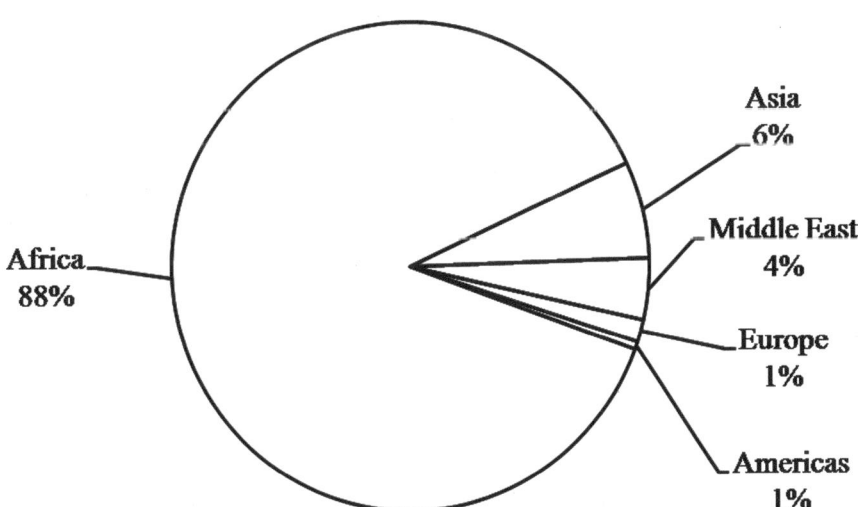

Figure 1.2   Post-Cold War conflict death tolls by region

their positions of power as they distributed these benefits through patronage networks composed of local elites.

The ending of the Cold War changed this. The strategic relevance and ideological importance of many such states declined, particularly in Africa, and Cold War superpowers lost their interest in propping up governments and rebel movements alike. Old patronage networks could no longer be maintained through external support from superpowers, and governments and rebel movements alike were forced to adapt. This saw the weakening of the formal state in many countries, as key players in domestic politics began to seek commercial control rather than territorial control. Rulers retreated to their capitals, shrank their bureaucracies (which, without foreign support, were increasingly seen as a burden and a potential source of challenge to their power base) and adjusted their patronage networks to ensure their survival, relying more on exploitation of resources through partnerships with foreign firms, and on access to loans from international financial institutions. Warlords, the 'hyenas' of the conflict zone (MacKinlay 2000, 55), rose to fill the power vacuum, taking advantage of the shrinking state and utilizing disorder to monopolize economic activity in a certain area, through violence or the threat thereof.

This state of affairs was rarely the result of mismanagement by inept rulers, and was certainly not a 'chaotic' consequence to the removal of Cold War superpower control as terms such as 'state failure' may suggest. It was rather a logical political strategy for survival, in response to rapidly changing political and economic environments, by rulers of weak states that traditionally relied on superpower support and patronage among elites, as opposed to popular support. Politically adept and innovative rulers, such as President Mobutu in Zaire, were able to adapt and survive. Deprived of the US support that he had relied on for so long, he weakened the army, encouraged conflict among potential rivals and instigated ethnic tensions as distractions, eventually lasting in power for eight years after the end of the Cold War. By the end of his reign he maintained control over little more than Kinshasa itself, which explains why Rwanda and Uganda, together with their rebel allies, found it so easy to cross and occupy the entire breadth of the country and take the capital in 1996–97. Other rulers were not so skilful (or lucky). President Siad Barre in Somalia had managed to alienate almost all of his potential supporters by the end of the Cold War and was quickly toppled. The same can be said of President Doe in Liberia, who was tortured and killed when overthrown.

These changes in international security dynamics accompanying the end of the Cold War led to what Mary Kaldor (2007) has termed 'new wars'. Although the nature of these conflicts is not necessarily a 'new' phenomenon, and although there are important differences among many of these conflicts (see Newman 2004), the argument does capture certain key elements. Perhaps the most notable aspects in this sense are the manipulation of fear and hatred, the decentralized nature of actors involved, and the globalization of war economies: factors that are consistent with warlordism. These conflicts tend to contrast with those involving Western countries, which have typically involved short term, highly destructive long-range aerial bombing, as seen in Iraq (in 1998 and 2003), in Yugoslavia (over Kosovo) and Afghanistan, with friendly casualty avoidance considered a high priority. NATO's offensive against Yugoslavia, for example, relied solely on high-altitude bombing, in a bid to avoid any casualties at all on their part. The terrorist attacks on the USA in 2001 made Western countries (the USA in particular) less casualty-averse in waging conflict, and more likely to commit to long-term conflicts, as seen in their ground occupation of Iraq in particular, but superior technology, training and support continue to result in considerably higher casualties among their opponents. Furthermore, the high ratio of violent deaths compared to nonviolent deaths is in distinct contrast to most other conflict situations in the world.

Warlordism

Although the formal state weakened in many cases, 'shadow states' emerged and took up a more prominent role in the political economy (Reno 1999, 2). In such shadow states, the key actors are officially recognized governments (whose behaviour in many ways may resemble that of warlords), local warlords, foreign firms (particularly in the fields of resource extraction and security) and even international financial institutions, whose policies aimed at securing repayment of foreign debt ironically encourage shrinking state control (see Reno 1999, 15–44; Dunn 2001, 50–62). This state of affairs could also be found, to a certain extent, during the Cold War: the effective territorial and border control in most states had always been absent in many weak states (Herbst 2000, 17–22). But the end of the Cold War significantly accelerated the rise of such warlord politics. In many ways, such warlordism has become one of the defining features of the majority of post-Cold War conflicts, and has dominated conflict in countries such as the DRC, Somalia, Liberia, Afghanistan, Colombia and Myanmar.

Warlords thrive because they are able to control, extract and market high-value resources, and the conflicts they produce also come to depend upon the exploitation of these resources. Several conflicts whose continuation had been made possible by the financial and military support of Cold War patrons came to an end when this support ceased. Those that did not, and those that began in the post-Cold War environment, were very often linked to the exploitation of resources in some form. Warlords and rebel movements in Angola and Sierra Leone financed their war efforts through control of the diamond fields in those countries, while in Liberia it was diamonds smuggled in from Sierra Leone and timber that financed conflict. A wide variety of resources in the DRC, including diamonds, gold, coltan, cobalt, copper, timber and even wildlife, supported warlords, armed groups and intervening forces both for and against the government. Production of and trade in illicit drugs (opium in Afghanistan and Myanmar, and cocaine in Colombia and Peru) supported armed movements. Strong links between chocolate (cocoa production) and conflict have also been revealed in Côte d'Ivoire. Even humanitarian aid has served as a source of funding and sustenance for armed movements, most notably in eastern Zaire, Sudan and Somalia. On the other hand, control of oil production in Angola and Sudan allowed the governments in those countries to stave off rebellions.

The degree to which the presence of these resources in itself serves as one of the prime causes of conflict is open to debate: Botswana, for example, is also rich in diamonds but has enjoyed peace since independence; but it is clear that conflict could not have been sustained to the degree it has been in many conflict areas without these resources. As Hannelie de Beer and Virginia Gamba (2000, 78) observe of two attempts at peaceful resolution to conflicts at the close of the Cold War: 'The question begs to be asked whether the different results of UN operations in Angola and Mozambique – one failed, one successful – were at least in part related to the fact that Mozambique is rich in prawns and peanuts, while Angola is rich in oil and diamonds.'

With the ability to control resource exploitation achieved through violence and intimidation, warlords (unlike traditional insurgents) generally neither seek nor receive popular support, with the responsibility for the civilian population seen as a 'needless burden' (Young 2002, 25–7). Even within government armed forces, unpaid or underpaid soldiers in conflict zones may typically 'live off the land', which effectively means looting and stealing from the civilian population. On top of this, a general culture of impunity allows rape and other human rights abuse to become rife. Civilians may also be coerced by warlords into providing labour for the extraction of resources. Others may be killed because of suspected support or sympathy for a rival group. Unable to attract fighters from the adult population, who are unsympathetic to the objectives of the warlords, a preference has emerged for child soldiers, who are seen to be easier to recruit and train to kill (often through terror, brutalization and drugs), as well as more energetic and brutal (see also Honwana 2001, 123–42). This kind of environment is ideal for warlords to thrive, as a culture of fear cements their control over resource-rich areas and unnecessary civilians cooperate, are killed, or are forced to leave. Thus violence (including sexual violence), terror and the removal of the civilian population is less a by-product of conflict, and more a part of the very purpose of the conflict.

Increased access to weaponry, particularly small arms, has also been a factor in conflict. During the Cold War, superpowers supplied their client states and rebel groups with large amounts of heavy weaponry (including tanks, artillery and jets), but as the Cold War ended, superpower patron states lost interest in such expensive military support (particularly in Africa), and were instead eager to offload the large amounts of small arms they had accumulated but no longer needed. Conflict zones thus became flooded with inexpensive small arms that have made it easier for armed groups to organize, challenge authorities and dominate society. The fact that such arms may often be traded directly for diamonds, timber or other extractable resources is further evidence of the link between resources and armed conflict.

The end result is the mass movement of population and the destruction of social services vital to the support of healthy human life. Farmers are forced from their land by violence, landmines or the pillaging of their livestock and crops, and those in villages and towns are also forced to leave because of violence and looting. Doctors, nurses and pharmacists, together with those trading in food and supplies, are among those who flee. For those who flee, many may end up in inhospitable environments such as deserts or jungles infested with malaria-carrying mosquitoes, often with little more than the clothes on their backs. For those who stay, their access to clean water, sanitation and health care services may not exist, and they may live under constant threat from armed elements that control their environment. Disease and starvation have thus become the factors that lead to a high proportion of nonviolent deaths in today's conflicts. Nonviolent deaths become particularly prominent when a situation of this nature continues unchecked: with the warlord grip on resources tight enough to allow complete indifference to the plight of civilians, without resolution of the violence, and without sufficient levels of outside scrutiny or basic humanitarian assistance.

Internal Conflicts?

It is a commonly held notion that the end of the Cold War saw a shift from interstate to intrastate conflicts. This perception is in a number of ways misleading. Looking simply at the numbers of conflicts since World War II, interstate conflicts have always been relatively few and intrastate conflicts much greater in number. It is true that the number of intrastate conflicts did increase in the early post-Cold War period, but they had already been rising steadily in number since World War II, perhaps beginning most notably in the mid-1970s. This number peaked in the early 1990s and began decreasing; although many new conflicts had been ignited, many other conflicts came to an end as superpower support declined (see Harbom and Wallensteen 2007, 625). But more importantly, labelling conflicts as intrastate or internal tends to create the impression that they are strictly domestic affairs that are not particularly impacted by, and do not have a significant impact on, the affairs of places and actors beyond the borders of that state. This is by no means the case.

To the extent that the majority of conflicts rarely see nations declaring war on each other and publicly sending their armies to face off directly against each other, the notion that interstate conflicts are rare is true. But direct clashes between forces from different countries on foreign soil, although rare, are not necessarily a thing of the past. A coalition of West African states fought against forces in de facto control of the state in Sierra Leone; Western coalitions of states fought against other state forces in Iraq, Yugoslavia and Afghanistan; Angolan troops helped a rebellion to power against government forces in the Republic of Congo; forces from as many as eight foreign states fought in the DRC; Ethiopia and Eritrea fought each other in trench warfare; and Ethiopian troops fought their way to the capital of Somalia against the Council of Islamic Courts who were in de facto control of the country. There have also been a significant number of cases in which forces in otherwise 'internal' conflicts receive military support from foreign forces: so-called internationalized intrastate conflicts. In the period from 1989 to 2006, these have accounted for more than 30 percent of all conflicts (Harbom and Wallensteen 2007, 624). In addition, external financial and logistic support for parties to conflict has been found in at least three-quarters of conflicts since the end of the Cold War (623).

In the vast majority of cases, rebellions are not contained within the borders of a single country. Most rely on sympathetic neighbouring countries for support in terms of weaponry and/or logistics and supply, or at least turning a blind eye to the use of their territory for bases or sanctuary (Clapham 1998, 15). Zaire/DRC has been host to bases for rebellions from Angola, Sudan, Uganda, Rwanda and Burundi (whether inadvertently because of lack of central government control over the territory or by design). Similarly, there were complex webs of foreign bases and support in many West African countries for 'internal' conflicts in Sierra Leone, Liberia and Côte d'Ivoire, as there were in East Africa for conflicts in Somalia and Sudan.

It is not only states that support parties to conflict. One of the rebel groups in the DRC (the MLC), for example, has provided troops and military support for the government of the neighbouring Central African Republic; and a rebel group in Colombia received support in the past from the Irish Republican Army. Large numbers of individual foreign fighters (particularly from the Middle East) have been involved in conflicts in Afghanistan and Iraq. The post-Cold War era has also seen the emergence of global private security firms (traditionally known as mercenaries), who have been active in conflict zones from Papua New Guinea to Angola and Sierra Leone, protecting governments and/or mining and oil installations (often in return for mining concessions), and who in some cases have been instrumental in halting rebellions (see Cilliers and Mason 1999).

The warlord in particular has become a truly global player, as John MacKinlay (2000, 55) notes: 'in his new environment he [the warlord] could no longer ignore the attractions of global compression and its tendency to reach into the sanctuary of his territory.' This global compression included the ability to export extractable resources to, and import arms from, almost anywhere in the world, often through the same companies. Diamond exports from Liberia jumped, despite little increase in production, as diamonds mined by rebels in Sierra Leone were smuggled to Liberia and other neighbouring countries (Pugh, Cooper and Goodhand 2004, 105–8). Foreign multinational companies are key enablers of warlordism in this regard. A UN panel of experts identified companies from more than 20 countries as being involved in some way in the illicit trade in resources connected to the conflict in the DRC (UN Document, 2004). In a separate study in that country, bullets found in the Ituri region were traced to arms manufacturers in China, Greece, Russia, South Africa, Serbia and the USA (see Afrol News 2006; and Amnesty International 2005). Illicit drug imports into the USA and Europe are a major factor in conflict and warlordism in Colombia, Afghanistan and Myanmar. There are also networks of diasporas in foreign countries that use wealth generated there to support groups in conflicts in their home countries, as seen in Sri Lanka, for example.

It is difficult to label any conflicts in the post-Cold War world as being truly internal. Through both formal and informal networks and relationships, almost all conflicts have international dimensions and/or have gone global in some manner, and the continuation of most would not even be possible without extensive international involvement. The rarity of direct state-on-state conflicts should not be misinterpreted as a sign that conflicts have shrunk and withdrawn to the extent that they are simply domestic affairs. They are instead better seen as being indicative of the decline in importance of the formal state as an actor in such conflicts, and of the concurrent rise of a variety of non-state actors. The state of conflict in the world today in this sense casts doubts on the utility of categorizing conflicts into clear-cut cases of interstate and intrastate conflicts, even when an additional category for internationalized intrastate conflicts is added. It also casts doubts on the utility of limiting the counting of conflicts to those in which officially recognized government forces are involved.

A Note on Identity

Identity based on ethnicity, religion, tribe, clan or other perceived group difference also plays a role in many conflicts, but this role is frequently exaggerated and misinterpreted. Many conflicts are seen, for example, as the result of 'ancient tribal hatreds', 'spontaneous ethnically-driven savagery' or 'genocidal chaos' that cannot be understood by outsiders. The genocide in Rwanda was, for example, commonly described in such stereotypical terms. Yet there was very little that was 'chaotic' about it: the very fact that as many as 800,000 people were killed within a mere 100 days was the result of meticulous planning, coordination and mastery of propaganda (rivalling that of Nazi Germany during World War II) by the elites in that society. Furthermore, the genocide was less the result of spontaneous tribal hatreds, and more the manipulation of ethnic factors by the elites over access to power and resources.

It is important to note that ethnicity, having no biological basis, is a socially constructed phenomenon (Allen and Seaton 1999, 3; Allen 1999, 26–33). The same can be said of the notion of 'tribes': a term with racist overtones suggesting 'primitive' or 'uncivilized' societies. In the case of Africa, this happened to a large degree during the colonial era, as colonial powers sought to categorize their subjects into groups (based on perceived similarities that, in many cases, had been until then largely irrelevant) for ease of administrative rule, and as Christian missionaries sought to translate Bibles into local languages for evangelization. The eruption of so-called ethnic conflicts is typically reliant on a combination of the work of 'ethnic activists' (individuals who feel a strong need for identification with a particular group) and 'political entrepreneurs' (who manipulate ethnic identity and social divisions for their own political power) (Wolff 2007, 82–4). The exploitation of ethnic identities and conflicts to consolidate power and influence is a tactic that has been used throughout history by elites including colonial powers, Cold War superpowers and local leaders.

Of course by the time conflict erupts, the notion of 'identity' has become very real for the perpetrators and victims of what becomes a cycle of violence that serves to reinforce these so-called identities. It can largely be said, however, that 'Inflamed ethnic passions are not the cause of political conflict, but its consequence' (Berkeley 2001, 15). Emphasis on the role of ethnic or other forms of identity in observing conflict, results in the marginalization of the political and economic factors that are usually much more significant.

> To suggest that people kill each other in Bosnia because Muslims are Muslims, Serbs are Serbs and Croats are Croats is no more insightful than to suggest that the Iran-Iraq war was fought because the Iranians were Iranians and the Iraqis were Iraqis. The challenge is to explain why various forms of ethnicity become so significant at certain times and in certain places (Allen 1999, 29).

The factors behind these conflicts can be seen in light of the struggle for power and resources in an environment in which the power of the official state is in decline, resulting in an apparent blurring between state and warlord, ends and means, conflict and peace, and conflict and crime. For Bill Berkeley (2001, 15), 'Ethnic conflict in

Africa is a form of organised crime. The "culture" driving Africa's conflicts is akin to that of the Sicilian Mafia, or of the Crips and Bloods in Los Angeles. Africa's warring factions are best understood not as "tribes" but as racketeering enterprises.'

A Note on Terrorism

Finally, the issue of terrorism, together with the so-called 'war on terror' (despite having become an overwhelmingly high-profile concern and political obsession in the West) needs to be put into perspective when examining conflict. There appears to be a widely held assumption that the incidence of terrorism has risen considerably; many even go as far as to make the alarming claim that the world has entered an 'age of terror' (see Talbot and Chanda 2002; Gray 2007). Studies suggest, however, that although the number of incidents of international terrorism has risen since the late 1990s, it is still lower than the number of such incidents in the 1980s. Furthermore, this apparent rise in international terrorism is driven almost entirely by incidents in the Middle East and South Asia, the bulk of them occurring in Iraq. International terrorist incidents in the rest of the world have declined considerably since the end of the Cold War (see Human Security Brief 2006, 15–16).

But the utility of isolating international terrorism from domestic terrorism is questionable: how does one determine whether a particular suicide bombing in Iraq is 'international' in origin, for example, and does that clarification make it worse (or more important) than a case of a suicide bombing that is deemed to be home-grown? Perhaps more importantly, it is necessary to clarify what we mean by the term 'terrorism'. From the perspective of those who claim to be waging a war on terror, terrorism seems to be a term specifically referring to the apparently random use of violence (particularly the use of explosives) by what are perceived as Islamic extremists, directed primarily against Western civilian targets or interests. If this is the case, on a global scale, the level of violence and death tolls are quite low: at a level not comparable to that of most major conflicts in the world, although reference (in doomsday scenarios) is frequently made to the potential level of damage that such attacks might cause. In any case, such extreme selectivity hardly makes for viable definition.

If a broader and more objective definition is applied, the situation is altered considerably. While definitions of terrorism remain controversial in the current highly charged political environment, a UN panel has recommended that it be defined as:

> any action ... that is intended to cause death or serious bodily harm to civilians or non-combatants, when the purpose of such act, by its nature or context, is to intimidate a population, or to compel a Government or an international organization to do or to abstain from doing any act (UN Document 2004, 52).

Under such a definition, terrorism would most certainly apply to militia and soldiers entering villages and towns and killing, mutilating and/or raping civilians, in a bid to 'terrorize' them into complying with their demands or leaving the area: a situation that applies, probably without exception, to all warlord-dominated conflict zones throughout the world. It would also apply to the use of bombing campaigns that include civilian targets, as well as the besieging of cities. In short, it would apply to acts by participants of virtually every conflict in the world. Under this interpretation, there really is no logical difference in the application of such terminology to a series of bombs on civilian buses and the subway in the UK and to a series of rebel attacks on civilian villages in the DRC, Burundi or Sierra Leone; both are clearly violent methods that use terror to achieve certain political objectives. As such, the utility of focusing intently on the issue of terrorism as a method, and isolating it from the broader implications of conflicts (of which terrorism is usually a part), appears questionable. In any case, both terrorism and the so-called war on terror require careful scrutiny, and certainly need to be kept in perspective.

Chapter 2

Conflict Consciousness and Stealth Conflicts

The previous chapter has presented as objective as possible a picture of the state of conflict in the post-Cold War world (based on scale) in terms of estimated death tolls. It is clear that the African continent has been the host of the vast majority of the world's conflict-related deaths. The most deadly conflict has been concentrated in the Great Lakes region, which alone has been responsible for more conflict-related death than the rest of the world's conflicts combined. Furthermore, in most cases the vast majority of conflict-related deaths are nonviolent, resulting from the effects of conflict, rather than from the acts of violence themselves. One of the defining characteristics of most conflicts appears to be warlordism, in which leaders achieve and sustain control over valuable resources in an environment of insecurity: a situation made possible by the global trade in arms and valuable natural resources and other commodities.

This is the state of conflict in the world. But as the following chapters will demonstrate, this is not at all how the state of conflict in the world is seen. Individuals and institutions alike have a tendency to display awareness of and concern for a very select number of conflicts, apparently with little consideration at all for conflict scale. How is it that our perceptions can be so far detached from reality? To answer this question, it is necessary to look at the various factors that determine the development of our consciousness of conflict, as individuals and as institutions, and how the agendas of institutions interact and influence one another. This chapter aims to set out a broad outline of this process, a process that culminates in the assimilation of the agendas of key actors towards conflicts in a disproportionate manner, with a select few conflicts being seemingly chosen for concentrated attention, and the remaining conflicts being largely ignored.

Individual Consciousness of Conflict

Consciousness of the World

Before examining the consciousness of individuals pertaining to conflict, it is important first to look at how individuals view the world as a whole and the people in it, as it is closely related to how individuals view conflict. From the perspective of an individual human being, the world is a massive place, it is round and it is inhabited by billions of people, the vast majority of whom we will never meet, see or hear from in our lifetime. Given the sheer scale of the world and of humanity, the ability of the human brain to comprehend the world and its people in its entirety is highly limited: thus, 'Because people's ability to process information is limited, they must perceive the world selectively in order to operate effectively in it' (Lepgold and Nincic 2001, 3). 'Filter' or 'bottleneck' theories suggest that we respond to excessive volumes of information by sorting it and deciding what is important and what thus demands our attention, while 'attentional resource' theories hold that there is only a finite amount of attention for us to allocate (see S. Cohen 2001, 46).

Whether we filter or allocate attention, the end result is that we apply copious amounts of selectivity, generalization, simplification and categorization as coping mechanisms to help us to better 'understand' the world and its people. To a certain degree our understanding of the world thus becomes our particular perception of reality, which is inevitably a distortion of reality. This perception, which is most likely closely linked to our particular identity (or identities), is shaped by such factors as geographical location, disposition, cultural and social upbringing, education, interaction with family, friends, acquaintances and teachers, the media, policymakers and other public figures, and access to information in general (Kegley and Wittkopf 1999, 6–7). We even have a tendency to interpret new information depending on how well it fits with our pre-existing beliefs, values and perspectives, deciding whether to accept, reject, or mould it to fit accordingly.[1]

The fact that the world is round presents an initial problem in conceptualization because we are unable to see it in its entirety at the one time. To overcome this, we have 'flattened' and stretched the world, making rectangular two-dimensional maps that show the entire world on one page. The problem is that, however projected, such maps can never accurately show the true dimensions of the world, and inevitably involve a compromise among factors such as area, direction and distance. The Mercator projection, which was first produced in the 1500s, remains the most widely used map projection in much of the world. According to this projection, the further away from the equator the region is, the more it is inflated, or 'stretched'. Furthermore, the northern hemisphere is projected as being much larger than the southern hemisphere. Thus, Europe, for example, appears considerably larger than it actually is. On the Mercator projection, Greenland appears similar in size to the African continent, despite the fact that Africa is in fact 13 times larger than Greenland.

This projection is increasingly being rejected in favour of more balanced projections, such as the Winkel Tripel projection, which attempts to compromise equally regarding distortions on area, direction and distance.[2] The effect of a particular map projection on perception can be considerable. When US strategists

---

1   Cognitive dissonance theory holds that we suffer discomfort when we encounter new information that contradicts what we already know or believe, and seek to alleviate this discomfort either by changing our pre-existing beliefs (accommodating the new information), or by rejecting or moulding the new information to fit what we already know or believe (assimilation). Accommodation is more difficult than assimilation, particularly when the knowledge or belief is deeply entrenched (see Festinger 1957).

2   The use of the Mercator projection, and other rectangular world maps, was at last rejected by the American Cartographic Association in 1989 and 1990. In 1998 the National Geographic Society adopted the use of the Winkel Tripel projection for all its world maps.

began using North Pole-centred maps, as opposed to equator-based Mercator maps during the Cold War, 'Russia "suddenly" became a close, even immediate neighbor of the United States – across a broad front in the vast Arctic region, not merely at the narrow Bering Strait between American Alaska and Russian Siberia' (Henrikson 2002, 454).

The shape of the world aside, distance in itself distorts our perspective of the world. Technological advances in transport and communications and the ongoing process of globalization have gone a long way towards reducing the perceived importance of physical distances between countries and peoples in a number of ways, but the world is geographically vast and these distances do remain both great and relevant to our understanding of the world beyond our immediate surroundings. Other forms of distance can also serve to distort such physical distance. Alan Henrikson (2002) identifies three other types of distance: gravitational distance (the distortion of distance by the economic, military or cultural power of a country), topographical distance (the distortion of distance by the presence of other countries in between), and attributional distance (the distortion of distance by characteristics or values attributed to other countries or peoples). These types of distance are used in the context of policymakers' views of the world, but they are also relevant to individuals in general.

Attempting to 'perceive' the peoples inhabiting the world is also a critical issue. Through the process of social categorization, we have a tendency to perceive people in groups rather than perceiving each individual in isolation from others. Such groups are socially constructed and may include divisions made according to race, nation, state, language, religion, socioeconomic status, profession, political leaning or even sporting teams and hobbies. Social identity theory holds that humans attempt to identify themselves with a particular group, which for them becomes the in-group. They then favour their in-group over out-groups (those belonging to groups that they perceive to be different from their group) 'in order to maintain or enhance their own self-esteem' (Devine 1995, 513). Each individual may align him/herself with multiple groups, attaching varying degrees of importance to each group. When viewing out-groups, the greater the distance, and the less available the knowledge about a particular group, the more vague the divisions become.

Most groupings are so large that the 'members' will only ever see or know a small minority of their fellow members, so the common bond between them has to be imagined and then constantly remembered through the production and reproduction of flattering stereotypes for it to have any meaning (see Anderson 1983). Eric Hobsbawm (1997, 7) notes that 'Myth and invention are essential to the politics of identity by which groups of people today, defining themselves by ethnicity, religion or the past and present borders of states, try to find some certainty in an uncertain and shaking world by saying, "We are different from and better than the Others."'

In historical terms, nations, for example, are relatively recent 'ideological creations' (Billig 1995, 24), and 'national identity in established nations is remembered because it is embedded in routines of life, which constantly remind, or "flag", nationhood', such as the presence of flags, national anthems, speeches of leaders, media coverage and references, and sporting events. Such 'remembering is simultaneously a collective forgetting: the nation, which celebrates its antiquity, forgets its historical recency. Moreover, nations forget the violence which brought them into existence' (38). Yet nationalism has become a highly pervasive ideology by which individuals and institutions see a world broken down primarily into units of nations. It has also been argued that nationalism is a modern or civil form of religion (Marvin and Ingle 1996; Bellah 1992). Through such a nation-centric lens, individuals and institutions are taught to see 'foreign' affairs in terms of how they affect their own nation. Whatever map projection is used, for example, the cartographers in countries producing world maps inevitably place their own countries in the central position of the map. Acceleration in globalization in recent decades appears to have had little effect on the power of nationalism. Studies show that national identities among people in Western Europe, for example, despite fifty years of integration, have not been dented or replaced in any way by a European identity (Tarrow 2005, 70–72).

Conflicts and Identities

Most of the world's conflict is distant from most of us and does not appear to have an immediate impact on our lives. If bombs are falling in our neighbourhood, killing family members, friends, and neighbours, if those we know are putting on uniforms and going off to kill and/or be killed, or if refugees are pitching tents near where we live, that particular conflict will be very real for us and we are likely to pay attention to it, its causes and its consequences. But very few (for many of us none at all) of the world's conflicts affect us directly in this way, so twenty or thirty conflicts lie beyond our immediate scope of consciousness. Each of these conflicts is most likely highly complex, with multiple causes (visible and hidden), multiple groups of participants and external influences, and is surrounded by strong and conflicting emotions and varying levels of propaganda. Even if we are genuinely interested and put in considerable effort, gaining a comprehensive understanding of each of these conflicts will most likely escape us.

But most of us have enough troubles and issues of concern of our own to think about (issues that directly affect our daily lives) and do not actively seek to understand the complexities of the world's conflicts. In the words of Stanley Cohen (2001, 160), it is 'quite abnormal to know or care very much about the problems of distant places'. We thus rely on pre-filtered information about conflict that is presented to us and employ the same techniques of selectivity, generalization, simplification and categorization based largely on identities (such as race, religion, nationality, ethnicity, and language) to help us 'understand' the multitude of foreign conflicts.

Identities serve as lenses that help us filter and expose information on conflicts that is deemed important to us and requiring our attention. When receiving new information about conflicts, the question of how this affects us (our particular in-group) is likely to be a factor in our decision on what level of importance to attach to that information. While the physical distance of the conflict from 'home' is an important factor, the attributional distance is also key. At an individual level, any number of examples may be given for how perceived identification and affiliation with people who belong to a particular group (beyond those one personally knows) affect the determination of what makes a conflict important. An American may consider the lives of fellow Americans involved in foreign conflicts more important than those of other nationalities affected by the same conflict. A Muslim in Indonesia may be more concerned about fellow Muslims suffering in Kosovo than those of other faiths suffering in Sri Lanka. A Portuguese-speaking black farmer in Mozambique may identify more with a persecuted black farmer in Angola than with an English-speaking persecuted white farmer in Zimbabwe, while for a white Australian farmer the reverse may well be true. The strength of identification with a particular group will depend on a wide range of socially constructed factors. Nationalism is a form of identity that has considerable bearing on attention to conflict in this sense. National armies are founded and maintained on the premise that its soldiers are willing to kill and die for the interests of their countries.

In terms of race, a study in the USA, for example, found white audiences attached more importance to unemployment as a national issue after seeing the plight of an unemployed white man than those who saw the plight of an unemployed black man (Iyengar and Kinder 1987, 41). Another study found apparent evidence of the influence of the location, race and religion of an endangered population in decisions to support hypothetical military intervention in certain conflict situations (Boettcher 2004). When former US President Bill Clinton used genocide to justify going to war against Yugoslavia, it was not just genocide per se that was seen as important, it was 'genocide in the heart of Europe – not in 1945, but in 1995. Not in some grainy newsreel from our parents' and grandparents' time, but in our own time, testing our humanity and our resolve' (BBC News 1999). The association with the Holocaust was clearly used to emphasize the magnitude of the situation, but the racial connotations were also apparent. Victor Davis Hanson (2003, 451) notes that 'We in the West still shudder at the carnage of World War II largely because it took the lives of so many Westerners'. Whether individuals can identify with those involved in a conflict or not, race and other forms of identity help individuals to simplify their perception of that conflict. A conflict that appears to involve blacks versus whites, or Arabs versus blacks, or Christians versus Muslims, for example, is immediately easier to simplify than conflicts perceived to be occurring among members of the same race or religion.

Conflicts and Frames

Another way in which individuals process and prioritize conflicts is by using a 'frame': something that can outline the context within which the conflict is being fought, provide a point of focus, and perhaps even an enemy to which we, as distant observers, can direct our indignation. For more than four decades, the Cold War provided such a frame. The Cold War saw most of the world become a battlefield between the two superpowers for influence and dominance, and any conflict that involved the superpowers directly or indirectly could be explained as part of that struggle. Participants in proxy conflicts learnt to frame their conflicts in such a context, becoming experts at playing superpowers off against each other in a bid for support. For distant observers, conflicts made sense in that light.

As the Cold War ended, policymakers, the media, academics, and the public struggled to find a replacement for this frame. Although US policymakers declared a 'new world order', this didn't seem to fit correctly, particularly as new conflicts broke out in places such as the Balkans, Somalia, Liberia, and parts of the former Soviet Union. Officials in the USA experimented with other frames, such as 'rogue states', 'axis of evil', and 'outposts of tyranny', but these frames referred largely to states (or perhaps more accurately, leaders of states) that that country perceived as hostile to its own interests. A frame also emerged from academia, when Samuel Huntington (1996) proposed that the world was going to experience a 'clash of civilizations'. A much more accessible frame for individuals (particularly in the West) came after the terrorist attacks on the USA in 2001 when that country declared a general 'war on terror'. As logically strained as it is (declaring war on a method of violence, rather than on a particular opponent), terrorism became the new frame through which people in the West could 'understand' conflict and security threats throughout the world (see McLaughlin 2002, 206). Although the frame of terrorism had global reverberations and in many states considerable impact, and although many leaders of states saw its emergence as a frame as an opportunity to enhance their security and support by labelling their opponents as terrorists, the frame appeared to be primarily intended to refer to attacks by radical Islamists aimed at Western targets.

More importantly, valid frames were not found or popularized that could represent in some way the vast majority of the world's conflicts. Given the emphasis on analyzing the world at the level of countries, frames such as 'state failure' and 'state collapse' did emerge, along with many other labels (Dunn 2001, 46). As to what was going on within those states, frames such as 'internal conflict', 'ethnic cleansing', 'tribal conflict', and 'chaos' were among those frequently raised. The use of such frames (particularly those including 'failure', 'internal', 'tribal' and 'chaos') has the unfortunate effect of discouraging attention and understanding. This is because they help maintain the appearance that 1) the conflict will be limited within the borders of that particular state, and 2) the conflict is beyond external comprehension and assistance: it is ancient tribal bloodletting that can only be allowed to run its tragic, yet inevitable course, and outsiders would best look away. Some parties to conflict take advantage of this effect, portraying conflict in this light to discourage outside attention and response (see Keen 1999, 91).

Another frame that has been applied to certain conflicts, with considerable effect, is 'genocide'. Its effect stems from the human tendency to attach importance to groups of people, rather than individuals (as noted above). Thus an assault focusing on a particular group of people appears more threatening than one that does not necessarily appear to differentiate according to easily understood definitions of ethnicity, or language, religion or nation, regardless of what the actual levels of killing are. Even though the death and destruction caused by what is labelled a genocide may be far less than that caused by a conflict which cannot be framed as an attempt to destroy a particular group of people, the term genocide appears to have a cataclysmic and compelling ring to it (Prunier 2006). The *New York Times* columnist, Nicholas Kristof, who is a proponent of the use of the term genocide in referring to conflict in Darfur (see Kristof 2004), justifies his strong focus on the conflict in Darfur, as opposed to that in the DRC (while acknowledging that the latter is far more deadly than the former), with the assertion that 'human evil' is greater in Darfur, because it is 'about an ethnic group in the government using its military force to kill other groups', whereas conflict in the DRC is 'a tale of chaos and poverty and civil war' (Kristof 2007).

The notion that targeting a particular group should be distinguished from, and considered more pressing (or more 'evil') than, other forms of killing, appears to be widely shared, and is commonly used to enhance calls to action, including those by policymakers, the media, activists and celebrities (see ABC News 2006). Along similar lines, when Iraq invaded Kuwait, former US President George Bush, although not suggesting the existence of genocide, appealed for support for the military intervention on the grounds that a 'nation' was being 'raped, pillaged and plundered': the implication being that the nation is something much more important than individuals (see Billig 1995, 1).

The use of the genocide frame is also effective because of guilt over past failures to stop genocide, most notably during World War II in Europe and in Rwanda in 1994. Certain powerful states strongly resisted the use of the term to describe the killings in Rwanda in 1994, because they were well aware of the legal, and perhaps more importantly, 'moral' duties associated with the acknowledgement of genocide, and were determined not to get involved. There were no such qualms about conflict in Kosovo, and the same US administration that had baulked over Rwanda explicitly used the term genocide as justification for its war on Yugoslavia (BBC News 1999). Attempts to label the conflict in Darfur as genocide have sparked intense debate over whether the term is applicable or not (see Straus 2005; Mennecke 2007), but these attempts had particular impact because conflict in Darfur coincided with the commemoration of the tenth anniversary of the genocide in Rwanda. Many observers made a clear connection, along the lines of, 'we said "never again" after Rwanda, but now it has started again in Darfur', as if there had been no conflict or killing worthy of outrage in Africa in the ten years in between; as if the millions of deaths in the DRC, southern Sudan and Angola had not been meaningful because the conflicts didn't fit the simplified frame in which all the victims appeared to belong to the same particular ethnic group.

Conflicts and Sympathy

The perceived innocence or blamelessness of the victims has considerable bearing on the level of sympathy, or the level of importance attached to their plight (S. Cohen 2001, 177). If a conflict is perceived as being 'tribal' or 'chaotic', victims are unlikely to attract sympathy, because they are seen as somehow tainted by a mutually sustained cycle of violence. From a political perspective, some victims may be 'worthy' and others 'unworthy'. Their affiliation with (or stance against) groups relative to those one belongs to affects their worthiness (Herman and Chomsky 1994, 35). Kurdish groups fighting against Iraqi oppression in the 1990s, for example, were able to attract attention and sympathy in the West, whereas Kurdish groups fighting against Turkish oppression were not. Deaths among groups perceived as having 'terrorists' in the midst are unlikely to attract sympathy. During the Cold War, the difference between 'communist' victims, or 'capitalist' victims (depending on which side one was on) was important in determining sympathy for the victims of conflict.

Whether a group is able to attract sympathy or not is usually a matter of how their situation is perceived by the outside viewers, and may be closely related to identity and affiliation. But this does not necessarily mean that parties to a conflict or victims are at the mercy of outside perception: they may actively attempt to shape it in a bid to attract sympathy and support. For some groups, this may mean launching attacks against a stronger opponent that provoke an overreaction, giving them the status of victim in an apparently one-sided campaign of oppression. This appeared to be effective for rebel groups in Kosovo and in Darfur. They may also attempt to link their conflict or struggle to other issues that are already key concerns of external actors, such that their plight is seen as part of a struggle against environmental degradation or against globalization and poverty, as seen in conflicts in Nigeria and Mexico (Bob 2005). Sympathy may also be related to factors on a more personal level. Putting a single human face on suffering that affects many can be an effective way of attracting concern for the plight of those suffering because of conflict: a technique frequently employed by the media and NGOs (see Jenni and Loewenstein 1997). Image, charisma and communication skills of a leader can often have considerable impact on the sympathy levels for groups in both conflict and non-conflict situations (see Bob 2005, 46–51). The image of Myanmar's democracy leader Aung San Suu Kyi, for example, as an attractive, frail female, yet one who is resolute, charismatic and English-speaking, has undoubtedly contributed greatly to levels of sympathy for her cause in the outside world (see Brooten 2005).

The sheer numbers of deaths that result from a conflict, or the conflict scale, do not generally appear to have a major bearing on the levels of sympathy, or the importance that individuals attach to particular conflicts. The deaths of tens of thousands, hundreds of thousands, or even millions, of people from conflict in Africa is often not enough to spark such a response: 'The value we attach to numbers is often arbitrary. The element of race has a way of coloring our judgement' (Berkeley 2001, 18–19). And as noted in Chapter 1, there is a certain moral dysfunction associated with large numbers of human lives, such that we find it difficult to conceive the true magnitude of anything more than a few thousand lives. Joseph Stalin's famous observation that a single death is a tragedy, but a million deaths is a statistic, is sadly close to the truth from the psychological point of view. As the following chapters will show, the discrepancies in the death tolls of conflicts and the outrage expressed in response to them are considerable.

Studies have suggested that the manner of death can be more important than the numbers of dead, with a gruesome and pitiful manner of death attracting more attention and sympathy than a higher death toll (S. Cohen 2001, 211). Sympathy may also be sparked or boosted by a particular event that serves as a tipping point for attention to a conflict, such as an atrocity that happens to be caught by the media. One example is the boosted response to conflict in Bosnia, following the release of graphic footage of the aftermath of a mortar bomb that exploded in a crowded marketplace in Sarajevo in 1994 (Robinson 2002, 86–92). The discovery of an alleged execution site in Racak, Kosovo, in January 1999, is another example, although there was no evidence that the victims had suffered execution, and it was discovered that most of the victims were combatants (Parenti 2000, 104–7). Parties to the conflict often play a role in boosting the visibility of (and in some cases even staging) such events, in an attempt to draw sympathy to their cause. On the other hand, the mutilation (particularly the deliberate cutting off of limbs) of thousands of adults and children in Sierra Leone did seemingly little to attract the attention or sympathy of the outside world.

Animals affected by conflict are at times also able to attract considerable amounts of attention and sympathy (sometimes more so than human victims), largely because of their perceived innocence and blamelessness. A campaign for 'gorilla-friendly' mobile phones (phones made without using coltan from the DRC, where the mining of the mineral was linked to conflict that threatened the gorilla and its habitat), for example, sought to spark consumer action based on sympathy for what was seen as an innocent yet endangered animal, rather than on sympathy for the millions of humans killed or affected by the conflict. Similarly, a lion in the Kabul zoo became the object of considerable sympathy and attention when it was injured by a hand grenade attack, partly because of the novelty of the story (the attacker was attempting to avenge the death of his brother who had entered the enclosure and been killed by the lion), but also partly because of its perceived blamelessness as an innocent animal caught up in a web of human aggression and violence.

Conflicts and Helplessness

Another element that must be considered when looking at the individual's consciousness regarding conflict is the sense of the ability to do something as opposed to the sense of helplessness. According to Stanley Cohen, three conditions must be met to avoid a sense of helplessness setting in when observing suffering: 1) that something can be done, 2) that we can do it, and 3) that we can make a difference. 'Much passivity results not from lacking the right feelings, but from perceiving that an ordinary person like me can do nothing about such a monstrous problem' (2001, 219). When helplessness does set in, it is uncomfortable for us to continue to react to the suffering we may see with sympathy, outrage and with a drive to do something to stop it, so we have a tendency to switch off our senses to these stimuli. We may react with 'implicatory' denial: we don't necessarily deny the facts regarding what is going on, and we may still care, but we pretend not to see or know, justifying our silence with the belief that there is nothing we can do about it (8–9).

This tendency to switch off our senses and sympathies may ironically be exacerbated by too much stimulation or too much information designed to attract attention, in what has been called 'compassion fatigue'. When bombarded with concentrated images of distant human suffering framed in such a way to attract an emotional response,

> The public screams, 'Stop those images!' – meaning: 'Do something!' but also, sometimes, meaning: 'I don't want to know any more.' Didactic images can overload the senses. A single child at risk commands our attention and prompts our action. But one child, and then another, and another, and another and on and on and on is too much. A crowd of people in danger is faceless. Numbers alone can numb. All those starving brown babies over the years blur together (Moeller 1999, 36).

Some dispute, however, that there is a finite amount of compassion that can be exhausted by providing too much emotional stimulation, suggesting instead that this phenomenon results from a misreading of the human capacity for compassion by those providing the information and stimuli (S. Cohen 2001, 290). In any case, such 'fatigue' is most likely closely related to a sense of helplessness and ability to identify.

In summary, the volume of information that would be required for us as individuals to properly understand all of the world's many conflicts is simply too great to process, even if that information is presented to us (and most of it is usually not). We therefore are necessarily selective about the information we take in regarding foreign conflicts that do not have a direct bearing on our daily lives. We filter information and frame conflicts according to their perceived nature and their participants for ease of categorization. Most of the time we rely on pre-filtered and pre-packaged information that is presented to us, without actively seeking out information. We prioritize the information we receive, attaching varying levels of importance to each conflict, feeling outrage and a need to 'do something' towards some, and shutting out and switching off to others. The importance we attach to conflicts may in some rare cases be somehow related to the scale or severity, but other factors appear to be far more important in most cases: factors such as how close to 'home' it is, how well we can identify with the participants and victims (in terms of race, religion, nation, ethnicity), how well we can understand the problem, how blameless or 'worthy' the victims appear to us, and whether or not we think we can do something about it.

Institutional Consciousness of Conflict

In terms of response to conflict, it is institutions, rather than individuals, that generally have the power and influence to 'do something', so it is important to look at how institutions view and react to conflict. Depending on the institution and on the individual, however, individual influence at the higher levels within an institution can be considerable, and institutions are essentially made up of individuals, so many of the factors that apply to individual consciousness also apply, to a certain extent, to institutional consciousness. But institutions are established to fulfil specific purposes, are governed by certain rules and regulations, operate within fixed parameters, and are generally designed to serve a specific group of people. These factors shape an institution's consciousness of and response to conflict, including the information they gather, how they process and utilize that information, and what actions they decide to take (or not to take).

Conflicts and Institutions

There is a wide range of institutions that have an interest in, and that respond (in varying degrees) to foreign conflict. For the purposes of this study these institutions are divided into four broad categories: policymakers, the media, the public and academia. There is considerable diversity within each of these categories. Policymakers here include international organizations (bodies representing both states and bureaucracies), as well as the executive and legislative branches of national governments and their bureaucracies. The media includes print and broadcast media, news agencies and the Internet. The public here refers to the general public, plus NGOs, interest and pressure groups and corporations. Academia includes universities, think tanks and other research institutes that are active in the study of international relations, international security, history and international affairs in general.

Each of these 'actors' exists for different purposes and works according to different principles. While international organizations, for example, were created to protect their member states and/or the inhabitants of the world or of particular regions, policymakers in national governments are tasked with protecting and promoting only the interests of their nations and the people who are recognized as citizens of those nations. The media may see it as its role to relate reality to the public the way it is, or to keep a watchful eye over figures in authority to make sure that they are honest and in line with the people's expectations. NGOs may see themselves as duty-bound to rescue those in need that have been neglected by other actors (particularly governments). Interest and pressure groups, on the other hand, exist to promote the wellbeing or interests of a particular group of people, and corporations aim to maximize their profits and expand their operations. Academic institutions may determine that their role is to reveal the mechanics behind international affairs, record history as they see it, or to assist the policymakers in their particular countries to come up with wise policies and strategies that further the national interest.

Within each of the actor groupings, there is wide variety of finer institutional differences. Different governmental systems and power balances can mean variations in perspective and stance, as can attachment to a particular political party. Furthermore, a bureaucrat is likely to see the 'national interest' in a different light from a politician representing the same country. Political parties, media corporations, and academic institutions differ according to their political leanings. Individual news media corporations are numerous, as are their styles of reporting, which may include one or more of the following: entertaining, sensational, patriotic, serious, objective or critical of authority. NGOs may focus on a region close to home, or they may attempt to be global in their reach. Advocacy groups may follow a diplomatic approach towards policymakers or they may be more aggressive and make use of public demonstrations and performances designed to work through the general public.

The consciousness of institutions regarding foreign conflicts is determined by their interests regarding conflict in general as well as that of specific conflicts. The UN Security Council is charged with the maintenance of international peace and security, so it is duty-bound to hold a high level of consciousness about all conflicts occurring in the world, while regional security organizations are also established specifically to be concerned with conflicts occurring in and around the region they represent. For most other institutions, consciousness of and response to conflicts in the world is 'voluntary' (as long as the conflict does not directly affect the institution), although countries may be legally bound, through treaties, to act in response to certain conflicts, in mutual defence, or in response to genocide in general. In a more general sense, each member state of the UN, according to Article 2 of the UN Charter, also pledges to settle international disputes peacefully, refrain from the threat or use of force, and to 'fulfill in good faith the obligations assumed by them in accordance with' the UN Charter. Non-state institutions' interest in conflict is primarily self-imposed, and depends initially on what the purposes of the institution are.

There are a number of views on where the responsibility lies to protect people threatened by violence and the equally deadly consequences of violence. While the primary responsibility to protect resides with the state in which those threatened are situated, this ceases to function when the state is unable or unwilling to do so (or may even be the party that is threatening the people). In this case other states take on the 'residual responsibility' (ICISS 2001, 148). There appear to be three views on the manner in which such responsibility should be allocated: 1) those with the greatest economic and military power have the greatest responsibility; 2) states have equal responsibility, but the execution should be in proportion to their economic and military capacity; and 3) past actions (such as those under colonialism, under the Cold War or other forms of intervention) that have a bearing on the conflict affect the allocation of responsibility.

For state and non-state institutions alike, interest in conflict arises, to varying degrees and for varying reasons, beyond any legal or even moral obligations. Governments take an interest in conflict if it is perceived to affect their national interests (in terms of security, economics and/or ideology), if it affects the interests of their allies, or if their reputation would be damaged by not taking an interest, particularly where others are showing a strong interest. Media corporations may take an interest in conflict because they believe it is their duty to inform their consumers about events that are taking place in the world, particularly those events that are perceived to affect or interest those consumers. This interest is usually contingent on the ability to make a profit in gathering, packaging and presenting such news. NGOs centred on humanitarian work take an interest in conflict because it is a major cause of large-scale humanitarian suffering, but this interest is also contingent on the ability to find people or other institutions willing to donate money to allow them to conduct their activities. Academic institutions may take an interest in conflict in the sociological sense, in attempting to understand organized violence as a human phenomenon, or in a political sense, in attempting to understand the implications for the country or region in which the institution is situated, or perhaps for international security in a broader sense. Furthermore, in any institution, personal interest by individuals in key decision-making positions in certain conflicts can have a considerable influence on the consciousness of the institution.

In any case, the ability of the majority of the world's institutions to maintain a high level of awareness about all of the world's conflicts is limited. Most states do not have the resources (or interest) to maintain permanent diplomatic representation in all other countries. With the exception of some news agencies, the presence of individual media corporations is sparse in most of the world: even those that have a global audience and focus on international news maintain as few as two bureaux on some continents. As with individuals, institutions employ selectivity, filtering and prioritization to establish their consciousness on conflict in the world, depending on their interests, on the circumstances and on other actors. The 'close to home' and the 'ability to identify' principles apply not only to individuals but also to institutions during this filtering process. As with individuals, the sheer scale of the conflict does not usually appear to be a major factor in consciousness for most institutions.

Conflicts and Agenda-Setting

The process of establishing consciousness, which involves first awareness and then ranking the relative importance of each item, that may then lead to decisions or actions in response, is known as agenda-setting. The point is not what an institution's opinion or stance is towards a particular issue, nor how effective or otherwise its choice of response may be, but rather, how important that issue is to that institution: agenda-setting is about issue salience. Two different institutions may vehemently disagree on a particular issue and how it should be handled, but the issue is perceived as being equally important for both institutions. And while individual institutions have their own internal dynamics (functions, interests, and management structures) that contribute to the setting of their agendas, they do not exist in a vacuum, and their agendas are influenced inevitably to some degree by the agendas of other institutions.

Agenda-setting research looks at how actors interact with and influence each other in determining the perceived importance of issues. It initially focused on the influence of the media on the public, but studies linking the media and policymakers also began to be conducted. Other research emerged, focusing on how issues originate in the first place (known as agenda-building), and how individuals tend to match their own priorities to those of a group of which they are a part (known as agenda-melding). As Maxwell McCombs (2004, 141–5) points out, however, these terms fit under the basic core of the term agenda-setting, in the sense that they are concerned with the transfer of salience from one agenda to another, and can thus be applied at any level and in a variety of fields. This expanded view of agenda-setting primarily deals with the relationships among the agendas of the policymakers, the media and the general public, and the relationship between these agendas and real-world factors. Numerous studies have found evidence of significant influences being exercised between the media and the general public (see McCombs and Shaw 1972; Iyengar and Kinder 1987), between the media and the policymakers (see Hallin 1986; and Bennett 1990), and between the general public and policymakers (see Hill 1998). In fact, a close look at each of the actors reveals that each has an influence on each of the others in more ways than one, although admittedly in varying degrees.

Academia, for the purposes of this study, has been added for examination on to the three groups of actors traditionally studied (policymakers, media and public), given its relevant role in foreign policy issues and in the recording of human history. As Richard Haass (2002, 5) points out, of the influences on foreign policy formulation, 'the role of think tanks is among the most important and least appreciated'. It should not be forgotten that within individual actor groups there is also considerable peer pressure, with different players exerting influence on each other. Governments, for example, influence other governments, some branches of government influence other branches of the same government, media corporations eagerly compare what they are covering with what their rivals are covering, and academic institutions take an interest in the work of other academic institutions.

Studies to date have looked at agenda-setting from a wide variety of angles, such as domestic policy issues including inflation, budget deficit, social security and crime; and international policy issues such as military intervention in foreign conflicts and nuclear disarmament. This study, however, will concentrate on agenda-setting from the perspective of response to foreign conflict. Most studies looking from this perspective focus on the media as an influence in 'pushing' policymakers to intervene militarily, or 'pulling' policymakers to withdraw their forces, but this is a very narrow perspective. Military intervention is an extreme and exceptional response to armed conflict, and many other responses have far more regular and broader-reaching impacts on foreign conflict. Humanitarian aid, for example, is one response that applies to almost all conflicts at one point or another, and those giving aid have been shown to be influenced in many ways by the agendas of other actors, perhaps most notably the media (see Jakobsen 2000). Mediation between the parties is another response to conflict, as are the application of pressure through sanctions and the threat of sanctions. Even making public statements on a conflict, such as calling upon parties to refrain from certain actions, is a form of response. Such responses also warrant an examination when looking at agenda-setting as it pertains to foreign conflict.

The fact that this perspective on agenda-setting looks solely at response to foreign conflict means that the model proposed below for looking at the various influences within and among the actors is slightly different from other agenda-setting models that have been proposed, although it builds upon them.[3] In this expanded agenda-setting model, each of the four agendas (policy, media, public and academic) is shown to have a direct influence on each of the other agendas. Real-world factors refer here to the presence and progress of foreign conflict, and are thus shown outside the web of influence among agendas. These real-world factors can potentially influence each of the four actors' agendas, but only policymakers and parts of the public agenda (primarily NGOs) have the potential to influence real-world factors through various forms of intervention in the foreign conflict. Of course it can be argued that the media can potentially influence the conduct of foreign conflict through their coverage (with some parties to conflict forced to alter their tactics because of the watchful eye of coverage, and others taking advantage of the attention to advance their cause at the expense of their opponents), but the media and academics are essentially observers, and are not in a position to intervene. They can influence real-world factors by influencing the policy and public agendas.

As noted above, actors are not single and homogeneous groups and neither are their agendas. The arrows in the model may apply in some cases and not in others. In response to foreign conflict, the policy agenda, for example, may appear to affect the general public's agenda only through the media (or other domestic real-world factors)

---

3   In Stuart Soroka's (2002) model (which is primarily designed to examine domestic politics), for example, the policy, media and public agendas influence each other, but the policy agenda influences the public agenda only through real-world factors (as domestic political and economic issues change as a result of government policies) and through the media, not directly. The policy agenda also influences the media agenda through these real-world factors, which is placed in the centre of the model.

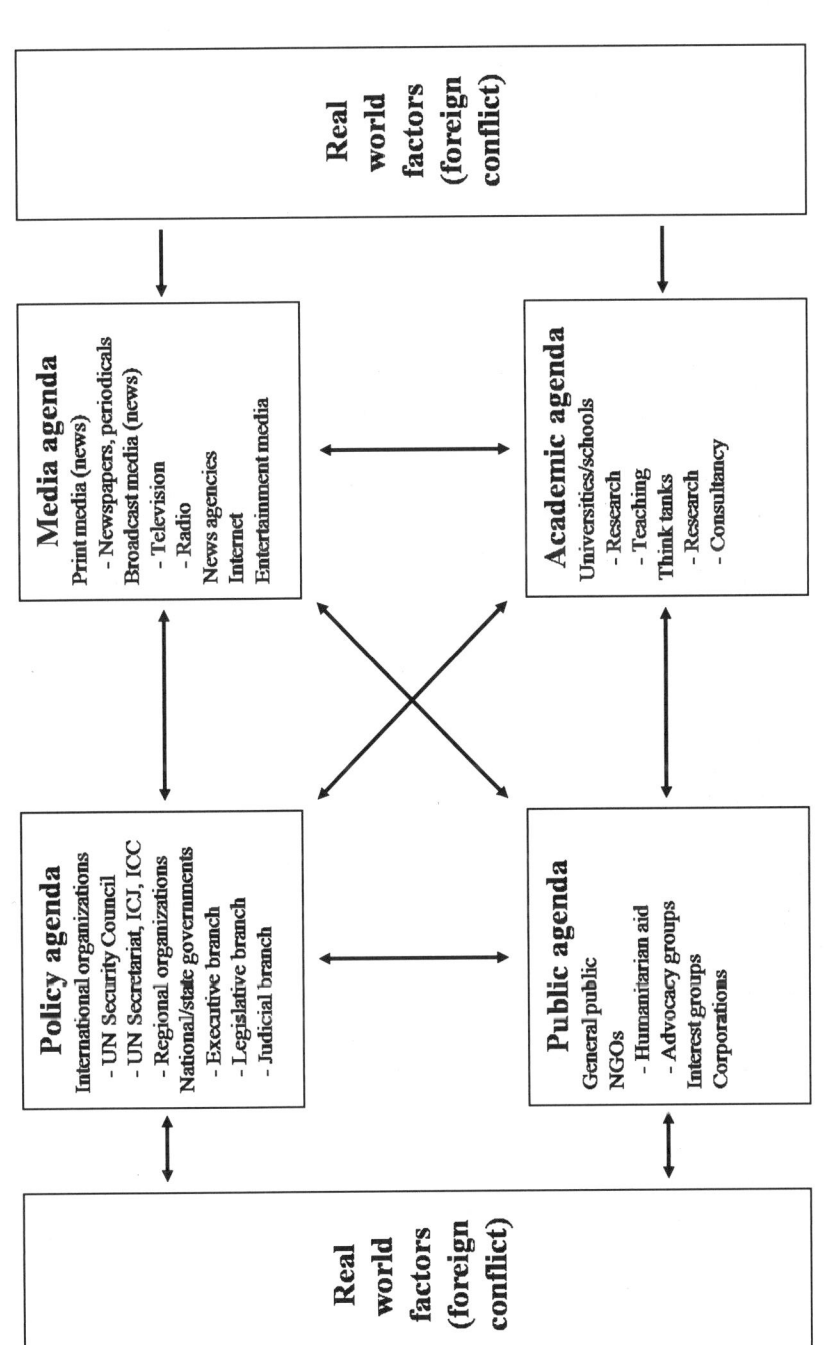

Figure 2.1   Expanded agenda-setting model: response to foreign conflict

as Stuart Soroka suggests (2002, 269–70), but the policy agenda does directly affect other components of the public agenda, namely NGOs, as governments provide direct funding for much of the emergency humanitarian work carried out by such organizations. The legislative branches of government may also have a direct effect on corporations, legally blocking economic activities conducted by them in areas affected by conflict. Nor does this model show the web of influence within each of the four groups' agendas. The public agenda, for example, is made up of a variety of potentially conflicting groups. It is assumed that the agendas that emerge from these four groups are formed through a variety of internal influences as well as external ones. In short, the model is a grand simplification of a highly complex process. The details of these internal and external webs of influence will be discussed in the following chapters.

Assuming that each of these organizations has an agenda, or a set of priorities that reflect what is important to that organization in terms of foreign conflict, the necessary question is, how can we see and measure these agendas? The agendas of actors are not generally written down or presented for all to see. Governments do not announce a list of foreign conflicts each month in order of importance to them, and speaking of the media agenda does not suggest that all media groups come together and hammer out an agenda of important issues for consideration. Agendas can also be highly fluid, changing together with real-world factors, internal dynamics and external influences.

To a large extent, the agendas of institutions reveal themselves through the words and actions of those institutions applied to certain conflicts. For international organizations and governments, priorities may be seen in the public statements they make, the diplomacy they engage in, the resources devoted for humanitarian assistance and the numbers of troops dispatched for military intervention. For the media, priorities can be gauged from the quantity of coverage produced on a particular conflict or region, or from the positioning of correspondents. The agenda of the general public can be measured through public opinion polls, whereas for NGOs the allocation of resources for humanitarian projects or advocacy outputs may be an appropriate measure. Academic agendas can be seen by measuring the output of work (the number of journal articles, books, and quantity of coverage devoted to certain conflicts and regions within books), as well as by the types of academic programs established at institutions.

As noted above, research shows considerable linkages among the agendas of the various actors. When bringing together the agendas, or consciousness, of the four groups of actors in relation to foreign conflict and comparing them, some obvious patterns across the agendas of all of the actors emerge, and while this involves a considerable amount of generalization, the patterns are clear nonetheless. The resulting overall agenda may be called 'international consciousness', although many of the actors that contribute to this agenda transcend national boundaries and do not fit the 'nation as central unit for analysis' type of thinking. In this sense, 'global consciousness' may be a more appropriate term. It may be somewhat presumptuous, however, to use either of these terms without fully gauging the consciousness of representative institutions among policymakers, the media, the public and academia the whole world over. To use such terms without doing so may be akin to using the term 'international community' when actually referring only to a small proportion of the world's governments – albeit often the most powerful (as is frequently the case among policymakers, the media and academics). As Thomas Weiss (2001, 423) points out, 'There is no "community" if this word implies shared values and common convictions'.

Unfortunately, this study does not manage to cover the entire globe in its analysis of conflict consciousness and response. It focuses instead primarily on what might be called the Western world or perhaps the Northern world (in socioeconomic terms): chiefly the industrialized countries of northern America and Europe, Japan and Australia (as well as the institutions that are based therein), with a particular focus on the wealthier countries. It chooses this focus because, by virtue of their wealth, these regions and their institutions have the greatest influence on other actors and the greatest capacity to respond to foreign conflict. In this sense, 'Western consciousness' or 'Northern consciousness' may be more appropriate terms for the resulting shared consciousness which results from the web of internal and external influences making up the agenda-setting and decision-making process. Where possible, this study also examines the agendas of institutions based in countries outside these industrialized areas, but the focus remains primarily in the West/North.

It must be noted that bringing together the agendas of these four groups of actors in this study is by no means intended to imply that there is a singular and unified perception of reality pertaining to conflict throughout the world. There exists a broad and diverse set of influential actors, and they possess many and varied priorities and agendas that are fluid and multifaceted. To a large degree, however, interdependence, mutual influence and divergence of consciousness on the issue of foreign conflict can be observed within and among them, and certain obvious trends emerge. These will be examined below.

Chosen Conflicts and Stealth Conflicts

Chosen Conflicts

One general trend that can be observed in agendas of policymakers, the media, the public and academia, is a tendency for the various actors to focus their collective attention on just one or two at a time of the twenty or thirty ongoing conflicts in the world. The agendas of most of the actors in these groups appear to be largely assimilated on this point across the board, and the conflicts that are the subject of this attention are almost invariably the same for each of the actors at the same time. The levels of attention bestowed upon those particular conflicts can become so intense that even actors that may not otherwise have a significant interest in them will be forced to take notice and attribute importance to them. During the temporary absences of such conflicts, the agendas of some actors may attract only moderate levels of influence from other key actors and their priorities may diverge to a degree, but as attention for a particular conflict gathers momentum among the more influential actors, the so-called gravitational distance shrinks among the various agendas, and actors find their attention being 'pulled' ever more strongly towards a particular conflict.

While there may be a great divergence of views on what the nature of the conflict is and on what the appropriate response should be, the point is that all attention is focused on that conflict in one way or another: it becomes the 'main event' on the world stage. Policymakers will make statements about the conflict with increasing frequency and emotion. They may push for action in some form in the UN Security Council or elsewhere. The various media corporations will send more reporters and cameras and boost the quantity and prominence of their coverage, which is likely to become increasingly emotive. The general public will also become both knowledgeable and emotional about the conflict, with people privately and publicly expressing their concern or outrage, while NGOs will step up their humanitarian support for the victims of the conflict. Academics will be called upon to give their views on the political background and to ponder likely future scenarios, and articles will begin to appear in international affairs journals. The snowball effect takes hold across and within the various groups of actors and the 'importance' of the conflict grows exponentially.

I will refer to such conflicts as 'chosen' conflicts. Looking at conflict consciousness in recent years, we can see the emergence of such chosen conflicts: those that stand out far above all others. From late 1998, Kosovo was the conflict dominating attention, culminating in the attacks by NATO on Yugoslavia in 1999. In late 1999 East Timor briefly emerged to prominence, and in 2000 limited fighting in Israel-Palestine led to that conflict being chosen. The terrorist attacks on the USA in September 2001 dominated consciousness from that point on, and this attention continued through the Western military response to those attacks in Afghanistan. Iraq rose to sole prominence in anticipation of the invasion in 2003, and with the occupation of that country by foreign forces and the continuing violence, Iraq has remained as the key chosen conflict up to the present, although Israel's invasion of southern Lebanon in 2006 briefly resulted in that conflict being a chosen one. While the factors behind the 'choosing' of conflicts will be discussed in the following chapters, one common thread among these conflicts that is immediately obvious is the direct participation of key Western countries in the conflicts in one way or another, or at the very least a strong interest by such countries.

As already noted, conflicts are too numerous and complex for all of them to be the recipients of significant levels of attention; a certain degree of selectivity is inevitable for any actor, particularly considering that most actors devote only a small percentage of their time, energies and resources to observing and responding to foreign conflicts. The phenomenon of chosen conflicts is problematic, not because of selectivity per se: only a certain percentage of the world's conflict-related suffering can be stopped, and any lives threatened by conflict that are saved because of foreign attention of some form make such attention worthwhile. Chosen conflicts are problematic because: 1) the levels of attention given to chosen conflicts are so intense that they leave little room for attention for all of the other conflicts (it is a winner-takes-all situation), and 2) the chosen conflicts are rarely (if ever) among the most deadly, and may even be relatively quite minor in terms of scale. Both of these problems represent issues of proportion: chosen conflicts receive disproportionately large amounts of attention compared to all the others, and smaller conflicts receive disproportionately large amounts of attention compared to conflicts that are greater in scale. The levels of disproportion can be staggering.

Intense focus on a single conflict at the expense of most others, and an apparent disregard for conflict scale in determining that focus may be understandable if a particular actor acknowledges that its allocation of attention is connected to national interest (strategic, political or economic), or to racial, ethnic or religious ties between observer and victim. But claims that motives are truly humanitarian are unsustainable under such circumstances, considering that the scale of humanitarian need is not the determining factor in the allocation of attention, and that the vast majority of actors share the same narrow focus. Attention and response to conflict today reflect a chronic case of 'selective indignation' by most actors (Schnabel and Thakur 2000). As Ian Smillie and Larry Minear (2004, 1), discussing the unbalanced allocation of humanitarian aid, point out, 'The humanitarian "imperative" is difficult to take seriously when its application is so tattered.'

The ongoing twenty or thirty conflicts have not only to compete, so to speak, with each other for outside attention. Potential conflicts, threats or hot spots also serve to distract attention from actual conflicts, particularly when the potential damage from the potential conflict is perceived as being great. The tense relations between North and South Korea across the most militarized border in the world, or the sabre-rattling between China and Taiwan, are two such security issues, as is speculation of further US attacks in the Middle East, namely against Iran and/or Syria. Even in Kosovo, before NATO's attacks, some observers asserted that that conflict, left unattended to, threatened to spill over, sparking broader conflict through other parts of the Balkans and even as far as Greece and Turkey. Such assertions served to strengthen the focus on that conflict also. But since the September 11 attacks on the USA, it is the potential threat of terrorist attacks on Western targets, in every manner imaginable, that has distracted much potential attention from very real and ongoing conflicts elsewhere in the world.

The Concept of Stealth Conflicts

So what becomes of the other conflicts (including the most deadly in the world): those that are not chosen? Some do attract an intermediate level of attention, playing a kind of supporting role to the chosen conflict for a time. They then have the potential to rise to the position of chosen conflict, or fade away from consciousness. Russia's forceful re-entry into Chechnya attracted a considerable degree of sustained attention in 1999, as has the conflict in the Darfur region of Sudan since 2004, but not quite at the all-dominating level of a chosen conflict. The Israel-Palestine conflict (or any conflict involving Israel, for that matter) appears to be in the privileged position of permanent intermediate-level conflict: all developments (however minor) are consistently and closely monitored, and significant attention is paid to its progress. When there is a conflagration, it can quickly rise to the level of chosen conflict, as it did in 2000, and with Israel's conflict with Lebanon in 2006.

The remainder of the world's conflicts may briefly become the recipients of outside attention, flash-in-the-pan style, when there is a major conflagration, or novel/odd incident or twist, but to a large extent they, their progress, and the damage they cause, are ignored by the outside world. These conflicts may be left to take their 'natural' course, and little of them is seen, and less recorded. This is, of course, a generalization – not all actors completely ignore these conflicts. While the US government may attach some importance to the progress of the conflict in Colombia, for example, the media and the general public usually do not. And while Western mining corporations may show a good deal of interest in the conflict in the DRC, most other actors do not. Token steps may also be taken by some actors to give the appearance that a conflict is not being ignored. On the whole, however, the majority of the world's conflicts (including the most deadly) are largely ignored by most of the external actors most of the time. Oddly enough, with very few exceptions, conflicts on the continent of Africa, despite comprising the vast majority of the world's conflict-related deaths, and despite the unparalleled scale of human suffering, are generally left to languish in the category of the conflicts that are ignored or marginalized: 'There are two humanitarian policies, one for Africa and one for the rest of the world' (Weiss and Collins 2000, 133).

Observers have offered a variety of terms for conflicts or complex emergencies that remain unseen or unrecognized: forgotten, orphan, third-class, silent, neglected, ignored and hidden.[4] All of these terms serve in different ways to capture much of this problem, but, at the risk of further burdening the nomenclature in this area, I would like to propose a term that perhaps better expresses the essence of such conflicts from the perspective of the attention they receive.

'Forgotten' is probably one of the terms used most frequently in describing conflicts that fail to attract outside attention. But the term is misleading: for a conflict to have been forgotten, it must first have been remembered. The conflict in Somalia in the early 1990s certainly fits this description, and, to a certain degree, Angola and Haiti do as well. These conflicts 'enjoyed' a period of outside attention and concern, but were later forgotten. But conflicts in Burundi, and the DRC, for example, were never remembered to begin with, and hence can hardly be called forgotten conflicts. The same applies to the term 'orphan' conflicts. Unless a conflict once had 'parents' who were at one point attentive and concerned with the situation, it is difficult to suggest that, in the absence of attention and concern, they are now orphaned.

Ian Smillie and Larry Minear (2003, 144–5) divide humanitarian emergencies into three categories: 'first-class', for which there is the 'lavishing of abundant military and economic assistance'; 'second-class', which attract an intermediate level of interest and involvement; and 'third-class', which are the neglected emergencies, or 'the canary in the world's humanitarian coal mine', and serve to 'demonstrate that the system is in routine violation of its core principles, particularly those of humanity, universality, and impartiality'. Dividing conflicts or humanitarian emergencies into classes certainly helps to vividly convey a sense of inequality in response. And while this perspective applies very well to imbalances in the allocation of military and

---

4   For the use of the term 'forgotten', see Holm (2002); for 'orphan', Boutros-Ghali (1996); for 'third-class', Smillie and Minear (2004); for 'silent', Weiss and Collins (2000); for 'neglected', Bookstein (2003); for 'ignored', Hampson and Malone (2002); and 'hidden', Save the Children (2003).

economic responses, it doesn't quite capture the withholding of attentional resources over such conflicts in the agendas of a wider set of actors.

Calling a conflict 'silent' seems to put the onus for being noticed on the conflicts themselves, such that it appears that such conflicts fail to attract attention because they are inherently silent, whereas conflicts that attract attention are inherently loud or noisy. That is, it does not suggest an outside role in the marginalization process. The term 'neglected' certainly conveys the idea that outside parties are responsible for the marginalization of a particular conflict, but it suggests that the conflicts are not noticed out of indifference or carelessness. Like the terms silent and forgotten, it creates the impression that, for some reason or other, the conflicts have simply slipped the minds of those with the power to respond. As will be seen from the discussion below, it can hardly be claimed that this is so in most such cases. 'Ignored' and 'hidden' are terms that better convey the sense that the existence of a conflict is known, and that the denying or withholding of attention and response is therefore something that is done knowingly and consciously. In this sense, they are probably the most appropriate among the terms raised so far.

This study will use the term 'stealth' conflicts to refer to those that do not attract attention or response from the outside world. The term is not necessarily used to suggest that the parties to such conflicts themselves act with stealth, although many do indeed attempt to hide or downplay their involvement (such as Rwanda in the DRC, or Angola in the Republic of Congo). In a way, it can be said that it is the conflicts themselves that act with stealth, appearing inconspicuous but actually causing grave and deadly effects on a grand scale, although this is a somewhat abstract concept, considering that conflicts do not have conscious agency. Perhaps more importantly, the term is used to refer to the actions – hiding, ignoring or downplaying – of those outside actors who have the ability (and/or duty) to respond to conflict, or at least to acknowledge its existence and effects. There are a number of reasons why stealth would seem to describe the state of these conflicts in this sense better than the existing terminology.

Firstly, it conveys the notion that these conflicts are knowingly deprived of attention and response: that it suits the interests of those in a position to respond not to do so. By depriving them of attention, these actors ensure that such conflicts steal along below the range of outside consciousness: unseen, unheard and unchecked, as they extract their deadly tolls. In the case of policymakers, keeping quiet on a conflict may stem from a desire to protect allies and/or strategic or economic interests, while for the media it may be because of an editorial decision that the conflict will not sell well as news, or that it may even hinder sales. There is a wide variety of reasons (which will be explored in later chapters), but for most actors, the failure to respond to major conflicts is not accidental or inadvertent: it is based on a series of deliberate and conscious decisions, which could be interpreted as surreptitious or underhanded. Actors in a position to respond to foreign conflict cannot claim, for example, that they did not know about the existence of conflict in the DRC, or its scale, for that matter. Surveys have provided updates of the death toll there on several occasions, million by million. While it may be somehow understandable that the general public have been unaware of this conflict, given that they are largely at the mercy of the media for information about the outside world (although news of the conflict and its death toll have appeared in the media, however inconspicuously), this claim is hardly sustainable for policymakers, media, relevant NGOs and academia. It is inconceivable that the continued marginalization of a conflict of such magnitude could be construed as accidental or unintentional.

Secondly, the term suggests that the covert or furtive nature of the action is what makes it so effective or 'successful'. This is certainly the case in such conflicts. To a large degree, the world's deadliest conflicts become so deadly precisely because they are marginalized and ignored. The vast majority of the deaths resulting from such conflicts are nonviolent. Death is not by noisy gunshots or explosions, but by the silent factors of starvation and/or preventable and treatable diseases. While the appropriateness and effectiveness of the many forms of attention and response to conflict vary greatly, the more commensurate attention and response are with the scale of the conflict, the greater the chances are, generally speaking, of limiting the extent of (or even stopping) the violence, reducing its adverse social effects, and raising the survivability of those displaced or otherwise affected by the violence. In the absence of attention and response, on the other hand, the silent results of violence are unchecked, and such conflicts typically become exponentially more deadly; thus there is a clear link between the act of choosing to ignore or downplay a conflict, and the level of death and damage that it causes. Disproportionately high levels of nonviolent deaths are usually a tell-tale sign of the lack of attention and response to a particular conflict.

Finally, the use of this term is conceptually useful because of parallels with the current use of the term for military technology. Bombers equipped with stealth technology, for example, are able to remain virtually undetected on radar as they bomb their targets. Like the stealth bomber, stealth conflicts cause considerable amounts of death and destruction, while somehow remaining virtually undetected, in this case on the 'radar screens' – or consciousness – of individuals and institutions in the outside world. In both cases, it is the furtive aspect of the action that enhances the ability to cause the damage and destruction. The radar analogy is already being used in a similar manner by some militaries in their operations. Israel, for example, conducts what are known as 'low signature operations': a term originating from the field of radar, and used in this case to refer to military strikes conducted in such a manner as to be not easily witnessed by the media, and therefore less likely to attract unwanted attention; the operations thus remain 'off the radar' of other actors (Wolfsfeld 2001, 114–115).

Stealth conflicts may not always be that way. Something may happen that facilitates a particular conflict's rise to an intermediate or even a chosen conflict. The protracted conflict in Afghanistan, for example, could have been classified as a stealth conflict for most of the 1990s, with little interest shown in the violence and humanitarian suffering, but following US involvement in the aftermath of the terrorist attacks on the USA in 2001 it rose to prominence as a chosen conflict. But cycles of attention for foreign conflict have a tendency to be short (particularly when key interests are not involved), and so conversely, chosen conflicts may drop off the radar of consciousness and become stealth conflicts, after the so-called 'occasional carnival of charity' has left town and moved on to the next emergency (see Bauman 2001, 148; Coker 2001, 129). Somalia in the early 1990s is the prime example of this situation, where external forces withdrew mid-conflict, leaving that country and its people to solve their own problems of conflict and governance.

Even within conflicts that are able to attract some attention, and in fact even within some chosen conflicts, there may be elements of stealth. The Israeli low signature operations mentioned above are a case in point, but there are many other examples. While operations aimed at achieving 'ethnic cleansing' by Serbs during the Bosnian conflict were treated with considerable concern and outrage in the Western world, Operation Storm conducted by Croatia with similar objectives – one of the largest 'ethnic cleansing' operations in the former Yugoslavia – was given scant attention. When the USA, UK and Australia invaded Iraq, the media meticulously covered the southern prong of the invasion, with hour upon hour of live media coverage broadcast from 'embedded' journalists (embeds) of tanks doing little but driving north, while at the same time the western prong of the invasion was off-limits to these embeds, and the conduct and progress of that part of the invasion was largely hidden from sight.

In a similar vein, policies employed to punish a particular belligerent can lead to the 'disappearance' of a portion of a conflict. Attempts by much of the outside world (including UN agencies) to isolate the UNITA rebels in Angola after 1999 meant that humanitarian aid and even the ability to observe the conflict itself were cut off from most of the territory beyond government control. Thus, 'Without witnesses, the war could unfold at leisure with all the violence "required" or authorized by the two sides. Some 80–90 percent of the territory situated outside the "security perimeters" drawn between 5 and 30 km around government-controlled towns and villages remained beyond the reach of humanitarian organisations' (Messiant 2004, 118). But elements of stealth do not necessarily make stealth conflicts. Stealth conflicts are those whose very existence is absent from the collective consciousness of the key actors in the outside world.

The Context of Stealth Conflicts

Stealth conflicts exist within the context of a world in which some areas are obviously marginalized by the most influential actors in the various groups. Donald Snow (1997) categorizes the world's countries (not necessarily conflicts) as 'First Tier' and 'Second Tier' (with sub-tiers in the Second Tier according to the level of development), and discusses the problem of the marginalization of conflict in the Second Tier in a global system that is dominated by the First Tier. According to Christopher Coker (2001, 115), since the end of the Cold War, which was a 'struggle between communism and capitalism for the high-ground of history', the world is now perceived as being divided into two historical time zones – one for those with a history and a future, and another for those without. Those without are the marginalized, poor: an 'underclass', who at best 'are seen as useless; at worst, threatening' (129). For Stanley Cohen (2001, 293), these populations and their problems are excluded and segregated, forming 'enclaves of losers and redundant populations, living in the modern version of ghettos, remote enough to become "out of sight, out of mind", separated from enclaves of winners'. Hence the line of thinking popularized in the 1990s, 'African solutions for African problems', which appeared to be an attempt to somehow absolve the world outside of Africa from any responsibility of applying humanitarian principles to the humans on that continent (see Weiss and Collins 2000, 157).

In attempts to explain the marginalization of many of the world's conflicts, the term 'triage' sometimes appears. Christopher Coker (2001, 115) notes that 'If one has to limit the occasions on which one intervenes, it is better to fight for those people with a future. That is the logic of triage, of humanitarian warfare.' Susan Moeller (1999, 8) also comments that 'Like emergency-room triage, triage of emergencies does not necessarily mean that the sickest case gets the first and most help. Sometimes the sickest case is the most hopeless case, and receives little more than a Band-Aid of care – just enough so the hemorrhaging is not embarrassing.' Martin Bell lamented that the DRC was the only conflict he knew in which the worse it became, the more it was ignored (BBC World Service 2006). For such countries as these, whose problems 'seem to lie far beyond the pale of assistance and solution', this kind of fatalism 'is convenient for international political expediency. It allows western politicians to shake their heads in pity while keeping a "tragic" and perhaps "intractable" humanitarian crisis firmly at the bottom of the foreign policy priority list' (Slim and Visman 1995, 148).

It is not only a triage of humanitarian aid: it is also a triage of attention and consciousness. It would be difficult to allocate only paltry or token sums of humanitarian aid, designed perhaps to assuage any guilt arising, while at the same time being fully aware of the magnitude of the humanitarian crisis and the suffering that is going on in such large-scale conflicts. There must be some form of implicatory denial; we can get the conflicts out of mind by putting them out of sight, pretending not to know about them. A stealth conflict becomes 'a bit like a tree falling in the middle of a forest. If it falls and no one hears, it's like it never happened' (Moeller 1999, 12). Oddly enough, this seems to hold generally across the spectrum of actors involved in international affairs. While it may be easy to explain why policymakers keep at the bottom of their agendas conflicts that do not threaten their interests, it is less easy to explain why the media, NGOs and academics generally keep the same conflicts at the bottom of their agendas, particularly when they are not supposedly bound by the so-called 'national interest', and instead are based on the lofty principles of universal truth or humanitarianism.

It is equally difficult to explain the phenomenon of stealth conflicts when considering the information and communication technology available and systems in place in this day and age. With jet airplanes, television, fax machines, increasingly portable video recorders, computers, e-mail, the Internet, satellite videophones and all other manner of technological innovations, our ability to gather, process and disseminate any amount of information literally from anywhere in the world, and deliver it, often in real time, to anywhere in the world, is at a level unprecedented in human history. Powerful governments have extensive and hi-tech webs throughout the globe for gathering information, a number of news agencies have a presence in more than one hundred countries, and information on what is going on in almost any part of the world is freely and effortlessly available with just a few clicks of a mouse in the living rooms of most people in the Western world, thanks to the rapidly expanding Internet.

Nevertheless, in reality a chronic lack of consciousness characterizes outside response to most of the world's major conflicts. Despite all of the modern trappings of globalization and communications technology, and an unprecedented level of global awareness, stealth conflicts abound, and many are in danger of being marginalized even in the history books – left out of our collective memories. The following chapters will attempt to discover why this is so. They will first examine the responses of the various actors to foreign conflict, and then analyze the internal dynamics and external influences that can help explain these responses.

Chapter 3

Policymakers

The term 'policymaker' refers here to a wide variety of actors. At a supranational level, it includes international and regional organizations (both the state members and the bureaucracies), particularly the UN and its agencies. At the national level, it includes the executive and legislative branches of government (and at times even the judicial branch), as well as the bureaucracies and even political parties. This chapter will examine how these policymakers have responded to conflict in recent years with the various means at their disposal: statements, diplomacy/mediation, humanitarian aid, sanctions, military intervention and judicial measures. It will then analyze the internal dynamics of this group of actors: the workings and concerns of international organizations, as well as state interests (security and economic) and their reputations. Finally, it will examine how external actors (the media, public and academia) influence policymakers, enabling a better understanding of the responses they choose (or choose not) to make.

Responses to Conflict

Policymakers, when compared to the other actors in international affairs, have at their disposal the broadest range of responses to conflict. They may express through statements their position on a particular foreign conflict, engage in diplomacy and mediation, and provide humanitarian aid to alleviate the suffering by the victims of the conflict. On a more aggressive note, policymakers have the power to impose sanctions on parties to conflict, and even engage in some form of military intervention (or threat thereof), either to enforce a particular course of action or to prevent further violence. They may also use judicial means (usually after the conflict) to bring to justice those perceived to have perpetrated the violence. It can perhaps be said that in some cases, an ideal response to conflict is one that incorporates elements of each of these responses. Statements, diplomacy and mediation serve as both pressure and facilitation for a settlement (as do sanctions on recalcitrant parties), and military intervention, particularly in the form of peacekeeping or peace enforcement, bolsters the implementation of agreements. Bringing to justice the perpetrators most responsible for crimes during the hostilities may deter future perpetrators, although this may ironically discourage some parties from coming to the peace table.

Statements

At the low end of the spectrum, policymakers can make statements, directly to other policymakers, interest groups and parties to conflicts, through the media, or directly to the general population through the publication of policy papers. Through such statements, policymakers can express their dissatisfaction with parties to a conflict, which may serve as pressure on them to implement or refrain from certain actions. Statements may also serve to influence their fellow policymakers or other actors to take note of a situation, and recognize its importance, raising its position on the agenda and encouraging further action. A look at how policymakers express themselves in this way can, to a certain degree, give an indication of the level of importance their institutions attach to certain conflicts.

As the prime body charged with the maintenance of international peace and security, the UN Security Council is an important institution to observe in this regard. Two key forms of Security Council expression are presidential statements (agreed-upon expressions of policy) and resolutions (voted-upon decisions). We have already seen that Africa is host to the vast majority of the world's major conflicts, and accounts for almost 90 percent of the world's conflict-related deaths. Diplomats at the UN have often claimed that the Security Council devotes 70 percent of its work to dealing with African conflicts (anonymous, interviews with the author 1998, 2000), but the output of the Council does not necessarily reflect such a supposedly high priority. Looking at the numbers of presidential statements and resolutions the Council adopted in the 1990s, 25 percent of statements and 32 percent of resolutions were concerning African conflicts (Hawkins 2004, 49–53). In comparison, 19 percent of all resolutions in the 1990s were adopted on matters pertaining to the conflict in the former Yugoslavia alone (not including the later conflict over Kosovo). Compared to the 124 resolutions adopted in the 1990s on the former Yugoslavia, the Council managed to adopt only 10 on Sierra Leone, 7 on Zaire/DRC and 4 on Burundi. Throughout this decade the Council failed to adopt a single resolution on the conflicts in the Sudan, Sri Lanka, and Colombia, among others. This disproportionate situation appeared to improve somewhat in the 2000s (although engagement levels were arguably still noticeably low), with Africa's 'share' of both Council statements and resolutions rising to 45 percent each in the period from 2000 to 2006.

The timeliness of such expressions by the Council can also give an indication of the importance attributed to a conflict. Terrorist attacks aimed at Western targets attract particularly rapid responses. Security Council resolution 1530, in response to the coordinated bombings on Spanish trains in 2004, was adopted within hours of the event – so quickly that it mistakenly held the Basque separatist group responsible (see O'Donnell 2007). Such rapid responses contrast starkly with those for African conflicts. The Council adopted its first resolution six years after fighting broke out in Sierra Leone, two years after in Burundi, and eight months after in the DRC. The government of the DRC complained bitterly about perceived neglect by the Council after being invaded by Rwanda and Uganda in 1998, despite having repeatedly requested the engagement of the Council. The then serving Ambassador of the DRC to the UN, André Mwamba Kapanga, lamented that both the Council and the UN Secretariat seemed to show little interest in this invasion and its humanitarian consequences, as well as in the conflict in Sierra Leone, citing a 'total neglect of the African region', and observing that the Council at the time was 'totally paralysed by the Iraqi problem', with the rest of the world being 'non-existent' (UN Press Briefing 1999).

Still, the numbers of statements and resolutions cannot be taken at face value as a reflection of interest. The Security Council represents a great diversity of views, and expressions are the product of compromise by its members. Veto-wielding members of the Council can block even the discussion of an item in spite of interest by other members, and the content, or value, of resolutions can range from an expression of concern, a mild warning, or a simple extension of the mandate of a peacekeeping operation, to the authorization of comprehensive sanctions, the deployment of a large-scale peacekeeping operation, or the use of all-out force to reverse aggression. Expressions of the Council may be made simply to give the impression of concern. Thus, while the numbers of statements and resolutions can give an idea as to the seriousness of policymakers, looking at the seriousness of the contents of such decisions is also important. As Pierre Schori, the outgoing Secretary-General's Special Representative to Côte d'Ivoire, observed in February 2007, despite 22 resolutions and 20 presidential statements, the peace process in that country was 'still at square one' (UN News Service 2007).

Crucial aspects when judging the content of resolutions include whether or not a threat to the peace has been recognized by the Council, usually by invoking Chapter VII of the UN Charter, and whether or not action (in the form of sanctions or military intervention) has been authorized. The Council failed in the 1990s, for example, to find the existence of a threat to the peace for many of the major conflicts, most notably for the conflict in southern Sudan. Even when it did find the existence of a threat to the peace, this recognition often came up to a year or more after the outbreak of hostilities, and after tens of thousands of lives had been lost. In the same decade, resolutions authorizing some form of action in response to conflict appeared to be lacking proportion. In the 1990s the Council 'was willing to respond at almost the same frequency to minor conflicts as to major conflicts', but at the same time was 'unwilling, or unable, to take action in response to two-thirds of the world's major conflicts' (Hawkins 2004, 64–5).

Expressions by the UN Secretariat, or bureaucracy of the UN, on its internet website can also be revealing. The Kosovo conflict, for example, prompted a special link to the situation in Kosovo from the main page, with vast amounts of information on that conflict, unlike that available for any other conflict. After the air strikes had ended and the UN Mission in Kosovo (UNMIK) was deployed, only the website for UMIK differed from the standard format of all of the other UN missions at the time. It was the only mission page with a cover page (featuring emotive pictures of a crowd of refugees reaching for humanitarian aid) and contained a wealth of information unseen in the others. The UN main homepage, as well as its Peace and Security section, for many years have featured special links to information on the situations in Iraq, the Middle East roadmap, the question of Palestine and terrorism, but rarely any on African conflicts. On the other hand, the choice of the DRC as the destination for UN Secretary-General Ban Ki-Moon's first official overseas visit as Secretary-General also serves as a statement of interest. On the same trip to Africa, he stated that Darfur was on the top of his agenda (BBC News 2007).

Statements by individual states can also give an idea of which situations, conflicts or potential conflicts are considered important to those countries. In 2006, the website of the US Department of State, for example, under the heading of 'Issues and Press' contained links to conflicts and issues in Afghanistan, Darfur, Iran, Iraq, Middle East peace, and North Korea. The USA also named six countries as 'outposts of tyranny' in 2005: Cuba, Myanmar (Burma), North Korea, Iran, Belarus and Zimbabwe – signalling their importance for that country (Kralev 2005). In Australia's Foreign and Trade Policy White Paper (2003), that government identifies terrorism as a key concern, and notes (in separate chapters) the importance of its relations with Asia, the USA, the Pacific and Europe. In a chapter on 'Wider Global Interests', which lists the interests in the other regions of the world, the government notes that security in the Middle East is important to Australia. Africa is the last region mentioned, with Zimbabwe singled out as a cause for deep concern. Another indicator may be the total number of statements released by a government. According to its website, the Ministry of Foreign Affairs of Japan, for example, released a total of 27 statements on the issue of the DRC between 2000 and 2006, while over the same period it released 214 statements on the issue of Palestine. Edward Luck (2001, 198) noted the disparity between the 'soaring rhetoric heard in some capitals' on the conflicts in Kosovo and East Timor and the international community's being 'so reticent to speak out – let alone act – in dozens of other raging conflicts'.

Diplomacy/Mediation

Diplomacy or pressure applied by outside parties in conflict situations is not an easy indicator to examine. Although policymakers may choose to berate parties to conflict, warn of possible repercussions for continued belligerent conduct, or make demands through public diplomacy as part of their response to conflict, diplomacy and mediation designed to change a conflict situation are more often conducted behind the scenes. In fact the success of such diplomacy may well depend upon its being hidden from the scrutiny of the public eye. Parties to a conflict need to be able to effectively communicate with each other without having always to be demonstrating their strong posture to their own side or 'playing to the gallery'. Parties also need to ensure that they can save face when making the inevitable compromises that such negotiations require. Privacy may also be important for mediators who would rather not show their constituencies the deals they are making with warlords or dictators with brutal track records, particularly when peace is given preference over justice.

On the other hand, those engaging in diplomacy and mediation may be more concerned with protecting their own vested interests (or those of a key ally) than the achievement of a lasting conflict resolution, particularly if they are acting as a 'principal' mediator. Principal mediators can use carrots or sticks to make an agreement more attractive to the parties, giving them more leeway to control how the negotiations will end, but such mediators usually have some direct or indirect interest in the conflict. 'Neutral' mediators, on the other hand, rely upon their lack of interest in the conflict to give them the necessary credibility with the parties, but their power is generally limited to enhancing direct interaction between those parties to ensure correct communication between the parties (Princen 1992, 11–31).

Because of the prevalence of behind-the-scenes diplomacy and mediation, it can be difficult to determine to what extent policymakers have been involved in actively responding to conflict using these means. Still, while the contents of the negotiations may be private, the fact that negotiations are being held is not necessarily hidden, particularly when it is prominent policymakers that are serving as the mediators. Conflicts in the Middle East and Europe particularly appear to attract the involvement of such prominent Western policymakers. The US government, for example, routinely engages in direct diplomacy and mediation, at the presidential level, on the issue of Israel-Palestine. The UN Secretary-General personally held negotiations with former Iraqi President Saddam Hussein over the issue of weapons of mass destruction in an attempt to prevent the outbreak of hostilities. The conflicts in the Balkans have also been the object of high-level negotiations by Western policymakers, both in Europe (such as the Rambouillet talks over the conflict in Kosovo) and in the USA (such as the Dayton peace talks over the conflict in Bosnia-Herzegovina).

Such high-profile diplomacy in conflicts outside these regions has been in quite short supply, most notably in Africa, with the guiding principle of 'African solutions for African problems' appearing to apply. Although there may be some support and pressure from external sources, and mid-level Western policymakers are often involved in diplomacy in some form, high-level mediators in African peace processes are almost invariably African. Former Botswana President Quett Masire's role in the peace process in the DRC, and former Tanzanian President Julius Nyerere and later, former South African President Nelson Mandela, in Burundi, are key examples. The AU (as an organization) and standing presidents from Zambia, Nigeria, South Africa and Libya have also tried their hands at mediation in various conflicts on the continent in recent years, including those in the DRC, Côte d'Ivoire and Darfur.

The purpose here is not to suggest patronizingly that mediation from external sources should replace that conducted by African leaders. Although the perceived interests of some African leaders in nearby conflicts may jeopardize their credibility as neutral brokers, the same can be said for many Western would-be mediators (France in Rwanda, for example), and in many cases African mediators may have the advantage of a deeper understanding of the regional politics associated with a particular conflict. It should be noted, however, that the carrots and sticks that Western mediators can bring to bear on parties to conflict in encouraging a settlement are considerably greater than those of their African counterparts, provided that the interests of such mediators do not endanger the process. Nor should the fact be ignored that a considerable amount of historical responsibility for factors leading to many such conflicts lies with many of the Western powers.

Nor is it the purpose to suggest that there have been no notable diplomatic initiatives or mediation by Western countries in conflicts beyond Europe and the Middle East. France, for example, took the lead in negotiating a settlement between the government and key rebel groups from Côte d'Ivoire in Marcoussis in 2003, albeit one that didn't last. The USA played a key role in bringing about a settlement to the conflict in southern Sudan. Although in these cases, mediation was essentially that conducted by 'principals', or parties with some interest in the conflict, Norway has attempted to act as a 'neutral' mediator in brokering peace in Sri Lanka. The UN Secretary-General, together with the US Secretary of State, also visited Darfur in

2004 on a peacemaking mission. But these examples are in many ways exceptions to the rule, with a general trend that shows a lack of serious attempts to engage in diplomacy and mediation in many of the world's major conflicts.

The DRC is a case in point. Although the UK did hold mediation meetings between Uganda and Rwanda when, having together invaded and occupied most of eastern DRC, they fell out over territorial control there and began fighting each other in Kisangani, these were described by Francois Grignon (2003) as 'little more than photo opportunities over cups of tea'. And while the USA did eventually begin to apply some pressure on Rwanda to withdraw its troops from the DRC, this came years after the invasion and occupation. Overall, the response to this conflict by the world outside the continent, particularly the great powers most seriously concerned with Africa (the USA, UK and France), was characterized by a striking 'silence' (ICG 1999, 34), with these countries remaining 'resolutely on the sidelines' (Arnold 2005, 898). Even in the lead-up to the first invasion of the then Zaire in 1996, Vice-President and Defence Minister of Rwanda, Paul Kagame, visited the USA to inform that country of Rwanda's intentions: so that they 'would not be taken by surprise'. According to Kagame, 'Their response was really no response. And yet, I was not disheartened by it' (quoted in Huliaras 2004, 283).

Visits by state officials to countries affected by (or involved in) conflict also serve as a form of diplomacy, even if not accompanied by lengthy and involved mediation attempts, and can also be an indicator of the importance of a particular issue. The US Secretary of State under President Clinton, for example, made 26 visits to the Middle East before visiting any country in Africa. A similar display of priorities was seen when US Secretary of State Condoleezza Rice cancelled a visit to the DRC in July 2007, dropping Africa from a planned overseas trip in order to focus on Iraq and Middle East peace efforts. Had she followed through with the African trip, it would have been the first time in ten years that such a high-level US official had visited the DRC.

It is also important to stress that support for peace agreements after they have been reached is critical. As Fen Osler Hampson (1996, 541) notes, 'Negotiated peace agreements are little more than a road map to the peace process. A settlement indicates the direction the parties must move if they are to consolidate the peace, but it usually does not tell them how to get there except in very general terms.' It is these ambiguities, compromises, and details that are usually brushed over in an attempt to reach a settlement, that are likely to resurface and undermine the implementation of the peace process in the not-so-glamorous implementation phase that comes after the ink has dried on the peace agreement (see also Hoddie and Hartzell 2003). Thus, support for peace settlements, politically, financially and possibly militarily, is a critical follow-up to what may appear to be 'successful' diplomatic activity and mediation in conflict situations.

Humanitarian Aid

Even if policymakers choose not to become involved in mediation efforts or take more aggressive courses of action in response to conflict, there remains the option of providing humanitarian aid to at least alleviate the suffering of the victims of conflict. This response is not designed to achieve conflict resolution and cannot hope to be effective in such a way. In fact it may well serve to exacerbate the conflict. Depending on the nature of the recipients, the control over distribution and the security situation, humanitarian aid can contribute to feeding militants and their supporters (allowing them to continue fighting), it can contribute to the war economy, and even provide legitimacy to militants. According to Sarah Kenyon Lischer (2003, 101), 'impartial and indiscriminate humanitarian assistance becomes a building block for successful rebel movements.' This was seen most clearly in eastern Zaire after the genocide in Rwanda, where militants who had fled from Rwanda were supported by humanitarian aid and used refugee camps as bases for recruiting and strengthening their forces before re-crossing the border to launch attacks on Rwanda (see Terry 2002; 2004). It was also seen in Somalia and Sudan, among other conflict zones.

Setting aside these negative consequences and assuming positive intentions by the donors in the provision of humanitarian aid, the levels of funding for such aid can give an indication of the attention being given to the plight of those affected by conflict. That being said, there are certain obstacles, particularly considering that humanitarian assistance is 'notoriously difficult to track: data is patchy and not easily available; there is no official global calculation of total aid flows; and definitions vary and are inconsistent' (Buchanan-Smith and Randel 2002, 1). Data on humanitarian aid channelled through the UN is readily available, however, and a certain amount of data can also be found on other aid that is channelled by policymakers bilaterally or multilaterally outside the UN system. A cursory look at such data shows enormous contrasts between humanitarian need and humanitarian aid, and between chosen conflicts and stealth conflicts. Given that there is a broad range in the period of conflict (some may start and finish within the space of less than one year, while others may continue for decades), many of the statistics used below examine the amounts of aid given in a single year for ease of comparison.

Humanitarian assistance for complex emergencies that is channelled through the UN system goes through what is known as the Consolidated Appeal Process (CAP), whereby UN agencies provide needs assessments based on which donors (both at state level and individual/organization level) may voluntarily contribute funding for specific appeals among those established through the CAP. The results of such needs assessments (the sum total of the funding requested by the agencies) can be revealing, as seen in Table 3.1.[1] The highest request for funding in a single year since 1999 was that for Iraq in 2003, at over 2 billion US dollars. Although Sudan is second with roughly 1.9 billion US dollars in 2005, it should be noted that this was essentially a response to two conflicts: post-conflict assistance after the peace deal in southern Sudan and the ongoing conflict in the Darfur region. Other chosen conflicts also feature high on the list. In comparison, the highest amount requested for the DRC was 695 million,[2] for Liberia, 145 million, and for Sierra Leone, 126 million.

---

1   All figures on the CAP were obtained through the Financial Tracking System (FTS) maintained by the Office for the Coordination of Humanitarian Affairs (OCHA), and have been rounded off to the nearest million US dollars.

2   It should be noted that some additional aid for the DRC is included in the appeal for the Great Lakes.

The response by donors to these CAP appeals is also revealing. The appeal for the emergency in Lebanon in 2006 received funding reaching 120 percent of that requested, and although the appeal was minimal, the request for Timor-Leste in 2006 attracted 114 percent of the requested amount. Usually, however, such requests end up with a shortfall, to varying degrees. Despite an extraordinarily high request for Iraq, the appeal in 2003 was still funded at 91 percent. Looking at the total amounts requested and those actually received through the CAP over the period from 1999 to 2006, a number of appeals for emergencies were funded at less than half of that requested, including: Republic of Congo (34 percent), Central African Republic (47 percent), Burundi (47 percent) and Côte d'Ivoire (48 percent). Funding of the appeal for the DRC was at 54 percent.

Overall regional comparisons can also give an idea of the proportionality of humanitarian aid. In 1999 the CAP attracted more donor funds in response to complex emergencies for south-eastern Europe than it did for the entire African continent. The Table 3.2 compares the humanitarian aid distributed through the CAP in the Great Lakes region in Africa with that in the Balkans in Europe during a period of ten years from 1993 to 2002. The aid for the Great Lakes region included responses to the genocide in Rwanda, both multinational conflicts in Zaire/DRC, as well as long-running conflicts in Burundi and Uganda, while for the Balkans it was primarily the response to conflict in Bosnia and in Kosovo. The former group of conflicts cost the lives of almost 7 million, compared to roughly 70,000 in the latter

Table 3.1   Some emergency humanitarian aid requests: 1999–2006 ($US millions)*

Emergency	Average yearly amount requested (1999–2006)	No. of years requested	Max. amount requested in a single year	Year	Percentage of requests met
Iraq	2,223	1	2,223	2003	91%
Afghanistan	947	2	1,781	2002	66%
Sudan	669	8	1,910	2005	65%
S.E. Europe	546	4	929	1999	68%
Occupied Palestine	323	4	395	2006	64%
Angola	225	6	314	2003	63%
DRC	213	8	695	2006	54%
East Timor	199	1	199	1999	52%
Ethiopia-Eritrea	184	5	384	2001	57%
Great Lakes	142	8	292	2000	84%
Sierra Leone	70	6	126	2003	73%

* Includes only aid requested and received through the CAP

Data source: OCHA FTS

Table 3.2   **Aid received by the Great Lakes Region and Balkans: 1993–2002 ($US millions)***

The Great Lakes Region		The Balkans	
Great Lakes**	2,799	Former Yugoslavia	4,092
DRC	197	S.E. Europe	1,504
Burundi	143		
Uganda	95		
Rwanda	52		
TOTAL	**3,286**	TOTAL	**5,596**

* Total aid (including aid within and outside of the CAP)
** Includes Central Africa for 2000–2002
Data source: OCHA FTS

group. Yet the aid for the latter group far exceeds that for the former. Even if we include the four years beyond 2002 when aid for the DRC increased significantly, the total still does not reach that of the Balkan aid.

But aid channelled through the UN by no means accounts for all of the aid distributed by policymakers in response to conflict, and depending on the emergency, a large proportion of the total amount of aid may be provided bilaterally or by a group of nations outside the UN system. In most cases, the gap between chosen conflicts and stealth conflicts becomes even more pronounced when figures include the total amount of aid also provided outside the appeals.[3] Iraq received more than 3 billion US dollars in a single year, while Afghanistan, Sudan and south-eastern Europe (Kosovo) were also each able to attract more than 1 billion US dollars in a single year. The most the DRC received in a single year was 497 million US dollars (2007),[4] which was less than that received in a single year for the Occupied Palestinian territories (666 million in 2001), and that for Lebanon (526 million in 2006). Total humanitarian aid since 1999 for conflicts in Ethiopia-Eritrea, Liberia, Sierra Leone and Burundi failed to reach 150 million US dollars, even in the outside world's most generous years.

Equally as important as the amount that is raised in response to a particular conflict, is the timing of that aid. In too many cases, it would appear that humanitarian aid reaches significant levels only as the conflict subsides, with minimal levels of aid reaching the victims of conflict during years of protracted conflict. For the DRC, for example, 1999 and 2000 were two of the most deadly years of its conflict with a

---

3   The source of the figures provided here is the OCHA FTS, and includes all information provided to OCHA by donors and appealing agencies. The figures include only those from states, coalitions of states and international organizations, not private individuals or organizations.

4   It should be noted that some additional aid for the DRC is included in the appeal for the Great Lakes.

death toll well beyond one million, yet in those years it managed to attract only 12 and 27 million US dollars respectively, in humanitarian aid. In contrast, East Timor in 1999 received 157 million dollars in response to post-election violence resulting in roughly one thousand deaths. For Angola, which had managed to attract a moderate amount of aid throughout its conflict, its historic peace process in 2002 still managed to attract a rise in aid to only 260 million US dollars in that year. This was not the case in the former Yugoslavia, with a consistently high level of humanitarian aid being supplied throughout the conflict. Changes in the nature of the conflict may also change the conditions for aid. Humanitarian aid to Afghanistan, for example, was minimal during its internal violence in the 1990s, but it jumped following the foreign involvement in 2001.

Looking at such responses of individual countries to conflict can also make for interesting comparisons. The physical and attributional proximity of a donor appears to play a large role in the distribution of aid. Although the USA and European countries have a global reach in their humanitarian aid provision, they focus largely on conflicts occurring in Europe and the Middle East. According to Ian Smillie and Larry Minear (2004, 138–9), for example, 'German ties to Kosovo were so multifaceted and the scale of its military and economic assistance – bilateral and multilateral – so massive that some Kosovars viewed Bonn rather than Pristina as the country's capital.' Japan and Australia focus their attention on conflicts in Asia to a large extent. Middle Eastern countries such as Saudi Arabia, United Arab Emirates and Kuwait have made sizeable contributions of aid in response to conflicts in the Middle East, but little to other conflict situations.

But aid is not only regionally focused. Some countries make large contributions to the victims of conflict in areas that are distant both physically and attributionally. African conflicts, however, are usually not the major beneficiaries of such aid. According to the statistics provided by the FTS on total humanitarian aid, in 1999 Japan provided 89 million US dollars in humanitarian aid to south-eastern Europe in response to the Kosovo intervention – three times as much as it did in response to all of the conflicts in Africa combined. In 2004 Japan provided almost twice as much aid to the Occupied Palestinian Territories (20 million) as it did to the DRC and the Great Lakes combined. Countries such as UK, Denmark, Sweden, Germany, Canada, Ireland and Italy, countries on the other side of the world from East Timor, and with negligible historical or economic interests there, nevertheless all gave significantly more aid to that conflict in six months (1999–2000) than they did in response to conflict in the DRC in one year (2000).

However we choose to dissect, assemble and present the statistics for humanitarian aid (and there are any number of ways that this can be done), by the very fact that in many major conflicts more than 90 percent of conflict-related deaths are nonviolent deaths caused by hunger and disease, with the numbers of these deaths in the millions even in some single conflicts, we can easily conclude that humanitarian aid is horribly inadequate for these conflicts. And when the levels of aid in response to certain conflicts far outweigh those to conflicts with much larger death tolls and humanitarian suffering, we can also easily conclude that something is not quite humanitarian about humanitarian aid.

Sanctions

A more aggressive measure is the use of economic or diplomatic sanctions to coerce belligerent parties into ending conflict, and their application can provide an indication of the seriousness of the response of policymakers to conflict. Sanctions may range from travel bans against those in key leadership positions and bans on participation in international sporting events, to weapons bans and even comprehensive trade bans. This may be done unilaterally, or as a globally coordinated measure based on a UN Security Council resolution. It may be directed at a state or a party to a conflict within a state. Particularly in light of the massive humanitarian damage caused by the more than decade-long comprehensive trade ban on Iraq, a considerable amount of work has been done aimed at enhancing the targeted or 'smart' nature of sanctions: those that are able to 'hurt' the leadership of certain states or groups, encouraging or discouraging certain behaviour, without causing harm to the innocent population (see Watson Institute 2006; Weiss 1999).

While there are still many challenges in establishing and maintaining effective targeted sanctions (see Mack and Khan 2000), and while it is generally thought that they are genuinely effective only when powerful countries take serious measures to ensure their application and enforcement (see Cortright and Lopez 2000; Rogers 1996), the broader effect of sanctions also needs to be taken into consideration when examining their applicability and effectiveness. Sanctions may be better suited to containment rather than forcing a change in behaviour, and they may also be effective by their very application: as a show of solidarity against a type of behaviour, and as a form of stigmatization against the party in question, thereby also serving as a deterrent to others (Mack and Khan 2000, 285–6). In any case, an arms embargo may be a logical first step in response to armed conflict.

Since the end of the Cold War, the UN Security Council has applied sanctions in response to issues in Iraq-Kuwait, Somalia, Libya, the former Yugoslavia, Angola, Rwanda, Liberia, Kosovo, Sierra Leone, Sudan, Afghanistan, Ethiopia-Eritrea, DRC, the Democratic People's Republic of Korea (DPRK), Lebanon and Iran, as well as to terrorist groups. Arms sanctions are included in most of the sanctions applied to conflict situations, but there is also a range of increasingly targeted measures included in some sanctions regimes, including bans on travel and the freezing of the assets of key policymakers, and on trade in rough diamonds (in Liberia and Côte d'Ivoire), and timber products (in Liberia). Simply to look at the list above, it would appear that many of the most deadly conflicts in recent years were covered by sanctions at some point.

Yet the sanctions listed above against Sudan (southern) and Afghanistan, were not applied because of the major conflicts in those countries (in the case of southern Sudan, conflict that led to the loss of more than two million lives). In these cases they were applied over non-conflict issues (albeit issues that could potentially lead to broader conflicts): because of the failure of the authorities in those countries to extradite suspects in an attempted assassination and in terrorist acts. Ironically, the Council passed resolutions citing the refusal to hand over these suspects as constituting threats to international peace and security, while at the same time finding no such threat from, and being completely unresponsive to, large-scale conflicts ongoing in those countries. Similarly, sanctions were applied over non-conflict issues in the case of the assassination of the former prime minister of Lebanon, Rafiq Hariri, and over nuclear programs in DPRK and Iran. On the other hand, there were also numerous other major conflicts for which UN sanctions were never applied, including conflicts with death tolls of about 300,000 (Zaire and Burundi), about 100,000 (Algeria and Chechnya), and about 50,000 (Kashmir, Colombia, Sri Lanka and Tajikistan).

As with other responses to conflict, the timing of the application of sanctions (when they were applied) can be indicative of the seriousness of the response. Sanctions were applied over Kosovo roughly one month after the start of open conflict, in Lebanon roughly two months after the outbreak of hostilities with Israel, as they were against elements in Iraq also roughly two months after the invasion of that country (at the same time as the old sanctions regime was dismantled). The response was even more rapid for some non-conflict issues. Sanctions were applied on the DPRK six days after the nuclear test in that country, and to those implicated in the assassination of Lebanon's Hariri roughly twenty days after the report of the investigation into the assassination was published. In contrast, sanctions were applied over the conflicts in Côte d'Ivoire and Ethiopia-Eritrea roughly two years after the conflicts erupted, and in Sierra Leone and the DRC, sanctions were applied five years after conflict began in those countries. In the case of the DRC, the arms sanctions did not extend to cover Rwanda and Uganda, despite the fact that these were the countries that had invaded and occupied that country, and that continued to support the rebel groups there.

Individual countries (or groups of countries) may also choose to impose sanctions on parties to conflict. Such sanctions may be imposed by the executive or legislative branches of government, or even at the state level in some cases. This is particularly the case when those countries are unable to convince the UN Security Council to apply sanctions to certain countries or parties to conflict. The USA and the EU have imposed a broad variety of trade sanctions against countries and groups involved in conflict, most notably against terrorist groups. They have also imposed sanctions against Sudan and Myanmar, although the latter appeared to be more over the issue of democracy than other internal conflicts in that country. The EU did impose its own sanctions against the DRC prior to the UN Security Council in October 2002, but this was still roughly four years after the conflict began. Although it was not a conflict situation, the EU imposed sanctions against Zimbabwe, as did Australia. These countries, together with Japan (among other countries), also imposed sanctions against Yugoslavia over the issue of Kosovo, and the DPRK over its ballistic missile and nuclear programs. Within Africa, some countries and coalitions imposed their own sanctions in conflict situations; ECOWAS, for example, imposed its own sanctions on Sierra Leone and Liberia. A number of neighbouring countries imposed their own sanctions on Burundi following the *coup d'état* in that country.

Military Intervention

Military intervention is the most extreme or serious form of response to conflict, but its application can vary greatly in strength and determination, and it may often be, in effect, a response to peace rather than to conflict. It may range from the dispatching of observers to monitor a ceasefire to all-out offensive action to overturn an action by a party, with other forms of intervention (peacekeeping and peace enforcement) falling somewhere in between. Shades of peacekeeping and peace enforcement (or peace support operations) became frequently used responses to conflict in the aftermath of the Cold War, sparking considerable debate over their application, and development in both doctrine and implementation. While their use waned in the mid to late 1990s, the number of missions and troops increased considerably once again in the 2000s. Needless to say, there were numerous conflict and post-conflict situations in which no external peacekeeping, peace enforcement or any other form of stabilization interventions were attempted at all, including those in Zaire, Republic of Congo, Uganda, Sri Lanka, Kashmir and Colombia.

Peacekeeping was originally intended as a confidence-building measure, and peacekeepers positioned themselves between two clearly defined adversaries, with the solid consent of both parties. They were typically lightly armed and their greatest assets were their neutrality and the fact that they would not use force. Such measures were adopted under what was colloquially called 'Chapter VI-and-a-half' of the UN Charter, because peacekeeping is not specifically provided for in the Charter: Chapter VI of the UN Charter regulates peacemaking and other measures for peacefully resolving conflicts, while Chapter VII deals with more robust responses (sanctions and interventions) to threats and breaches of the peace and acts of aggression. In the post-Cold War world, peacekeepers were more often than not being sent into situations where adversaries, front lines and consent were unclear. That is, peacekeepers were being sent where there was little peace to keep. This was seen in Somalia, Bosnia and Rwanda, and later in Sierra Leone and the DRC.

Peacekeeping in its traditional sense was ill-suited for such situations, and stronger measures, which came to be known as 'robust peacekeeping' or 'peace enforcement' began to be introduced into mandates for intervention forces (under Chapter VII of the UN Charter). This meant that the intervening group would use their force strength and the threat of force (but limited actual use of force) as a tool to deter aggressors and spoilers and maintain peace. Robust peacekeeping generally referred to cases in which forces were able to use force to defend themselves, their freedom of movement, and often civilians under direct threat of violence. Peace enforcement was stronger, and such forces were permitted to use any necessary means to uphold the mandate under which they were operating, although the credible threat of such action was considered more critical to the success of the mission than the actual use of force (see Malan 1998; Daniel, Hayes and Oudraat 1999). The authorization of all-out force (essentially war-fighting) to overturn the status quo (or restore a violated status quo) has been authorized only twice by the Security Council since the end of the Cold War: against Iraq over its invasion and occupation of Kuwait, and against Haiti to eject the military dictatorship.

Forces authorized by the Security Council to respond to conflict through peacekeeping, robust peacekeeping or peace enforcement came to be divided into those sub-contracted to member states of the UN for implementation, and those conducted under the command of the UN Secretariat (so-called blue helmets). The result has been, to a large extent, two standards or grades of intervention: one for which highly trained troops and abundant resources, equipment and logistics are supplied; and the other, lacking resources, equipment and logistics, and struggling to cobble together adequate numbers of trained forces. Some operations for which authority has been delegated to member states also fall under the second category of operations: namely those conducted by African coalitions.

The first category of peace support operations consists primarily of those in which Western countries participate, which are almost invariably under strong peace enforcement mandates, under Western state leadership, and usually built to ensure overwhelming force superiority over any possible adversary, particularly after bitter experiences in the early 1990s by the USA in Somalia (the loss of 18 troops in a raid gone awry), Belgium in Rwanda (the loss of 10 troops guarding the Prime Minister during the genocide), and the EU in Bosnia (troops taken hostage and used as human shields to protect installations). Troop levels in such operations are high, and are maintained years after the conclusion of hostilities to ensure a smooth transition to a state of stability and peace. Troop levels in Bosnia, for example, reached 54,000; in Kosovo, 50,000; in Afghanistan, 32,000; and in Haiti, 25,000. The troops in such operations are highly trained, adequately armed, equipped and supplied, and backed by abundant intelligence and logistical support. In many cases, ensuring the safety of the troops themselves is ironically one of the highest priorities of the mission.

Since the exit-under-fire of Western forces from Somalia in 1993–94, no such robust, long-term Western-led peace enforcement operations have been deployed in response to conflict situations in Africa. A Canadian-US force was planned and authorised to intervene in eastern Zaire in 1997, but was cancelled when Rwanda pre-emptively invaded Zaire (see Massey 1998). A number of peace enforcement missions led by Western forces have deployed in response to conflict in Africa, but they have been small scale and short term and with a clear fear of commitment in their deployment, despite their effectiveness. Those sending troops appear to be almost afraid to set foot on the continent at all, and once they have, are eager to show that they will not stay there long.

France's involvement in Côte d'Ivoire is one possible exception (but only in the sense that it is a long-term deployment), with 2,500 troops positioned, together with UN peacekeepers, in the capital and between government and rebel forces. The UK deployed a small force (1,000 that was later increased to 1,500) to Sierra Leone in 2000, initially to rescue Commonwealth citizens, but it went on to play a decisive role in repulsing RUF offensives and securing Freetown. In 2003, a 1,400-strong EU force served as a three-month stopgap force in the town of Bunia in the DRC to allow UN peacekeeping reinforcements to arrive as massacres were increasingly described as genocidal. A small EU force was also provided for security in Kinshasa during the DRC's 2006 elections, but most of the troops were stationed outside the DRC, and only 130 combat troops were available in Kinshasa for intervention. Reinforcements were sent when violence broke out, but they arrived after the violence had subsided (ICG 2006, 4–5). In the case of Liberia in 2003, US troops were stationed off the coast of Liberia, ready for the possibility of intervening as violence consumed the capital, but did not deploy. Residents of Monrovia expressed their displeasure at the failure of the USA to intervene in their plight by piling the bodies of those killed in the conflict outside the US Embassy (Campbell 2004, 221–2).

The doctrine of African solutions for African problems has led to a number of African attempts to engage in the resolution of conflict situations, but such interventions almost invariably fall short in terms of the availability of the resources required to perform such operations, as well as the capacity to move, sustain and support troops in the field, and are likely to rely upon the airlift and logistical support of Western countries to realize these interventions (see Rothchild 1997, 279–80). In fact, there are only a select few countries in the world that possess the logistical capacity for sustaining large-scale military interventions, and the USA stands far above all others in this regard.

ECOWAS has attempted a number of interventions, most notably in the cases of Liberia and Sierra Leone, but in these cases it relied upon some rear support from the USA and the UK respectively. Both missions were hampered nonetheless by logistical problems, and the Security Council gave its blessing to these missions only after they had already occurred. When a number of neighbouring countries answered the call from DRC President Laurent Kabila to defend his country against the invasion by Rwanda and Uganda, Namibia sent its contribution of troops by train across Angola – a journey of thousands of kilometres. Logistics has been a key challenge in the AU intervention in Darfur, with the entire budget for the operation being borne by external donors, without which it was feared that the operation would 'grind to a halt' (Appiah-Mensah 2005, 17). African operations also struggle in terms of troop contributions, as seen in the inability of the AU to find sufficient troop contributors even for a relatively small peacekeeping force for Somalia in the aftermath of the Ethiopian intervention there in 2006; at the AU summit in January 2007, African countries managed to pledge only 4,000 troops for a force for Somalia: half the number required.

Regardless of the motives of the parties that implement this type of strong intervention, the more aggressive in nature it is, the more difficult it can be to distinguish one implemented supposedly in response to conflict (meaning to stop it) from the beginning of a separate conflict, or from the joining of new parties in continuing the original conflict. This is particularly the case when the death toll following the interventions is greater than that preceding the intervention. The intervention of ECOWAS in Liberia in the 1990s is one such example. Although the intention had been to intervene as peacekeepers, they came under fire upon arrival, and soon became a separate party to the conflict, adopting conventional offensive strategies (Ero 1995). The intervention of NATO in Kosovo is another example. Ostensibly the intervention was intended to stop the already ongoing conflict that had cost approximately 2,000 lives, but it consisted solely of large-scale aerial bombardment, exacerbating the conflict and displacement of the population, possibly costing an additional 8,000 lives. NATO's Commanding General, Wesley Clark, admitted that the intervention had not been designed to block Serb 'ethnic cleansing' (quoted in N. Chomsky 1999, 36).

The other standard of peace support operations (usually under UN Secretariat command) generally consists of operations under robust peacekeeping (or grey area) mandates, not the stronger peace enforcement variety. Such operations are composed of troops primarily from developing countries who are often inadequately trained, equipped and supplied. The willingness of UN member states to contribute troops, supplies and logistics to such forces is often weak, and the UN Secretary-General is often forced to go door-to-door to member states to plead for contributions. The result is that, despite being endowed with a relatively strengthened mandate on paper, forces are rarely provided with adequate means to carry it out. Even with the mandate to protect their mission, their freedom of movement, and to protect civilians in immediate danger, the fact that forces generally lack the adequate strength, weaponry and logistics to realistically fulfil it, means that mandates are largely reinterpreted by the force commander and rules of engagement adjusted to a level more commensurate with the means actually available (see Wallace 1998; Hawkins 2004). The interpretation and execution of mandates also depend largely on the situation on the ground and can be quite fluid and flexible.

The force numbers authorized and provided for such missions are usually much lower than those for the first category of operations. The authorized strength of the military components of recent peacekeeping forces at their strongest is as follows: Darfur, 19,500; Sierra Leone, 17,500; DRC, 16,700; in Lebanon, 15,000; in Liberia, 15,000; Southern Sudan, 10,000; Côte d'Ivoire, 9,000; and Burundi, 5,700.[5] None of these forces reaches the size of the force authorized even for the relatively small country of Haiti in 1994, much less those for Kosovo or Bosnia. The force strength for the DRC (a country roughly the size of Western Europe) is revealing in this regard, with troops spread thinly over vast distances and often with considerable logistical difficulties. Even comparing numbers among UN-led missions, the forces in the DRC are roughly comparable to those authorized for Lebanon, a country that is tiny in comparison. The determination of these force sizes is usually the result of what Thomas Weiss calls 'mission cringe' (2001, 425), based on dangerously optimistic assessments of the situation on the ground. The dangers of the deployment of small numbers of troops (often ill-equipped and inadequately trained) into potentially hostile areas in this way were revealed in the capture of 500 peacekeepers by rebels in Sierra Leone, and in the inability of peacekeepers to quell large-scale violence in Bunia in the DRC, leading to the deployment of the stopgap EU force in that town, followed by an expanded UN force.

There are factors other than the authorized strength of the force that are indicative of interest in resolving a conflict. The timing of the authorization of the force and its deployment is also critical. After the outbreak of violence following elections in East Timor in 1999, for example, a peace enforcement operation (with a strength of 9,900) was authorized in just two weeks, and the Australian-led force began arriving five days after that. A 14,000-strong peacekeeping force arrived soon after a truce was reached in the former Yugoslavia (in what became independent Croatia) in January 1992, was expanded to cover Bosnia, and stayed the course of the conflict. The Dayton Agreement, which ended hostilities in Bosnia, was immediately followed by the deployment of the international Implementation Force (IFOR). Similarly, a ceasefire

---

5   The respective missions are: the UN-AU Mission in Darfur (UNAMID), the UN Mission in Sierra Leone (UNAMSIL), the UN Organization Mission in the Democratic Republic of the Congo (MONUC), the UN Interim Force in Lebanon (UNIFIL), the UN Mission in Liberia (UNMIL), the UN Mission in the Sudan (UNMIS), the UN Operation in Côte d'Ivoire (UNOCI) and the UN Operation in Burundi (ONUB).

to conflict in Lebanon immediately saw the peacekeeping force there upgraded to 15,000 in 2006. The rapid deployment of large-scale forces after ceasefires was also seen in Kosovo, Afghanistan and Iraq, although in these cases those deploying the forces were primarily led by belligerents in the conflicts.

By comparison, in conflict situations in Africa that did elicit a military response from the UN Security Council, it was usually a case of too little, too late. The conflict in Burundi, for example, could be characterized as on-off, yet no stabilization forces were authorized even in the relative calm of the off phases, to bolster ceasefire arrangements and peace and power-sharing agreements that were reached, much less as large-scale massacres were occurring. The small peacekeeping force was approved only in 2004: some eleven years after the conflict began. In the DRC, a peace agreement reached in Lusaka saw the authorization of 500 peace monitors in November 1999, more than one year after hostilities began. With security concerns preventing the monitors from doing their job, the deployment of roughly 5,000 peacekeepers specifically to protect these monitors was authorized in February 2000, but their deployment was also delayed by a full year. Further expansions of the force were authorized in December 2002, July 2003 and October 2004, but deployment was characterized again by delays. When the enlargement of the peacekeeping force in Sierra Leone to a record 17,500 was authorized in 2001 (years after the worst violence had been perpetrated), it took eight months for it to reach full strength.

The UN Assistance Mission for Rwanda (UNAMIR) is a classic example of an operation deprived of the means to do the job for which it was established. Force commander Romeo Dallaire lamented the meagre resources provided for the mission by the UN member states. He recalled that the initial planning for the mission was done without an office, with borrowed laptop computers and using a tourist map of Rwanda (2003, 55), and that because countries were unwilling to re-supply ammunition, during the genocide the force would only be able to sustain a fight of three or four minutes, after which it would be 'reduced to throwing rocks' (215). Vehicles, communications equipment and supplies in general were horribly inadequate, and much of what little did arrive in terms of equipment was either broken on arrival, lacking spare parts, or otherwise virtually unusable for any sustained activity (106–7, 203 and 331–2). Nor were countries with vital intelligence regarding the situation on the ground (namely France, the USA and Belgium) willing to supply any to the mission. The initial response of the Security Council to the outbreak of the genocide was not to strengthen the small force, but to reduce the number of troops to a mere skeleton force of 250. Troop levels were later increased, but when the troops finally arrived, six months had already elapsed since the end of the genocide, and they were no longer needed.

This situation has improved somewhat since that time, with strengthened capacity in the UN headquarters to conduct such operations, and the stockpiling of equipment,[6] but such blue helmet forces remain logistically weak, and, according to former UN Secretary-General Kofi Annan, the UN remains the only fire brigade that must go out

---

6 A number of improvements were made on the basis of the recommendations of the Report of the Panel on United Nations Peacekeeping Operations (UN Document 2000), or the so-called Brahimi Report, although many remain unrealized.

and buy a fire engine before it can respond to an emergency (quoted in *Economist* 2007, 21). Furthermore, the situation remains in which peace support operations can be divided into two classes, and in which there is a 'division of labour' for such operations, with Western countries contributing their well equipped and well trained forces to strong peace enforcement operations in certain locations, and developing countries providing their troops for weaker UN-led operations, usually in Africa. One exception to this trend in UN-led operations is the EU force that is forming the backbone of the strengthened peacekeeping force in Lebanon: the first time large Western forces have joined UN-led peace support operations since the conflict in Bosnia. These troop commitments have been made possible despite sizeable EU deployments in Afghanistan and the Balkans.

Judicial Measures

The International Court of Justice (ICJ) – the principal judicial body of the UN – was established at the inception of the UN. It is responsible for handling disputes between states only, and it may become involved in a dispute only if the states concerned agree to accept its jurisdiction. These two limitations considerably restrict its potential to respond to conflict, particularly in its current forms. The Court has, however, been able to make a number of useful judgements in response to certain conflicts, as well as to potential conflicts. The DRC, for example, brought a case against Uganda to the ICJ for violating its sovereignty when it invaded in 1998, claiming also that Uganda looted natural resources and committed human rights abuses. In 2005, the ICJ found Uganda guilty and ruled that it must pay compensation to the DRC. An ICJ ruling also saw the handing over of the oil-rich Bakassi Peninsular from Nigeria to Cameroon in a border dispute in 2006.

Bringing to justice those individuals that have perpetrated crimes related to conflict is a form of response to conflict that has the potential to serve a number of purposes beyond the punishment of a particular individual for a particular crime. It can assist in ending cultures of impunity for crimes in conflict zones and help deter parties to conflict from committing similar crimes in the future. The existence of some form of judicial measures may also help to break the cycles of violence and revenge that can flourish in the absence of justice. On the other hand, however, culpability in war crimes and the threat of being brought to justice for such crimes may be a disincentive for the leaders of parties to conflict to take the necessary steps towards bringing conflict to a close. Parties to a conflict may choose to continue the fight if the alternative is peace with arrest warrants hanging over the heads of their leaders. Furthermore, it is unrealistic to expect that powerful nations whose leaders have committed such war crimes will allow those leaders to be brought to justice, and any international justice system is likely to be unable to achieve justice in such instances.

Until the establishment of the International Criminal Court (ICC) in 2003, measures pertaining to criminal justice in conflict situations were conducted on an entirely ad hoc basis, and were thus highly selective. Tribunals were set up to deal with crimes perpetrated during specific conflicts only. In the 1990s the only judicial bodies that were established were the International Criminal Tribunal for the former Yugoslavia (ICTY) and its 'poorer cousin' (Berkeley 2001, 248), the International Criminal Tribunal for Rwanda (ICTR). An indictment against former Yugoslav President Slobodan Milosevic represented the first time that an arrest warrant had been issued against a serving head of state. Courts were also set up for East Timor (2002); Sierra Leone (2002) – a joint court involving both the UN and the Sierra Leone government, which eventually saw the indictment of former Liberian President Taylor; Cambodia (2003), where the court was set up to prosecute crimes committed by Khmer Rouge leaders in the 1970s; and Iraq (2005).

With an international criminal justice system dependent on such highly selective ad hoc arrangements, the argument that such tribunals can act as a deterrent to others in conflict situations is quite weak. The establishment of the permanent ICC with a virtually global reach (albeit one that can only prosecute crimes committed after 2002) will undoubtedly serve as a more effective deterrent to potential crime in conflict situations. The effectiveness of the ICC in this regard will, of course, depend on how universal its application of justice is and how it manages to realize the apprehension and prosecution of those it chooses to pursue. Although bringing to justice individuals from the world's more powerful states will remain beyond its jurisdiction, early signs of the work of the ICC appear positive in some ways. The first indictment filed by prosecutors at the ICC was against a warlord in the DRC, signalling that key players (warlords) in the world's worst conflict are not immune from the law (as they have been). Arrest warrants have also been issued against key leaders of the LRA in Uganda (although this has complicated peace negotiations underway on the conflict there). Furthermore, despite vehement opposition by the USA to its establishment and operation,[7] that country eventually grudgingly accepted the role of the ICC in bringing to justice those responsible for crimes in the conflict in Darfur.

Internal Dynamics

The above discussion on responses by policymakers to conflict appears to confirm that certain conflicts are given comparatively little attention by policymakers, and that the scale and level of humanitarian crisis appear to have little to do with the attention given to a conflict. So how do we explain this apparent lack of interest? While it can easily be said that this situation is caused by a lack of political will, the term 'political will' is considerably more complex than it may at first seem, and requires a more detailed examination. Setting aside, for a moment, the numerous external influences on policymakers, this section will examine the internal political factors affecting the decisions made by policymakers in responding (or not responding) to foreign conflict.

---

7 The USA, for example, accepted a Security Council resolution authorizing the peacekeeping force for Liberia in 2003 (UNMIL) only on the condition that a paragraph be inserted ensuring that US troops would not fall under the jurisdiction of the ICC. In 2004 it blocked for weeks a Security Council statement supporting an international investigation into the massacre of 163 people in Burundi (fearing the move would give legitimacy to the ICC), before finally accepting a compromise (see Reuters 2004).

International Organizations

It is first necessary to look at the internal politics of international organizations (as one group of policymakers): primarily the UN and its agencies. Among all policymakers in the field of international security and peace, it can be said that the UN has the greatest legitimacy, or moral clout. Yet the UN is a conglomeration of a number of organs that are diverse in their nature and in their power structures, rather than a single unified entity under the central control of a particular person or group, a fact that is often misunderstood by casual observers: particularly those observers who would make a scapegoat out of the organization for any perceived failures to prevent conflict and restore peace. On issues of peace and security, the lead organ is the Security Council, whereas the Secretariat, led by the Secretary-General, can be likened to the bureaucracy of the organization as a whole, and is charged with implementing decisions made by the Security Council. While the Secretary-General has the power to bring to the attention of the Council situations of concern, can attempt mediation through his 'good offices', and has a high level of moral authority, the actual power bestowed upon the Secretary-General is minimal.

The Security Council is a political body made up of fifteen member states of the UN: five of which are permanent (or non-elected), and the remaining ten are non-permanent members that are elected according to regional groupings for terms of two years. The decision-making process in the Council involves the forging of a consensus through negotiation and power politics among its members, and the end result (a resolution) is usually a compromise, with the opinions of the most powerful (and/or most interested) being most strongly reflected. The permanent members have the power to veto the adoption of resolutions, statements, and even the placing of an item on the agenda for discussion. Non-permanent members of the Council have less power, and becoming accustomed to the procedures and exertion of influence within the Council can be difficult in the two years available, particularly for those members with small diplomatic representation at the UN. The Council does have a tendency, however, to attempt to adopt resolutions by consensus, which can give non-permanent members greater power, and even countries with small representation can wield influence on certain decisions, depending on their preparation and diplomatic skill.

While any member state of the UN, the Secretary-General or other bodies may bring issues to the attention of the Council, it is up to the members of the Council to decide first whether to include the item on their agenda for discussion or not, and if so, how far the Council will go in response. Without an influential member that is actively interested in a matter raised before the Council and that is willing to 'champion' the cause of that conflict and lead it to high position of priority on the Council agenda, a conflict may not receive significant levels of attention. Discussions and decisions may not happen for months or even years, and the Council's response may end with a statement expressing concern or condemnation, without any action being taken at all. The lack of such an interested party in such a position on the Council has been a major contributing factor to the phenomenon of stealth conflicts where policymakers are concerned. A chosen conflict at its peak can also monopolize Council attention at the expense of most other conflicts, as noted with dismay by the

Ambassador of the DRC to the UN, when his attempts to draw a response from the Council to the invasion of his country failed.

But the lack of statements, resolutions or decisions by the Council on taking action in response to a conflict may not necessarily reflect a lack of interest by the Council or its members. It may be that certain powerful members (usually one or more permanent members with veto power) are too interested to allow the issue to be placed before the Council, even for discussion. The fact that no resolutions were adopted on the conflict in the Sudan in the 1990s, for example, does not necessarily reflect a lack of political interest, but rather a blocking of the item from the agenda by certain powerful veto-wielding members. The same can be said of conflicts in Chechnya, Algeria, Kashmir, Colombia and Sri Lanka, among others. Since 2000, a total of 13 official vetoes have been cast in the Security Council (ten by the USA, two by Russia and one by China),[8] but this is just the tip of the iceberg. Official vetoes are those cast in voting on resolutions in open meetings, and are usually avoided by permanent members of the Council (considering that they are damaging to their reputation) and by the Council in general. Public vetoes are usually only cast when other members bring a draft resolution to a vote in an attempt to force the veto, often to shame the casting member. But the threat of veto (or pocket veto) casts its shadow over the work of the Council at all levels, with the interests of permanent members having to be accommodated throughout the negotiation process until a resolution can be adopted. A simple suggestion by a permanent member that it will not accept something can significantly alter negotiations (see Hawkins 2004, 117–135).

When the Security Council decides to establish a peacekeeping force under the authority of the UN Secretariat, it is the Secretary-General who is responsible for bringing the force together, calling upon member states to pledge troops, equipment and logistics for the mission. Furthermore, while the Secretary-General may make recommendations as to the numbers of troops required for a mission and the mandate of the force, it is the Council that makes the decision. The UN Secretariat is often blamed for the failures and shortcomings of peacekeeping forces, but more often than not, the responsibility for shortcomings lies with the Council that has failed to authorize a sufficient number of troops with an appropriate mandate, and with the member states for not supporting the mission with adequate contributions of troops, equipment and logistical support. The UN Secretariat becomes an easy scapegoat for the general lack of political will among the member states of the UN.

In many ways, the allocation of humanitarian aid is also dominated by the donors (or states), despite the existence of UN agencies such as OCHA, the UN High Commissioner for Refugees (UNHCR) and the World Food Programme (WFP). Donor states provide much of their aid bilaterally, and when providing aid through the UN system, donors tend to 'earmark' their humanitarian aid so that it will go to a specific humanitarian emergency, agency and even project. It has been estimated,

---

8   This count was as of March 2008 (see Global Policy Forum). All vetoes cast by the USA were over draft resolutions on the issue of Israel-Palestine except one, which was concerning the peacekeeping mission in Bosnia and the immunity of US forces from prosecution by the ICC. Both China and Russia vetoed a draft resolution on Myanmar, and Russia also cast a veto on a draft resolution over the issue of Cyprus.

for example, that approximately 85 percent of donor funding to the UNHCR and the WFP is earmarked in this way (Smillie and Minear 2004, 187). The individual UN agencies do conduct their own needs assessment for each complex emergency, and these form the CAP that is presented to the donors, which would appear to give the UN agencies some control over the flow of aid, but to a large degree, the UN agencies are complicit in the favouring of certain high-profile conflicts and the marginalization of most others by the major donors. The Humanitarian Policy Group notes that the so-called needs assessments often play 'only a marginal role in the decision-making of agencies and donors' (Darcy and Hoffman 2003, 8). Because the assessments are used to substantiate a funding request by the agencies, they become largely supply driven, rather than demand (or needs) driven. Donors may also influence the aid process by making their contribution of aid contingent on the appointment of their citizens to positions of influence within an aid agency, or on the use of their own country's companies or NGOs as subcontractors for aid programs (see Smillie and Minear 2004, 167–9).

UN aid agencies are well aware of for which emergencies donors will and won't be willing to donate large sums of money, and adjust their requests accordingly. UN agencies, like any other organization, attach importance to their organizational survival, reputation and prestige, and the attraction of large sums of donor aid for high-profile emergencies can provide a considerable boost to these agencies in this regard. This can also lead to the inflation of requests for such emergencies. Thus the political interests of the donors and the marketing interests of the receiving agencies converge in a mutually beneficial blend, resulting in an 'apparently mutual tendency of agencies and donors to "construct" and "solve" crises' (Darcy and Hoffman 2003, 8), with seemingly little regard for the actual comparative needs of each emergency. It is largely because of these factors that funding requests by UN agencies appear highly disproportionate.

UN agencies may sometimes castigate donors for their failure to produce funds for major emergencies,[9] and may also valiantly push potential donors for funds for such emergencies, but they remain complicit to a large degree in the marginalization of stealth conflicts, as long as their appeals appear to be tailored to the interests of the donors rather than being proportionate to the actual needs of the emergencies, regardless of the realities of the contributions that can be expected. UN agencies may at times attempt to justify these disparities between the reality of needs and the funding available by downplaying the scale of the emergency and/or claiming that there is a lack of resources provided by the donors to adequately deal with the humanitarian needs. This type of response by certain UN agencies was seen in Sierra Leone in times of low donor interest (see Smillie and Minear 2004, 26), and in Angola when the largely unified external response was to isolate areas beyond

---

9   WFP Executive Director, for example, complained of the double standards and the marginalization of African emergencies (UN News Service 2003). UN Children's Fund (UNICEF) Executive Director Carol Bellamy made similar complaints (UN News Service 1999). Accusations of stinginess against the USA by UN Relief Coordinator Jan Egeland in the aftermath of the Indian Ocean Tsunami interestingly appeared to trigger a pledging race by a number of countries to see who could donate the most.

government control, providing neither aid nor witness to these areas (see Messiant 2004, 131).

Some improvements have been seen in recent years in humanitarian aid practices, by the introduction of measures to enhance the quality of decisions on the levels and allocation of humanitarian aid. The appeals for aid for some emergencies are now based on a Humanitarian Action Plan (HAP), which fully involves a broad range of humanitarian actors including the donors, aid agencies, NGOs and the countries themselves in the decision-making process. The use of such a plan was a factor in the tripling of the aid requested through the UN system for the DRC from 2005 to 2006, for example (Oxfam International 2006). Another measure is the introduction of the Central Emergency Relief Fund (CERF) in December 2005, which is a stand-by fund (without earmarks) that is used at the discretion of the Emergency Relief Coordinator on behalf of the UN Secretary-General. With the UN Secretariat, rather than donors, being in control of the fund, it means that conflicts unable to attract the interest of the donors (stealth conflicts) will still be able to attract significant levels of humanitarian aid, and because the funds are kept in advance, the response times to emergencies can improve dramatically. Grant facilities from the fund are possible up to 450 million US dollars. For the year 2007, 51 donors contributed a total 345 million US dollars. Some NGOs have, however, expressed concerns about the effectiveness of these funds, and it remains to be seen how it will improve the aid situation in the long term (IRIN 2006).

States and Security Interests

At the national level, several fundamental internal factors guide the response of policymakers to foreign conflict: most notably physical security (geopolitics), economic security (geoeconomics) and reputation, but also possibly personal friendships or animosities, as well as racial, cultural and/or historical ties (see Spanier and Wendzel 1996). While the sum total of these factors is often described as the 'national interest', the interpretation of such interest may differ considerably depending on the organ of government, as well as the position, affiliation and personal opinions of each individual policymaker. In making the final decisions, the internal factors are weighed by policymakers according to the perceived benefits, costs and risks of a potential course of action or inaction. The decision may reflect a compromise among the positions of various organs and policymakers within even the same government, with the result depending on how powerful each domestic actor is and how strongly it feels about the particular issue in question. Decisions on response are rarely the result of a single factor associated with national interest: they are more likely to be based on a combination of factors.

In terms of physical security, policymakers may be concerned about direct military attacks from foreign entities, the destabilizing effects of neighbouring conflict (or the possibility of being drawn in to that conflict), or the flow of refugees from neighbouring conflicts into their countries. Few countries outside the Western world are in a position to pose a direct military threat to Western countries, and Western vulnerability is low in this regard. Non-state entities, on the other hand, have shown the ability to directly attack Western countries, hence the highly concentrated

Western concern with the variety of terrorism that affects (or potentially affects) their own countries. Western countries are also concerned by conflicts that have the potential to cause waves of refugees to flee to their territories. This factor partially explains the European concern with Balkan conflicts, the US concern with Haiti, and the Australian concern with East Timor. Japan is concerned with the potential conflict on the Korean peninsular partially because of a perceived direct threat from a nuclear DPRK, but also because of the possibility of large-scale refugee flows in the event of a conflict there. Factors other than physical violence and refugees may be included in threat assessments regarding foreign conflicts, such as the involvement of narcotic drugs, which have a destabilizing effect on domestic communities. This helps to explain, for example, the billions of dollars' worth of US military support for the Colombian government (the USA being the primary consumer for Colombian cocaine).

African conflicts, on the other hand, appear to lack such elements of perceived threat for countries outside the continent. The rest of the world (most notably the centres of Western influence) appears to be largely insulated by distance, desert and sea from the physical influence of conflicts in sub-Saharan Africa in particular, although increasingly large numbers of African refugees (many economic refugees) are attempting the dangerous northbound journey to apparent safety and prosperity in Europe. Other African countries are not so insulated, however, and there is an almost invariably international threat and destabilization caused by supposedly internal conflicts within Africa. The prime example is the conflict in the DRC, which drew in military forces from as many as eight foreign countries. Since the threat of terrorism against the West began to take prominence on Western agendas, certain isolated conflicts in Africa, particularly that in largely forgotten Somalia, did, however, begin to spark interest in the threat perceptions of Western countries to a limited degree. This is not necessarily interest that prevents or resolves conflict, however, as it usually involves support for certain parties to conflict, or at least less criticism for governments involved in conflicts or human rights abuse, namely those that support the so-called war on terror. This was seen most dramatically in US support (including direct airstrikes) for an Ethiopian intervention in Somalia in 2006. A softened approach was also seen towards Sudan and Algeria, among others, because of their vocal support against terrorism (Malan 2002).

When discussing the issue of military intervention as a response, the element of practical possibility also needs to be taken into account, regardless of motives. Policymakers may have a desire to respond to conflict with military intervention, but this may not be a practical option, particularly when considering relative military strengths and other associated risks (most notably nuclear capability). No coalition of states, for example, could have intervened to stop the USA and UK from invading Iraq, because they would have been unable to match the military strength of these two countries, and would also have had to consider these countries' possession of nuclear weapons. Similarly, the risk of nuclear war would have made any attempt to intervene in conflict in Chechnya, Russia, impractical. The nuclear issue also makes attempts to intervene in conflict situations in Kashmir and Israel-Palestine impractical, as long as India and Israel respectively (backed by nuclear weapons) refuse to accept any form of intervention. Even in cases where intervention is militarily feasible, it may be rejected because of the perceived costs, risks, or because it is not seen as the most effective form of response.

States and Economic Interests

Economic interests are equally important determinants of responses to conflict at the national level. Access to oil, without which modern economies would be crippled, is the most obvious and frequently cited economic factor in response to conflict. The ability to guarantee access to (and control of) highly productive oilfields in the Middle East is certainly part of the high levels of interest in security issues in that region. Yet economic interest in a particular country does not necessarily translate into interest in, and response to, conflict in that country by policymakers. Conversely, lack of interest in a particular conflict may ironically persist despite economic interest. It is often presumed that African conflicts are ignored because Western countries have no economic interests there, but this is not necessarily the case. The USA imports more crude oil from Africa than it does from the Persian Gulf. Nigeria ranks behind only Saudi Arabia, Mexico, Canada and Venezuela in terms of the volume of US imports of the substance. Yet the growing conflict in the Niger Delta, targeting precisely the foreign-dominated oil industry (resulting in a drop of at least 25 percent in production) because of its perceived exploitation at the expense of the local population and apparent disregard for environmental damage caused, oddly remains comparatively low on the political agenda. Admittedly, the strategic importance of the region is increasingly being recognized by the USA of late, with diplomatic, economic and even military options being pursued to secure its interests there (see Rowell, Marriott and Stockman 2005, 172–207). During its large-scale conflict in the 1990s, Angola accounted for more than 7 percent of US oil imports and this share is now rapidly growing.[10]

Similarly, the DRC is a 'mineral storehouse, some [minerals] quite vital for US industry, and bordering on eight other central African states, the former Zaire holds a geo-strategic position for which the US invested greatly during the Cold War' (Clarke 1998, 73). Coltan for example, is a mineral of vital importance in the production of a number of electronic devices, including mobile phones and computing equipment, and approximately 65 percent of the world's coltan deposits are concentrated in the DRC. Demand for coltan peaked during the early years of the conflict in the DRC, and the struggle for control of its exploitation became a major source of conflict in eastern DRC. Because of shortages in the supply of coltan, the Japanese company Sony was unable to meet the massive demands for its new game console, Play Station 2, in Christmas 2000. In this light, with an economy largely dependent on the production of such electronic devices, it would seem odd that the Japanese government appeared to attach next to no importance to the massive conflict in that country. The diamond industry is also an extremely lucrative industry

---

10 US trade with Africa has been concentrated largely on oil, with South Africa, Nigeria, Angola and Gabon accounting for 80 percent of imports in the 1990s (see Gordon, Miller and Wolpe 1998, 81).

in the West, and diamonds have been closely linked to conflict in Sierra Leone, Angola and the DRC.

Yet economic interest and response to conflict by policymakers are not necessarily so closely linked. Even in the presence of economic interest, the value or benefit of this interest must be weighed against the costs and risks of responding to a conflict. If the perceived costs and risks are too high, a significant response will not occur. This is particularly the case when the conflict appears complex and protracted, and when there are alternative sources or means of obtaining the necessary natural resources, even at a greater cost. The conflict in Burundi was linked in many ways to its coffee industry (Oketch and Polzer 2002), but even without imports from Burundi, the West has many alternative sources of the crop. The perceived benefits of a response to a conflict may be low, even when the economic connection may seem lucrative. As Augusta Muchai (2002, 191) points out, despite recognizing the value of the natural resources in African conflict zones, Western countries 'stand to gain little, however, as long as the resources are controlled by local warlords who only seek to buy East European small arms, rather than capital equipment from Europe and the United States'.

In any case, there may well be means to guarantee access to resources and satisfy the economic interest within the country in question without the need for a response to an associated conflict by policymakers, particularly if the resource is easily extractable. Although rebel groups in the Niger Delta do directly threaten the production and export of Nigerian oil, Angolan oil is mostly offshore and hence the government was able to facilitate unfettered export during the conflict. During the conflict in the DRC, there was an international scramble for natural resources there, facilitated by warlords, foreign governments and foreign multinational corporations; access was made possible in spite of the conflict. The same can be said for diamonds in many African conflict zones. Furthermore, because the chain of supply of certain resources is sometimes quite complex, the effects of conflict on the access may not be so strongly felt by the policymakers on behalf of the corporations that bolster their economies. Coltan, for example, may exchange hands five times or more before reaching the high-tech manufacturers, passing from the miners to companies in the DRC, then to trading companies in Uganda or Rwanda, to processing companies, to tantalum capacitor manufacturers, before finally being bought by the manufacturers of the electronic devices (see Pugh, Cooper and Goodhand 2004, 28–9).

Economic interests may also blend with cultural or linguistic interests, as countries see such ties as a means of maintaining influence and strengthening economic relations. Such concerns may also influence how states respond to conflict. France appears to be particularly sensitive in this regard, and its policies reflect a struggle to protect the influence of its language and its culture against the ever-encroaching influence of the USA and the English language, across the French-speaking African countries in particular. This struggle has also been connected to a perceived threat to exclusive influence over Francophone Africa, as US diplomats have begun exerting pressure on Francophone leaders to sign contracts with American corporations. The French support for the Rwandan Hutu leadership (even during the genocide) was linked to the perceived threat of the rebel Rwandan Patriotic Front, which was comprised of long-term refugees in English-speaking Uganda, many of whom had grown up there (see Gnamo, 2004 90–91). Paul Kagame, who led the rebellion against the Hutus prior to and during the genocide, had been the Chief of Intelligence in Uganda (as a refugee warrior), and had received military training in the USA. French support for the Mobutu regime in Zaire as Kagame's forces invaded that country was also linked to this perceived threat (see Huliaras 2004, 293–8). Military cooperation between the USA and Algeria, aimed at containing terrorism, also 'set alarm bells ringing in Paris' (H. Roberts 2003, 285), and France proceeded to enhance its military ties with that country, against which it had fought a bloody war leading to independence some decades earlier.

States and Reputation

Reputation (how states are seen by their peers) can also be a critical factor in decisions relating to response to conflict by policymakers. National prestige, moral authority, and being seen as acting in accordance with international law and norms, as well as being generous and humanitarian, are forms of power that are generally appreciated by policymakers (see McElroy 1992, 29; Barnett 1998, 95), although sheer economic and military power can make such 'popularity' dispensable to a degree (see Chan 2003). As middle powers without high levels of economic or military clout, Scandinavian countries in particular have attempted to build reputations for developing international norms, peace brokering and high levels of aid (relative to their economic capacity), thereby enhancing their moral authority and diplomatic power (see Ingebritsen 2002).

Peer pressure and a bandwagon effect are a reflection of the role of reputation in international relations. Strong countries may apply pressure to weaker countries to support a policy in response to a certain conflict to which the strong country attaches importance, perhaps by issuing supportive statements, by voting in favour of a draft resolution in the UN Security Council, by providing humanitarian aid, or by contributing troops to a military intervention (even symbolically). Powerful members of the Security Council frequently apply various forms of pressure and persuasion on the weaker members to vote in a certain way. Former French President François Mitterrand apparently agreed to take part in the peacekeeping operation in Somalia in 1992 at least in part because he could not say 'no' to a US request (La Balme 2000, 273). It has also been suggested (although no evidence exists) that Canada offered to lead the aborted operation in Eastern Zaire in 1996 because of US and French pressure (Adelman and Baxter 2004, 263).

Even without explicit pressure from other states for a response to conflict, in the case of a high-profile conflict, the bandwagon effect may come into play, with policymakers feeling that supporting a popular response would enhance their reputation, or conversely, that failure to support such a response could be damaging to their reputation. The large amounts of Japanese humanitarian aid for Kosovo in 1999 (triple that for the entire African continent) can really only be explained as a measure of support for NATO and/or its member states with an expectation of an enhanced reputation and/or political or economic benefits, considering the negligible security or economic interests for Japan and the lack of any racial, religious, cultural or historic ties with that region. Any humanitarian motives are also clearly suspect, considering that the levels of aid were wildly disproportionate to the comparative needs (between Kosovo and Africa). The same can be said of large amounts of Japanese aid for Occupied Palestine, although violence there does affect the price of oil for Japan to a degree. Much of Australia's dogged support for US foreign interventions (both as an apparent response to conflict, and as an instigation of conflict) can be seen in a similar light, linked to expectations of political and/or economic support through enhanced reputation with the USA (see Feizkhah 2004; Armstrong 2003).

This effect also works in the opposite direction, such that in the case of a low-profile conflict, unilateral responses without the support of their peers may seem 'wasted' and out of place, with little expected benefit for responding. Such responses may even be perceived as dangerous if it means that that country may be expected to take the lead in responding to that conflict or to commit further resources in future. There is little incentive for responding if no other states are interested in doing so, and states are only likely to attempt to take the lead and rally support for a response if more important national interests are at stake. Even if states do respond to conflicts because of pressure from other sources, perhaps from UN agencies or non-policymaking actors, the response may stem simply from a desire to be seen 'doing something', when a failure to respond at all could be damaging to that state's reputation. In such a case a response is likely to be a token effort taken largely for appearances. Releasing a public statement, passing a resolution in the Security Council, or giving a minimal amount of humanitarian aid, often serve such a purpose.

In many cases humanitarian aid is seen as a tool to avoid engaging in political (or possibly military) responses aimed at bringing resolution to a conflict: a substitute for action (see A. Roberts 2001, 27–9). States can give the appearance of attaching importance to a conflict (or at least the humanitarian aspects of it), without engaging in any steps to assist in bringing about its conclusion. As Thomas Weiss (2000, 14) notes, 'The well-fed dead in Bosnia prior to Dayton aptly illustrate that a humanitarian veneer can help make collective spinelessness more palatable than collective defense or security.' In the case of the Rwandan refugee crisis in Eastern Zaire, Western states contributed aid in response to cholera outbreaks in the militarized refugee camps (from which attacks on Rwanda were being launched), thereby demonstrating their concern, but 'without committing themselves to the potentially dangerous task of dealing with the *genocidaires*' in a region 'deemed to be outside the foreign policy interests of the wealthier nations' (Terry 2004, 219). In any case, as has already been made clear, humanitarian aid is capable only of alleviating the suffering resulting from conflict, not of resolving the conflict, and in many cases it may conversely exacerbate conflict by serving as a source of supply for militant groups.

Response to conflict can also be related to attempts to restore damaged reputation. Aggressive Western response to conflict in Kosovo was partially related to failures to adequately respond to the conflict in Bosnia. Australian response to conflict in East Timor was partially related to a dubious past in relation to that region, in which Australia had turned a blind eye to large-scale conflict and human rights abuse committed by Indonesian forces in East Timor in the past. Humanitarian aid for refugees from Rwanda and the establishment of an ad hoc tribunal for crimes committed during the genocide were responses related to guilt over a failure to intervene to stop the genocide. Even the lack of response to (or failure to criticize)

Rwanda and Uganda's invasions of Zaire and the DRC can be partially tied to guilt over the Rwandan genocide, particularly as Rwanda claimed its invasions were conducted for the purpose of stopping the *genocidaires* from coming back to threaten Rwanda again: Rwanda was only protecting itself and doing what the outside world had failed to do for it in the past (Otunnu 2004, 49).

Reputations may also be damaged by perceptions of double standards, as Western countries, for example, profess humanitarian motives while responding disproportionately towards conflicts that appear to be related to their own strategic or economic interests. Responding to conflicts beyond these interests is one strategy that is used to deflect such criticism and restore damaged reputation, although such responses are likely to be token and superficial, to provide the appearance of 'doing something'. Concerning the US intervention in Somalia in the early 1990s, former US National Security Adviser, Brent Snowcroft, saw that the West had attracted a reputation for using the UN as an instrument to protect its own interests, and stated: 'Here's a chance to set that record straight. Here's an underdeveloped state, a Muslim state, a black state, and here's a chance to show the world that we are not acting in our self-interest' (quoted in Goldberg 2005). From this perspective, the intervention was calculated to restore damaged reputation. Similarly, responses to conflict in the DRC, Sierra Leone, as well as Ethiopia-Eritrea, appeared to be somewhat strengthened in and beyond 2000, including increases in humanitarian aid and the bolstering of weak peacekeeping forces, as criticism of double standards in the large-scale responses to relatively small-scale conflict in Kosovo and East Timor peaked. Responses to conflicts in Liberia and the DRC appeared to be strengthened again in the aftermath of the invasion of Iraq in 2003, with US forces temporarily and symbolically being stationed off the coast of Liberia.

Just as a failure to intervene militarily may not necessarily be out of a lack of strategic or economic interest, when military intervention is carried out, it may not necessarily be because of such interest. If the option of military intervention can be quick, cheap and painless, with a short and defined mandate, a clear exit strategy, the involvement of a small number of troops, and at a low risk to those intervening, intervention may be considered worth it, even if the interest is not necessarily compelling (Haass 1999, 70). For a relatively low cost, the reputation of the intervening state(s) can be enhanced, and criticisms of double standards can be deflected. The short-term, small-scale 'in-and-out' interventions by the UK in Sierra Leone (although this intervention was indeed effective), by the EU in Bunia, DRC, and in Kinshasa during the election period in the DRC can be seen in this light, as can the cancelled multinational intervention in Eastern Zaire and the US deployment of troops off the coast of Liberia.

Reputation can also function indirectly through the actions of allies. In this sense reputation can serve as a partial explanation for the failure of the West to respond to the Rwandan-Ugandan invasions of Zaire/DRC or to the conflict between Ethiopia and Eritrea. In the late 1990s, the leaders of Uganda, Rwanda and Ethiopia were being hailed as the representatives of a new generation of African leaders signalling the end of strongman politics and leading a so-called 'African renaissance'. Uganda in particular was seen as a success story for the International Financial Institutions (IFIs), a 'model pupil' of structural adjustment programs and other economic measures imposed upon developing countries by the World Bank and International Monetary Fund. The fact that all three key leaders of this supposedly new generation of leaders were participating in conflicts (largely of their own instigation) by the end of the 1990s was potentially damaging for the reputation of their Western backers and for the reputation of the structural adjustment programs. It thus served the interests of the West to remain quiet on the conflicts in which their allies were involved. Ill-gotten gains (namely the looting of natural resources) during its occupation of the DRC also served to improve Uganda's balance of trade and external accounts, which helped 'to keep the IFIs at bay' (Clark 2002, 7; see also Berkeley 2001, 237).

On the other hand, leaders of countries that appear hostile to Western interests can tarnish the reputation of Western countries by their vocal public criticism and attempts to rally anti-Western sentiments. This can also influence Western response to conflict or human rights abuse. Although it may be questionable to describe the violence against white farmers in Zimbabwe, or other limited political violence, as a conflict, Western response to the situation in Zimbabwe serves as a prime example. Although Zimbabwe poses virtually no physical or economic threat to Western interests, Western policymakers frequently single out that country for critical attention. The USA designated the government of President Robert Mugabe as one of the so-called 'outposts of tyranny', and the British Commonwealth imposed economic sanctions on the administration. Justification for such responses was generally humanitarian, despite the incomparable levels of humanitarian suffering in other countries for which response was muted. In imposing its sanctions, Australia (Department of Foreign Affairs and Trade 2002), for example, stated that it could not 'remain unmoved by the tragic situation unfolding in Zimbabwe' caused by human rights abuse and subversion of the rule of law, but it apparently was able to remain relatively unmoved by far greater levels of tragic humanitarian suffering in nearby Angola and the DRC. Nor did the Commonwealth impose sanctions on Uganda, despite its two-time invasion of its neighbour.

Interestingly, one of the world's most radically oppressive dictators, former President of Turkmenistan, Saparmurat Niyazov, who jailed and tortured thousands of political opponents and their relatives, established a personality cult not unlike that in North Korea, and ordered closed all hospitals outside the capital city, escaped serious criticism or even mention by the West. The fact that he had allowed Turkmenistan to be used for NATO bases during their attack on Afghanistan, combined with Turkmenistan's large share of natural gas reserves, in contrast with President Mugabe's vocal railings against the West, and his lack of control over resources, would appear to have been the key factors in determining whether or not a state of 'tyranny' existed, and whether the level of oppression required a response.

Complex Conflicts, Complex Policymaking

Strategic and economic interests and reputation aside, the apparent complexity of a conflict for policymakers may also be a factor that discourages attention or interest. As in the case of other individuals and institutions, the ability of policymakers to comprehend, or frame, the state of conflict in the world, was affected by the end of the Cold War. The apparent decline of the formal state authority and the rise to prominence of warlordism in many conflict zones has made the framing and categorization of conflict, and consequently the understanding of it, problematic. Incidences of terrorism against Western interests have provided policymakers with a new frame for application to some conflicts, but most remain beyond such a frame. As long as the motives (or even identities, for that matter) of an increasing number of participants in conflict cannot be confirmed or understood, and the 'good guys' separated from the 'bad guys', responding to those conflicts remains difficult. As Edward Luck (2001, 211) reminds us, 'Ambiguities breed ambivalence, and this subject is replete with both.' Walter Clarke (1998, 73) suggests, for example, that one of the major reasons for the apparent apathy of the outside world towards central Africa in the mid-1990s was that 'no government knew how to handle problems of such dimensions'. The fact that during the invasion of Zaire by Rwanda and Uganda, the US Ambassador in Zaire denounced the invasion at the same time as the US Ambassador in Rwanda was supporting it, suggests a policy towards the conflict that was confused and lacking in coordination (Otunnu 2004, 57).

As noted above, national governments are not necessarily unified in their perceptions of the 'national interest', and each organ of government may have very different views from the other organs on what is important for the state. The relative power of the ministries of foreign affairs has diminished in recent decades in many Western states, as growing globalization has sparked the entry onto the scene of a number of other government agencies (see Kleistra and Mayer 2001, 387, 396). As a general principle, government branches and agencies seek to preserve and strengthen their powers, resources and influence. According to the bureaucratic politics model, foreign policy choices are the result of bargaining and compromises among government agencies (Kegley and Wittkopf 1999, 62). The level of influence of the various branches of government and government agencies on the overall response to conflict varies according to the political power structure in the country in question, how strongly the branch or agency feels about a particular issue, and how effective they are in projecting their influence. The executive branch in a presidential system, for example, may have more power in decisions on foreign affairs than the executive in a parliamentary system, although in either case this may depend on the strength of the ruling party, and on what resources are required in the response. In any case, acceptability of a response to other policymakers is one factor that is usually considered by decision makers.

The influence of each branch or agency is likely to depend on the response to conflict being considered. While government organs may make statements, for example, considerations are likely to be made of the views of other organs in the interests of a coordinated policy. In terms of the allocation of humanitarian aid, the state-run aid agencies are able to exercise considerable control. The legislative or executive branches of government may be responsible for sanctions, while military intervention is usually under the control of the executive, although the legislative branch of government may be able to influence the executive by controlling the budget allocation. Differences of opinion and struggle for control between ministries can sometimes be seen contributing to a failure to coordinate policy in responding to conflict. In Belgium, for example, differences of opinion and tensions between the Ministry of Foreign Affairs and the Department of Development Cooperation, together with a lack of authoritative conflict analysis capacity, served to hinder the development and execution of response to conflict in Rwanda, Burundi and Zaire in the mid-1990s (see Verwimp and Vanheusden 2004). In the lead-up to the crisis in Rwanda, a split over policy between ministries responsible for foreign affairs and defence was observed in both France and Canada (see Dallaire 2003, 76, 85). As a result, Canada's policy towards Rwanda was comprised of 'only isolated departmental initiatives that in a time of crisis did not come together' (216). Advisers can also have a significant effect on decision makers. A number of studies have shown that negative political advice on otherwise positive policy options was sufficient to prevent decision makers from selecting that option, particularly in the case of military intervention decisions (see Mintz 2004; Redd 2002).

Finally, individual policymakers at various levels may genuinely feel strong indignation for the instigators of conflict and the perpetrators of crimes, together with sympathy for their victims. Such individuals may be the driving force behind isolated departmental initiatives and individual acts in response to conflict, even if such initiatives fail to grow and snowball into larger and more coordinated responses. The efforts of a single US sergeant at the Pentagon, for example, were largely responsible for the loaning of six US armoured personnel carriers to the UN peacekeeping force in Rwanda during the genocide (Dallaire 2003, 331–2), and some US senators made efforts to lobby the US executive over its response to the genocide (372). Similarly, some US senators have been on the frontlines of lobbying efforts for a greater international response to conflict in Darfur. Policymakers may also be motivated by personal friendships with (or animosities towards) policymakers who are involved (or have an interest) in a particular conflict. Race, religion, and/or cultural ties also likely play a role in the decision-making process of policymakers towards conflict, although this may be in part influenced by the constituencies they represent or the source of their campaign funds. Whatever the humanitarian professions of the key policymakers, however, as long as the humanitarian track record is so wildly disproportionate, it is clear that other factors are dominating the decision-making process.

External Influences

Policymakers are not only subject to the influence of other policymakers when determining the level and nature of their response (or lack thereof) to foreign conflict. Other actors in international affairs (the media, the public and academia) also have the capacity to influence the decisions of policymakers to a certain degree, although the influence is usually mutual in many ways. The following section examines the influence of these actors on the policymakers in the formulation of their response to foreign conflict.

Media Influence

There are a number of ways in which the media can influence policymakers in their response to foreign conflict. The media offers information to and requests information from policymakers in a direct manner. As the primary link between the general public and policymakers, the media can influence also through its interpretation and presentation of information. The influence of the media may be related to the position of a conflict on the agenda of the policymakers, which measures are taken in response, and how they are carried out. While critics of the influence of the media on policymakers maintain that the power of the media is exaggerated, they generally admit that the influence certainly exists.

This influence has increased over the past few decades, largely due to advances in information and communication technology that now enable the provision of information about conflicts and responses on a global scale, often in real time. Gone are the days when policymakers could make policy in response to high-profile conflicts outside the watchful glare of the media. Although the US Secretary of Defense at the time of the Cuban Missile Crisis, Robert McNamara, claimed that he did not turn on the television even once during the two weeks of that crisis (Moeller 1999, 225), such a situation is inconceivable in today's world. News and information from multiple television channels are closely monitored in real time by all of the relevant branches of government, particularly during conflicts that are considered to be of concern in terms of the interests of the state in question. The so-called 'silent room' outside the UN Security Council chambers and the room used for informal consultations, where diplomats take breaks and wait for the results of deliberations by the Council, is no longer so silent, with a television (usually tuned to a news channel) keeping the diplomats informed and entertained. Televisions are also installed in various strategic locations around the UN buildings, and groups of policymakers can be found huddled around them when news of interest to them breaks.

As the above examples demonstrate, the media has the power to influence policymakers, in the sense that it communicates directly with them. Like other individuals, policymakers are consumers of news. Watching the news on television or reading the newspapers becomes connected to their work, and it is also likely to make up a part of their lives at home. While the more powerful policymakers have access to their own sources of information and intelligence about the outside world, the media remains an important source of information. In some cases, policymakers themselves credit the media as a source of influence in their policy decisions. A US senator who had opposed the lifting of arms sanctions against Bosnia during the conflict there admitted that she had changed her mind and voted to lift sanctions (to allow Bosnian factions to defend themselves) after being moved by scenes of death from the conflict on the media (see Rotberg and Weiss 1996, 1). Former Canadian Prime Minister Jean Chretien claimed that he had decided to lead Operation Assurance in eastern Zaire (although Canada did not commit troops and the operation was later cancelled) after seeing disturbing images on the television (see Morrison and Blair 1999, 251).[11]

The media also has direct interaction with policymakers through press conferences and interviews. While the influence in such scenarios is no doubt mutual, and it can probably be said that if the influence could be measured, policymakers would have

---

11 While this is the official Canadian explanation for the decision, evidence is naturally elusive, and a number of other possible reasons have been raised (see Adelman and Baxter 2004, 262–4).

the upper hand, by the very fact that the media has the power to pose questions of their choice to policymakers on topics of their choice, they have a certain degree of influence. Journalists assigned to gather information from key policymakers spend long periods of time with them and travel together in the same aircraft en route to meetings and negotiations, discussing issues informally along the way. Former US Secretary of State Madeleine Albright stated that such a relationship with the media made them in some ways 'a team'.

> It's very interesting when I do a press conference and I see the people that I brought with me; there is obviously much more of a team activity. At the same time, the press that travels with me asks some pretty tough questions, and press people on the ground don't have a clue what they are talking about (Albright and Kralev 2001, 106).

This 'first-name-basis' level of proximity and sense of being a 'team' can make for a significant level of influence. An extreme example of this type of relationship was observed during the Kosovo conflict, in which the then spokesman for the US State Department, James Rubin, and the chief reporter on the conflict for Cable News Network (CNN), Christiane Amanpour, were, in fact, husband and wife.

The focus of greater attention in terms of media influence on policy, however, is its indirect effect: the notion that emotive and concentrated media coverage of a particular conflict designed to spark outrage among the general public is capable of causing sufficient pressure on policymakers (who would otherwise risk a damaged reputation) to respond to that conflict. Such coverage appears to gain effectiveness in mobilizing outrage, and directly calls for action by home governments, because it is often set in black-and-white clarity, identifying 'evil villains' and 'innocent victims', and calling for a 'hero' to come to the rescue of the victims. This indirect influence of the media, which gives it the apparent role of a link between policymakers and their constituencies, is often referred to as the 'CNN effect'.[12] The power of the media in this sense has been observed concerning the conflict and famine in Ethiopia in the 1980s (Annan 1994, 624), but has particularly attracted attention since the 1990s, with increasing claims that the media was responsible for prompting Western military interventions in conflicts such as that in northern Iraq after the Gulf War, in Somalia and Kosovo.

Policymaking elites, journalists and academics alike have stressed the effect that the media can have on policy decisions regarding foreign conflict. Former UN Secretary-General Boutros-Boutros Ghali called CNN the 16th member of the UN Security Council (see Minear, Scott and Weiss 1994, 4), and former US Secretary of State James Baker (1996, 7–8) also stated that the media sometimes determines vital national interest. John Simpson of the British Broadcasting Corporation (BBC) mused that the television media is a 'very curious beast [with] huge muscles' – albeit also with 'distinctly poor eyesight and a disturbingly short attention-span' (quoted in McLaughlin 2002, 186). Martin Shaw (1996) saw concentrated media coverage as the key factor behind a complete reversal of Western policy in the decision to

---

12 Although this label is frequently used, it by no means should be interpreted as meaning that that particular media corporation is solely, or even chiefly, responsible for this perceived media power.

intervene in the Kurdish refugee crisis in northern Iraq. In the case of Somalia, it was suggested by many that the media had not only been instrumental in prompting the US decision to intervene, but also the decision to withdraw when the aftermath of a raid resulting in heavy US casualties and images of a dead soldier being dragged through the streets of Mogadishu were extensively televised.

Studies appear to show, however, that the effect of the media in this sense may be considerably exaggerated, particularly in terms of military intervention decisions (see Robinson 2002). Timelines comparing the coverage of media with policy decisions show that policy decisions in fact preceded concentrated media coverage in cases in which it was assumed that the media had influenced policy. This was convincingly demonstrated in the case of Somalia, and the evidence suggests that in this case (and perhaps in many others) it was the policymakers influencing the media to respond, rather than the other way round (see Livingston and Eachus 1995; Mermin 1997). This intervention may well have been more about a desire to deflect criticisms of double standards (as seen earlier in the assertion by Brent Snowcroft), and as a means of creating a legacy for the outgoing US president. Similarly, although unfavourable media coverage has been connected to the withdrawal from Somalia, the decision to withdraw had already been made before the highly publicized failed raid in Mogadishu. In the cases of northern Iraq and Kosovo, it can also be argued that geopolitical concerns on the part of those intervening were also significant motivating factors, and that it therefore cannot be concluded that the media prompted the intervention decision.

Further evidence countering the notion that the media has the power to prompt military intervention can be found in cases in which there was no Western intervention, despite heavy media coverage calling for 'something to be done'. The Rwandan genocide received relatively heavy media coverage, but this pressure was resisted by all except the French, who finally intervened as the genocide was ending and were criticized for their self-interested assistance of the *genocidaires* in their intervention. Relatively concentrated Western media coverage of the conflict in Darfur in 2004 and 2006 managed to attract only a small and underfunded AU force, without Western presence. Heavy coverage of both phases of the conflict in Chechnya, and of conflict in Israel-Palestine, did not lead to any form of external intervention. While in the former two African cases, lack of geopolitical interest was clearly a factor, in the latter two cases, military intervention was not going to be practically feasible, in spite of Western interest. In all of these cases, national interests, as perceived by the policymakers, were followed, and saturated media attention was unable to move the policymakers to engage in military intervention in this way.

Although its power may be exaggerated, the media does play a role in intervention decisions, including those in Somalia, Bosnia and Kosovo, even if it is not necessarily the prime factor underlying the intervention. It is a factor that joins others (primarily perceptions of national interest) in the calculation of benefit, cost and risk that makes up the decision-making process. Its effect is greatest in this equation when there is policy uncertainty, or where there are divisions among policymakers (Robinson 2000). The proposed Western intervention in eastern Zaire (which was also thought to have been prompted largely by the media) was quickly cancelled after Rwanda invaded Zaire; and this was, according to a diplomat at UN Headquarters, largely because media interest had by then dissipated (anonymous, interview with the author December 2000). Furthermore, it is not only the intervention decisions themselves that are affected by media coverage, but also the manner in which interventions are carried out. A prime example is the Kosovo conflict, in which the NATO countries, assuming that there would be no stomach for friendly casualties at home, particularly casualties that would be televised, chose to rely solely on high-altitude aerial bombing. The fear of media influence during military interventions is also demonstrated by the lengths that intervening governments and their militaries will go to, to restrict and control media access to the conflict zones.

But the influence of the media on policymakers' response to foreign conflict goes far beyond military intervention decisions, which are a rare and somewhat extreme form of response. The overall effect is, in fact, much greater on responses that do not involve military intervention. Firstly, it can affect the process leading to the response, starting with the position that a particular conflict occupies on a policymaker's agenda; it can cause policymakers to reorder their priorities. The media may also function as an accelerant, shortening the response time in the decision-making process (Livingston 1997). Finally, and perhaps most importantly, media pressure may result in the adoption of token measures, or a minimalist approach, designed only to give the impression of concern and action, if national interests are not significantly affected: a response to the 'do something' syndrome. In such cases, measures that are less risky and less costly than military intervention are thus more likely to be the options that are chosen in response to demanding media coverage, and they are usually unlikely to have a significant impact on the conflict. Policymakers may, to ease media pressure, make statements expressing concern unilaterally or through the UN Security Council. They may bring the parties to the conflict together for talks, but are unlikely to apply serious pressure or offer significant incentives designed to bring the conflict to resolution.

Perhaps the most obvious result of media pressure can be seen in the allocation of humanitarian aid. Just as the media's handling of conflicts is highly selective, concentrated, and usually lasts only during the most violent phase of the conflict, so too is the allocation of humanitarian aid by policymakers. This results in the highly disproportionate allocations of aid to chosen conflicts, in contrast with little at all to stealth conflicts. Furthermore, if national interests are not at stake, the aid is likely to disappear as the media coverage fades, leaving little assistance for critical long-term peacebuilding or for response to a resurgence of fighting (Jakobsen 2000). Some acts of aid in response to conflict may appear to be little more than ineffective and token efforts aimed at gaining publicity in order to reduce pressure to take further action. During the Rwandan genocide, Bernard Kouchner, at the time the president of a French NGO, arranged, together with the French government, the evacuation of a group of orphans to Paris. This was despite the initial opposition of the UN force commander, who stressed that with the same funds, a much greater number of orphans could be cared for within Rwanda. The orphans, many of whom were seriously injured, were forced to wait for nine hours on a plane at Nairobi airport until a French military hospital aircraft arrived to take them to Paris. This delay ensured that the plane would arrive in Paris the following morning at a time guaranteeing 'maximum exposure in the press' (Dallaire 2003, 407).

Public Influence

The influence of the public on policymakers must be examined separately according to the different actors that make up the public agenda, as their roles and means of influence can be quite diverse. This section will look at the influence of the public divided into the following groups: general public, NGOs, interest groups and corporations.

In procedural democracies (where the public has the power to punish and reward politicians at election time based on their actions and their promises) the general public has influence over the policymakers through the ballot. Policymakers frequently conduct opinion polls, particularly in the lead-up to elections, in an attempt to gauge the feelings of the general public and learn how their reputation and popularity will be affected by taking (or not taking) a particular course of action in response to any given situation. There are also differences according to the political system, with parliamentary systems thought to allow for more influence by the public than presidential systems (see Isernia, Juhasz and Rattinger 2002, 204). But it is not only at election time when the general public can exert this influence (although at that time it may well be at its strongest). They can also lobby, petition, or use other forms of advocacy, to encourage their representatives to act in a certain way. In large enough numbers they can even influence policy by demonstrating on the streets if they feel strongly enough about an issue. In the case of a conflict or humanitarian crisis, the reputation of policymakers can be damaged through public disapproval if they choose not to respond to the conflict and remain idle. Celebrities may also join the cause, enhancing the visibility of the conflict and its effects. Civic leaders and NGOs may sprout from such movements. Public opinion may also work against responses by policymakers. The death of a single UN peacekeeper from Uruguay in Rwanda, for example, caused a swell of public discontent in Uruguay that almost cost the incumbent president the elections (Dallaire 2003, 429).

But the influence of the general public is limited in many ways. For the general public to exert influence on policymakers, a critical mass of discontent regarding the home government's handling (or lack thereof) of a foreign conflict must be reached, but reaching this level is quite rare. If it is at election time, the issue must become an election issue: something that will have an effect on the outcome. Beyond election time, the discontent must be sufficient to affect the general public approval ratings. If the issue in question is a conflict towards which resources (and possibly troops) have already been committed or pledged, it is likely that the public will have a sufficient level of interest to influence policymakers. If there is no prior commitment, however, and the conflict is not perceived as directly affecting the lives of the general public, it is extremely difficult to stimulate and unify public discontent to a level sufficient to have an impact on the policy agenda. Thus, for the vast majority of foreign conflicts which policymakers do not already treat with a degree of importance, the impact of the general public is highly limited. For the former US Assistant Secretary of State for African Affairs, Chester Crocker, the fact that foreign policy towards Africa was virtually immune from public pressure meant that policymaking could be conducted 'on its merits' (quoted in Berkeley 2001, 87).

The influence of the general public is also limited because the ability to gauge public opinion is limited. While policymakers do make extensive use of public opinion polls, these are used primarily to gauge opinion regarding matters that directly concern the general public, which automatically excludes the vast majority of the world's conflicts; polls are simply not taken in the West on conflict in the DRC, Angola or Burundi, and thus public opinion has little impact on policymakers in these situations. In the absence of public opinion polls, policymakers are likely to fall back on their own intuition or 'perceived public opinion', which is the 'convenient fiction observers use to characterize the comprehensive preferences of a majority of citizens' (Entmen 2000, 20). Perceived public opinion may in many ways be a creation by the media, a situation that gives the media the power to circumvent the influence of public opinion on policymakers (see Mutz and Soss 1997, 447). In any case, both public opinion polls and perceived public opinion are likely to differ from actual individual preferences and priorities: the trade-offs people would choose to make among available options (Entman 2000, 19–23).

Even if opinion polls can be considered accurate reflections of the public agenda, policymakers may well choose, for a number of reasons, to ignore the results. Policymakers may find that the results do not reflect the outcome they would have preferred, and may instead attempt to find (or create) results that better suit their plans. In many aid and intervention decisions, for example, policymakers often claim that they cannot commit aid or intervening forces because public opinion opposes it (despite evidence suggesting that public opinion solidly supports increased aid or military intervention). Such a contradictory citing of public opinion justifying lack of action was seen, for example, in Italy over intervention in Bosnia (Isernia 2000). The US decision to withdraw from Somalia was also seen as a misinterpretation by the US executive of the public's willingness to stay the course of the conflict (Kull 1995–96, 111–2). They may ignore public opinion in this way because they do not believe the response serves their notion of national interest, or because they anticipate that public opinion will turn against them if the response is not deemed a success in a short period of time. Conversely, where policymakers are determined to commit to a certain course of action in which they anticipate adverse public reaction, they may take time and certain measures to 'prepare' the general public for action to be taken.

NGOs also have the power to influence, in a number of ways, the response of policymakers to conflict. The very reason for being of some NGOs is, in fact, to influence policymakers through advocacy work. Such NGOs gather information on conflict situations and/or situations of human rights abuse, analyze it, and use this information to pressure policymakers, either directly, or through the general public using publicity campaigns. Many urge the general public to directly call or write to their political representatives. Some NGOs may target specific aspects of conflict, working towards a particular objective, while others have a broader focus. Some examples of such NGO influence are the successful campaign by the International Campaign to Ban Landmines (an umbrella group of NGOs), or the campaign against conflict diamonds by Global Witness. In Ireland, a bus driver who had watched a television program on East Timor was inspired to establish an advocacy NGO, which went on to influence the Irish government to become one of the most proactive members of the EU in the 1990s on the issue of East Timor (Smillie and Minear 2004, 60). At a broader level, the International Crisis Group provides analysis and advocacy to policymakers on the political implications of specific conflicts and the means to resolve them. Organizations such as Amnesty International and Human Rights Watch work to bring to light human rights abuse (in both conflict and non-conflict situations), pressuring policymakers to respond. Local NGOs in an environment of conflict and/or oppression may also join with NGOs in powerful countries, working together to pressure these policymakers, who in turn will apply pressure to the policymakers of the country in which the conflict/oppression is taking place, in what is known as 'the boomerang effect' (Tarrow 2005, 145–9).

Advocacy is not the only means by which NGOs can influence policymakers. NGOs may directly involve themselves in mediation attempts in conflict situations, the effects of which policymakers may have to factor into their own responses, depending on how prominent their role is in the overall peace process. Engagement in unofficial talks by non-government parties (which may include NGOs, corporations, academics and other groups) in peace negotiations (track-two diplomacy) has the power to complement the central peace process (see Lieberfeld 2002). Organizations that provide humanitarian assistance to the victims of conflict can also have an influence on policy decisions, depending on the size of their presence and the attention their activities manage to attract from other actors. Conflicts in Sudan and Angola, for example, managed to secure moderate levels of humanitarian aid in the late 1990s and beyond, despite insignificant media attention. It has been suggested that this was due to 'the existence of a long-lived and influential humanitarian presence and lobby networks directly engaged in these particular emergencies' (Olsen, Cartensen and Høyen 2002, 11). For some such NGOs, their presence may be designed to shame policymakers into action and attract funding for their activities. A novel attempt to influence the response of policymakers came in the form of an NGO that took the unprecedented step of raising private money to directly fund the activity of peacekeepers: the Genocide Intervention Fund was established in 2004 specifically to raise money to boost the AU force operating in Darfur.

Another factor that gives NGOs some influence on policymakers is the movement of personnel between governments and NGOs witnessed in recent years. Founder of *Médecins Sans Frontières* (MSF), Bernard Kouchner, for example, has moved in and out of key policymaking positions in the French government, international organizations, and NGOs, sometimes maintaining elements of each in his work. Similarly, former Australian Foreign Minister Gareth Evans currently heads the International Crisis Group; his former position as a policymaker no doubt gives greater influence to that NGO in policymaking circles.

Interest groups are groups specifically designed to exert influence over policymakers to protect and propel the interests of the group. Where their agendas are related to conflict situations, they have the potential to influence the response of policymakers. Diasporas in particular can exert a powerful influence (see T. Smith 2005), but so too can religious groups, and other unique interest groups. Such interest groups draw their strength from their organizational unity and political (in terms of placement and voter participation) and economic clout, and, in the case of diasporas, from a position that demonstrates integration into the host society yet with the maintenance of strong ties to the homeland. Interest groups can influence policymakers directly through their political placement, or through the injection or withholding of election campaign funds, and indirectly by organizing 'flak' campaigns encouraging members to express en masse their discontent with a policy (or lack thereof) by way of calls and correspondence.

One of the most powerful interest groups in the West is the Israel lobby group (used to refer to a loose coalition of pro-Israeli groups), which uses its prominent position in political, media and business spheres, as well as large amounts of election campaign fund contributions, to influence Western policy towards Israel and the Middle East. Adding to its power is the fact that it is made up not only of powerful Jewish groups, but also of some Christian groups who believe that the rebirth of Israel has biblical relevance. According to John Mearsheimer and Stephen Walt (2006), the powerful political influence of this group is responsible for a pro-Israeli US foreign policy: pro-Israeli to the extent that it has significantly jeopardized the USA's own interests, particularly in terms of oil security and the growth of terrorism. They assert that only the existence of such interest group influence can account for as much as one-fifth of that country's foreign aid budget going to Israel; for the more than 30 vetoes cast on its behalf in the UN Security Council (more than the vetoes cast by the other permanent members combined); for turning a blind eye to Israel's acquisition of nuclear weapons; and for its stance on Israel's conflicts with Palestine and Lebanon. Such pro-Israel lobbies appear to hold considerable sway in many other Western countries, but although they may constitute the most powerful ethnic lobby group, others wield significant power in particular conflict situations. Even in Australia, organized diasporas not only from faraway Israel, but also equally distant Lebanon, and the former Yugoslavia, for example, have played a significant role in Australia's response towards conflict in those countries.

Some interest groups have been active in influencing policy towards Africa. In the case of the conflict in southern Sudan, evangelizing Muslim lobby groups exerted influence over the policies of Muslim-dominated countries in favour of the northern-dominated government, while evangelizing Christian lobby groups in the West influenced Western policy in favour of the rebel Christian south, both in the name of defending their religion (see Lavergne and Weissman 2004, 159). During Uganda's invasion of Zaire, policymakers in Uganda were apparently afraid of the tens of thousands of citizens of Ugandan origin in the UK (most of whom were thought to be opposed to the Museveni regime) influencing UK policy towards Uganda to the detriment of their government (Otunnu 2004, 62), although significant influence did not materialize. TransAfrica, a Washington-based organization, was established to increase the voice of African-Americans in US foreign policy, but it focused primarily on ending apartheid in South Africa. The organization later turned its attention to Haiti and Nigeria, but it appeared to attract little mainstream support in the West (Berkeley 2001, 88–90). Another group to note in the USA was a loose grass-roots coalition known as Liberia Watch, which successfully lobbied the USA for a major aid package for Liberia in 2003. These examples are, to some extent, exceptions. As a whole, the influence of African diasporas in the West appears to be weak.

Interest groups other than those uniting people based on their national, ethnic or religious background can also influence policymakers on select issues. Certain groups in Japan that are unhappy with the foreign assistance that Japan gives to foreign countries carefully monitor the levels of aid to foreign countries and how it is used, mobilizing political pressure to expose and condemn any perceived shortcomings or weaknesses in that country's aid policy and implementation. The USA's National Rifle Association has served as a strong interest group on conflict-related issues beyond the borders of that country. In 2006, Sri Lanka's Ambassador to the UN, who was to chair a UN conference on progress made in curbing illegal trade in small arms, received over 100,000 letters from supporters of the National Rifle Association, who were led to believe that the UN conference would threaten their legal right to bear arms (Coultan 2006).

Corporations influence policymakers in a similar manner to other interest groups. While they are unlikely to organize street protests and open petitions, they directly lobby policymakers, contribute to election campaign funds and may organize flak campaigns. Policymakers have a number of incentives to accept the influence of powerful corporations. At a national interest level, they benefit from powerful corporations' contributions to a strong economy, employment, tax revenue and wealth in general. At a personal level, they may rely on the campaign contributions from corporations, and policymakers may even have interests themselves in business ventures that may be affected by foreign conflict. Such mutually advantageous high-level ties between corporations and policymakers can give corporations considerable leverage in conflict situations, particularly in the absence of government policy interest, restrictive policy frameworks, and other interested parties (including the media and general public); most notably it is Africa that fits this description (see Gordon, Miller and Wolpe 1998, 77).

Western oil companies proved to be powerful lobbying groups during the conflict in southern Sudan. Eager to gain access to oilfields controlled by the government (many of which had been taken by force from southern rebels), oil companies lobbied their governments to ease criticism on the Sudanese government and relax restrictions on doing business there. This put them in competition for influence with Christian lobby groups with opposing viewpoints.[13] During the invasion of Zaire in 1997, foreign mining and investment companies organized a meeting with the rebel groups and subsequently signed a number of large-scale contracts with the rebels, who they saw as having the upper hand in the conflict. It is interesting to note that the organizer of the meeting and the largest investor was American Mineral Fields, a company based in the hometown of the then US President Clinton. These links proved to be a powerful influence. Another company, Barrick Gold, which was linked to former US President George Bush and former Canadian Prime Minister Brian Mulroney, 'influenced policymakers in the US and Canada either to support or ignore armed intervention by Uganda and Rwanda' (Otunnu 2004, 52). On the other hand, US evangelist Pat Robertson, who had close ties with former Zairian President

---

13 US oil companies prevented from dealing with the Sudanese government were particularly concerned as less restricted companies from China, Malaysia, Europe and Canada signed oil deals with Sudan (see Lavergne and Weissman 2004 ,143).

Mobutu and business interests in Zaire, lobbied his government (albeit in vain) in support of Mobutu during the invasion. Robertson, this time with mining interests in Liberia, also lobbied (again in vain) in support of Liberian President Taylor during the conflict that eventually toppled him (see King 2001).

Academic Influence

Traditionally, a gap has existed between policymakers and academics in the field of international affairs. For policymakers, academic work has been seen as too abstract and based in theory rather than practice, with academics perceived as writing for their peers rather than as a means of contributing to policy. For academics, policymakers have been seen as being grounded too much in realist, balance-of-power mindsets, making decisions based on political considerations rather than objective analysis, and being prone to draw simplistic and inaccurate conclusions and historical parallels – comparing US intervention situations with previous US experiences in Vietnam, for example (see George 1993, 6–16; Lepgold and Nincic 2001, 173). This gap is now considered to have substantially eroded, with considerable interaction between the two worlds. This interaction brings with it mutual influence, and although that of academia is undoubtedly weaker than that of the policymakers, it can wield significant levels of influence on policy response towards conflict, both directly and indirectly.

Experts in the field of international relations, politics and security, for example, are commissioned by policymakers to conduct studies on security issues affecting their country or its interests, as part of the process of formulating foreign policy. Policymakers rely on scholars for academic background in preparing speeches and statements. Policymakers involved in foreign affairs are also likely to read journals, and op-ed pieces in the newspapers written by academics that are relevant to their policy interests. Policymakers take particular interest in academic studies that support their policies (see Wilson 2000, 115). The democratic peace theory, the notion that democracies do not go to war with other democracies, is one such example. This theory has sparked interest from Western policymakers who see it as providing justification for their aggressive promotion of democracy beyond their borders (see Walt 1998). Theories promoting so-called 'humanitarian intervention' also became subjects of interest for policymakers as they went to war over Kosovo. Perhaps more importantly, specialists with academic backgrounds in international affairs are increasingly being drawn in by bureaucracies and governments to serve as consultants and advisers. Such policy specialists, or 'technicians', serve as bridges between policymakers and academia. Governments also fund think tanks to encourage research in certain areas that will benefit the formulation of their policies. As a result of this process, many personnel tend to move between the two worlds, bringing influence with them. There are a number of high-profile policymakers who have come from academic backgrounds, including Sadako Ogata (former head of the UNHCR), Henry Kissinger, Madeleine Albright, and Condoleezza Rice (former and present US Secretaries of State).

One of the key weaknesses of academic influence on policy, however, is that the majority of academic contribution to policy appears to be demand driven.

Policymakers are more likely to turn to academics to provide support for policies that they already have in mind, than for strategies or ideas that have originated in academia (see Wilson 2000, 126). Academic input sought by policymakers is unlikely to serve as a significant influence on policymaking in response to conflicts that do not already appear on the policy radar. Academics do attempt, however, to independently inform or influence policy in relation to conflict. Academic institutions may conduct workshops and conferences on particular topics of their choice that bring together both academics and policymakers to debate on a particular foreign affairs topic, and may provide graduate training for future policymakers. Academics can take part in track-two peace processes, and may form alliances to offer academic pressure on issues that they feel strongly about. Academics have, for example, written petitions and open letters to leading policymakers to protest over certain policies. The Federation of American Scientists is an example of an academic lobby group.[14] Studies conducted by academics on conflicts may also have an effect on policymakers. Academic studies on death tolls from conflicts, for example, can have political implications. The reaction to the studies on deaths from the conflict in Iraq is a case in point, as was that to the study conducted by the IRC on deaths in the DRC, which 'became for many Congolese a tool in the political fight against the foreign occupiers, whose cruelty they served to demonstrate' (Le Pape 2004, 224).

Finally, key policymakers may rise to these positions in part out of ambition for power and influence, but they are also concerned about their legacy: how they will be remembered in history (particularly during the twilight periods of their terms in office). In this sense, it is not necessarily the active influence of academics on policymakers, but more the role itself of academics as the recorders of history that influences policymakers to attempt to contribute (or at least project the appearance of contributing) to the resolution of international issues for which they will be remembered in a positive light. The decision of former US President Bush to intervene in Somalia in the early 1990s can be seen as a reflection of the influence of legacy. Similarly, former UK Prime Minister Tony Blair's rhetoric on Africa in general (in his words a 'scar on the conscience of the world') may well have been a reflection of such a concern for his personal legacy, particularly given that despite the rhetoric, there are, according to Guy Arnold (2005, 967), 'few signs of any real changes in British-African policy'.

---

14 The Federation of American Scientists (FAS) was originally established by atomic scientists to influence policymakers on the nuclear weapon issue, but has since expanded its scope to a number of other policy issues.

Chapter 4

The Media

The media is an actor that 'speaks' rather than 'acts'. Its primary role in responding to conflict is to 'discover' and report on conflicts, informing other actors of their existence and keeping them updated with how the conflict is unfolding, as well as assessing and commenting on how other actors (particularly the policymakers) are performing in their response to it. In countries with freedom of the press, media corporations have the liberty to report about whatever (and in whatever manner) they see fit, within certain ethical boundaries. In theory, the media is thus able to independently pursue and report on stories, focusing on fulfilling their role as 'mirror', objectively reflecting the world and what is happening in it, and/or as 'watchdog', keeping an eye on authority and exposing abuse or failure by those in authority to act in response to matters that demand their attention. As will be seen in this chapter, with regard to foreign conflict, the media generally does a poor job as a mirror and as a watchdog, given its highly selective response to conflict that is generally neither objective nor proportionate. This chapter looks first at the media's response to conflict, assessing its selection of conflicts for coverage and the quantity and quality of that coverage. It then examines the internal factors that determine the media's choices: its shrinking foreign presence; focus on packaging, presentation and speed; danger and access; the close-to-home factor; the need for simplification; media convergence; and the effects of the Internet. Finally, it explores the influences of the policymakers, the public and academia on the media agenda.

Responses to Conflict

Limited Foreign Coverage

The first and most obvious point to note about the media's response to foreign conflict is that there is so little of it to begin with. As Peter Viggo Jakobsen (2000, 131) puts it, 'The media ignores most conflicts most of the time. The coverage of the pre- and post-violence phases is negligible at best and only a few armed conflicts are covered in the violence phase.' Media corporations targeting an audience within the borders of the country in which they are based have a tendency to clearly divide news into national and international, or local and foreign. Within that frame, local news dominates by far, and the space allocated to foreign news is usually not particularly large. For an evening television news program of 30 minutes, for example, time needs to be allocated for local news, foreign news, sports, weather and probably a light entertainment or gossip piece, interspersed with commercials. There may be time for only two or three short foreign news stories in a program. Newspapers, whose readership is steadily falling, are able to allocate more space to foreign news, providing more information and more stories, but it is still likely to be relatively little – almost certainly less than the information devoted to the results and analysis of local sports. Foreign news does not, of course, comprise only news on foreign conflict: politics, natural disasters, accidents and other events also make up foreign news.[1] Thus the news space available for foreign conflict is quite limited from the outset.

On top of already physically limited capacity for foreign news coverage, the interest among media corporations also appears to have fallen, with the share of foreign news in broadcast and print media decreasing significantly since the end of the Cold War (see Arnett 1998). Since the late 1980s voices were raised expressing concern about the falling space the media devotes to foreign news, and about the number of foreign correspondents responsible for gathering this news, who had become an 'endangered species' (Hamilton and Jenner 2002, 1). Whereas foreign news made up 45 percent of the time allocated for news on network television in the USA in the 1970s, for example, by 1995 this had become only 13.5 percent. During the same period, the length of each foreign story decreased from 1.7 to 1.2 minutes (Moisy 1996, 9). The quantity of foreign news in that country showed a tendency to increase at times in which its government was engaged in military conflict with foreign entities – during the Gulf War, Kosovo, the September 11 terrorist attacks, and the invasion of Afghanistan and Iraq, but the effect has been temporary, and the increase in coverage largely limited to the coverage of the particular events in question (see Stacks 2003–04, 14; Hamilton and Jenner 2002, 1–2). The quantity of foreign news in the West remains at low levels.

Furthermore, much of what is called 'foreign' news in fact refers to news focusing on how the home country interacts with foreign countries. One study found that one-third of all international stories in the USA was 'essentially about the United States in the world, rather than about the world' (Moeller 1999, 18). As Michael Marks (2002, 26–7) notes, in an era in which 'all-news cable channels are broadcast via satellite all around the globe, it can be especially baffling to the consumers of mass media that news programs produced in the United States, but intended for a global audience, do not take the global audience's perspective into account'. Priority in coverage is clearly given to foreign situations in which the home country has a stake. As such, stories for which there is no home connection or angle (media corporations may try to find or create such a connection) may well be unlikely to be covered at all.

The emergence of supposedly global cable news channels such as CNN and BBC, whose target audience includes people outside the country in which they are based, has not really brought about substantive changes in the coverage situation. Despite having the luxury of broadcasting news from around the world 24 hours a day and having an international focus, much of the world and most of its conflicts are still given scant, if any, coverage. Twenty-four-hour coverage does not necessarily mean that more of the world is covered. It generally means instead that stories are repeated in the following hours and updates are made as time goes on from the same

---

1   A Pew study in 1995 estimated that as much as 40 percent of foreign news could be associated with conflict (see Moeller 1999, 18).

locations. While the packaging, presentation and timing of delivery of the news may have changed and the provision of television images has increased, the crucial aspect of newsgathering has not been enhanced. The assertion that the media ignores most conflicts most of the time still stands.

Conflict Selection and Coverage Quantity

Within the highly limited amount of coverage of foreign conflicts, both print and broadcast media corporations practise high levels of selectivity, and are generally so selective in fact that 'the media in effect create a disaster when they recognize it' (S. Cohen 2001, 169). When a conflict appears that the media corporations believe will have a particularly strong effect on their target audience and/or their country, or that they believe is otherwise particularly newsworthy from their point of view, that conflict becomes a chosen one for the media, and they begin to focus their collective attention on that conflict with great intensity – to the extent that coverage of it begins to eclipse what little coverage there already was of the other twenty or thirty ongoing foreign conflicts. For the media, the scale and severity of the conflict appear to have very little at all to do with its selection. Looking at the chosen conflicts of the past decade (Kosovo, East Timor, Israel-Palestine, Afghanistan, Iraq and Israel-Lebanon), the involvement of large numbers of Western troops (mostly American), or at least of strong Western national interests, seem to be common characteristics.

The degree of coverage given to such chosen conflicts when compared to the other conflicts appears to defy any definition of proportion. In 2000, the year in which there was a conflagration of the conflict in Israel-Palestine, coverage of that conflict on CNN was not only the highest for any conflict for that year (as it was for most other Western media corporations), but the volume of coverage was also approximately five times that of the second most covered conflict. The second most covered conflict was that in the Philippines, focusing mostly on the plight of Western hostages captured by a rebel group. In the same year, coverage of the same conflict by the Japanese *Yomiuri* newspaper was more than four times that of the second most covered conflict; by the *New York Times* it was three times, and by the BBC and *Le Monde* newspaper it was two times greater.[2] This is particularly noteworthy given that the conflagration was relatively minor when compared to other major conflicts occurring (mostly in Africa) in that year. A search of the articles on the website of the German newspaper *Die Welt* covering the nine years from 1998 to 2006, found approximately 16,200 'hits' for Iraq, 10,600 for Israel, 7,100 for Afghanistan, 4,600 for Kosovo and 2,400 for Lebanon but other countries hosting conflict could barely reach 1,000 hits.

A look at the rise in coverage as a chosen conflict peaks also shows how other conflicts are eclipsed. In the three months leading up to NATO's bombing campaign

---

2   Data on coverage by BBC, CNN, *Le Monde,* the *New York Times* and the *Yomiuri* (Japanese version) newspapers for the year 2000 is sourced from Hawkins (2002). Coverage for BBC and CNN was measured in seconds for one complete news program per day, while daily newspaper coverage was determined by measuring the square area of articles on the front page and international pages.

over the Kosovo conflict, coverage of that conflict increased from 10 percent (in January 1999) to more than 18 percent (in March 1999) of the square area of international news coverage in the *New York Times*. At the same time, coverage in that newspaper of major conflicts in the DRC, Sierra Leone, Ethiopia-Eritrea and Angola combined decreased from 6 percent of coverage (in January) to less than 0.5 percent (in March).[3] The democratically elected government of the Central African Republic had the misfortune of being overthrown by rebels in 2003 as the US-UK invasion of Iraq was about to begin, and the media ignored its fall almost completely. For the duration of the Israel-Lebanon conflict in 2006, that conflict dominated most Western news corporations, including the *Australian* newspaper. On some days in July 2006, the world news page of the online version of that newspaper devoted eight or nine stories of the twelve stories displayed to coverage of that conflict alone. In choosing to focus so intently on this particular conflict during that month, key developments in other conflict situations were barely responded to at all, including historic elections in the DRC, peace talks between the Ugandan government and the rebel LRA, fresh attacks by the Sudanese government in Darfur, and renewed violence in Sri Lanka and Colombia.

Israel-Palestine occupies a unique position in the Western media. Any clashes between the parties to the conflict, bomb blasts, assassinations, tensions that may potentially lead to clashes, internal political developments, and all aspects of the peace process are closely monitored and carefully analyzed, frequently in real time, by Western media corporations. Reporters call and visit hospitals in areas affected, seeking out and reporting highly accurate death tolls down to the last individual. A significant conflagration in fighting involving Israel-Palestine inevitably propels that conflict to chosen conflict status, resulting in saturation coverage for a time, as was seen in the conflict in 2000, and also in the Israel-Lebanon conflict in 2006. Even when there are no major clashes, coverage of any developments is consistent, meticulous and treated with a high priority. It is not at all uncommon for there to be more media coverage, at any given time, of Israel-Palestine alone than there is of the entire African continent – in fact such a situation is probably the rule rather than the exception.

Behind the overwhelming saturation coverage that the media devotes to chosen conflicts, and the consistently high coverage for Israel-Palestine, are conflicts that attract intermediate levels of coverage, usually when chosen conflicts are not at their peak. Such conflicts may attract moderate levels of coverage over a long period of time, or they may be more intense over a shorter period of time, but do not manage to reach the intense levels of coverage that chosen conflicts do: that is, coverage capable of disrupting regular programming and occupying the majority of the total coverage allocated to international news. The two phases of the conflict in Chechnya in the 1990s and the conflict in Darfur are key examples. In the case of Darfur, although the conflict began in early 2003, the media first 'noticed' its existence in early 2004. Coverage grew through 2004, and faded somewhat in 2005

---

3   The period measured for March is up to March 24, when NATO's bombing commenced. Coverage of the Kosovo conflict jumped to an even higher level beyond this date (see Hawkins 2004, 142–3).

before reaching moderately high levels of coverage in 2006. During the British intervention, conflict in Sierra Leone attracted 'a brief CNN moment', but 'there were no protracted images of Sierra Leone on the television screens of Europe and North America' (Smillie and Minear 2004, 49). The conflict in Sri Lanka during the peak of its violence also was the subject of a moderate level of coverage.

As can already be gathered from some of the above examples, from the perspective of the media, conflicts in Africa, with very few exceptions, are of the stealth variety, despite their overwhelming scale and humanitarian cost. Many observers note that Africa is ignored in Western media coverage, but often qualify their statements with something like 'unless there is conflict or catastrophe' (Robins 2003, 30), or unless 'the body count clicks into the tens of thousands' (Harden 1990, 14–15). Looking at the actual quantity of media coverage, however, the existence of conflict, catastrophe and body counts in the hundreds of thousands (if not millions) appear to matter very little in the response of the media to such conflict. A journalist reporting on a crisis in refugee camps in northern Uganda in 2004, seeing that the government had been trying to downplay the magnitude of the crisis, stated that 'you can't hide 1.6 million people' (BBC World Service 2004b). Unfortunately, with a media beast that has such poor eyesight and a short attention span, 1.6 million people and more can and easily do go unnoticed.

Figure 4.1 compares the levels of coverage by a number of media corporations of the DRC and Israel-Palestine over the first two-year period of conflict.[4] In each case, coverage of Israel-Palestine is far greater than that for the DRC, ranging from roughly double (*Le Soir*) to 53 times greater (CNN). In the USA there is a newsroom truism stating that 'one dead fireman in Brooklyn is worth five English bobbies, who are worth 50 Arabs, who are worth 500 Africans' (Moeller 1999, 22). The unfortunate reality is, however, that in Western newsrooms, 500 Africans have nowhere near that level of value. The case of the DRC offers an extreme example. Over the first two years of conflict in the DRC, roughly 1,850,000 people died, compared to 2,000 Israelis and Palestinians, yet on CNN the coverage of the conflict in Israel-Palestine was roughly 53 times greater than that of the DRC. If such a scale of value existed in newsrooms, the value of 1 life from Israel-Palestine could be calculated as being equivalent to more than 49,000 Congolese lives. Morbid calculations aside, it would appear that media response is not calculated in this way, and that, in fact, scale is really not an issue at all. The point is that the media generally does not respond to conflict in Africa with any substantial quantity of coverage, regardless of the scale and however catastrophic the humanitarian costs are. Phillip Knightley (2003b, 14) reminds us that 'Although in most cases the camera does not lie directly, it can lie brilliantly by omission', and wittingly or unwittingly, it 'lies' about the state of conflict in the world, by appearing almost to ignore the very existence of the majority of the world's conflicts.

---

4 Data is based on the number of articles retrieved from LexisNexis searches (using 'Congo' and 'Israel' as search words), except for Le Soir, which is based on a search of articles on the *Le Soir* homepage. Results for CNN are from CNN Transcripts on LexisNexis. The timeframe for the search was 1 August 1998 to 31 July 2000 for Congo, and 28 September 2000 to 28 September 2002 for Israel.

The DRC, Angola and Burundi are prime examples of some of the world's most deadly conflicts that were virtually ignored by the Western media. An internet search covering the period of 1991 to 2006 of the articles on the website of the *International Herald Tribune*, which calls itself 'the world's daily newspaper', revealed just 611 hits for the term Congo (and a further 173 for Zaire), 413 for Angola, and 121 for Burundi. This was compared to 12,551 for Iraq and 6,928 for Israel. Considering that much of the fighting in the DRC has been concentrated in Ituri and the Kivus, searches were also conducted for these terms, which were compared with regions within other countries that have experienced conflict, although to a lesser degree. In the same paper, just 26 hits were found for Ituri and 18 for Kivu, while there were 680 hits for Darfur, 644 for Chechnya, 519 for Aceh, and 92 for Jaffna. Similarly, in the *New York Times* in 1999 and 2000 there was significantly more coverage devoted to East Timor (153 references) than there was to the DRC (91 references). In most of the Western media corporations (including the *New York Times* and *Die Welt*), Israel received far more media coverage in a single year (2006) than the DRC did in all of the nine years since its conflict began in 1998. Most of Africa and its conflicts have been and remain under a media blackout. The Japanese media was even worse. Although it did give some minimal amounts of coverage to Sierra Leone and Zimbabwe in 2000, the *Yomiuri* newspaper almost totally ignored the conflict

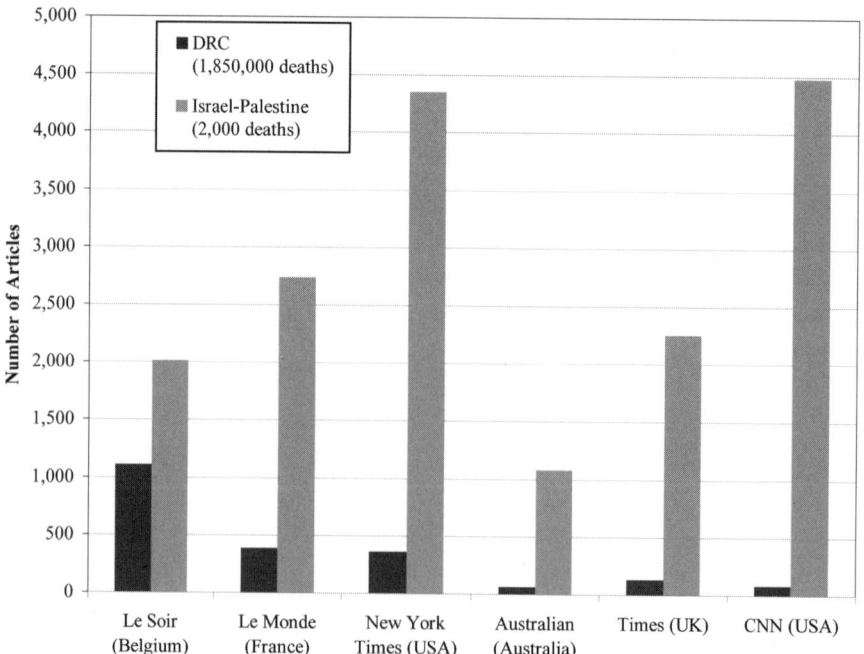

Figure 4.1   Comparative media coverage of DRC and Israel-Palestine (First two years of conflict)

in the DRC altogether, and devoted a total of just 1.9 percent of its international coverage to the African continent.

A look at coverage of Zimbabwe by the Western media also reveals some interesting patterns that somehow distinguish its response to that country from that to other conflicts, although it may be difficult to classify the attacks on white farmers in 2000 as a conflict. The BBC, for example, devoted more than four times the amount of coverage to conflict in Zimbabwe than it did to that in the DRC in 2000, while for CNN it was more than three times, although the overall amount of coverage was rather small in both cases. Similarly, the coverage of Zimbabwe in the *Australian* newspaper over the past ten years (to the end of 2006) was more than five times that for the DRC. In comparisons with nearby conflicts in the DRC, Angola and Burundi, the levels of coverage for Zimbabwe are completely out of proportion in terms of conflict scale, human rights abuse and even political and economic relevance.

The general trends observed above – highly disproportionate coverage characterized by intense concentration on select chosen conflicts of interest to the West, together with a general media blackout of major African conflicts – also appear to hold true for other English-language media sources, including radio and even the websites of the major global news agencies (otherwise known as the wire services). On BBC's World News radio program in the second half of 2005, for example, Iraq alone (11 percent of total coverage) was given greater coverage than was the entire African continent (10 percent, which was not much more than the coverage of 8 percent for Israel-Palestine).[5] In a one-hour discussion on the BBC World Service (2005e) Talking Point radio program to mark Human Rights Day, the focus for the first 30 minutes was entirely on the so-called 'war on terror' and Iraq, and the second half of the program dealt with a range of countries including China (Tibet), the DPRK, Myanmar, Vietnam, Pakistan, Indonesia and the Middle East. A brief discussion of Liberia (namely the issue of former President Taylor) was the only appearance of Africa in the entire program. An examination of the news stories featured over the first half of 2005 on the main page of each of the websites of the major global news agencies – Agence France-Presse (AFP), Associated Press (AP) and Reuters – revealed that Iraq and Israel-Palestine each were given considerably greater coverage than was the entire African continent by each of the agencies.[6]

It is not necessarily the case that these countries and their conflicts are completely ignored throughout their course, and individual incidents may be occasionally covered. However, it is the odd or dramatic incidents that are thought to stimulate curiosity (morbid or otherwise) that are more likely to attract a media response than 'mundane' developments in conflicts and peace processes. In the DRC, it was a volcanic eruption that had affected refugees in Goma, rather than the conflict itself, that attracted considerable media attention. Other rare events, such as a plane door

---

5   Study conducted by author, July to December 2005. Coverage was measured by counting the number of stories (by country and region) for one world news program per day.

6   Study conducted by author, January to June 2005. Coverage was measured by counting the number of stories (by country and region) from the main page of the homepage once per day. The English version of the AFP homepage and the UK version of the Reuters homepage were studied.

coming off in midair, attracted brief media attention where the conflict could not. In 2005, a number of people riding on top of an overloaded train in that country were swept off as it crossed a river. On the same day, the National Assembly of the DRC approved an amnesty for those involved in political crimes from 1996 to 2003: a major political development. The main news program of the BBC World Service (2005d) broadcast the former incident, with the latter development appearing only on the Focus on Africa program for African audiences. When a story came to light about a girl of Angolan origin being tortured after being accused of being a witch in the UK, the BBC sent a reporter to Angola specifically to investigate the story from the Angolan side (BBC World Service 2005c). Cost is apparently not an obstacle for such rare and sensational events.

Regional and Linguistic Differences

French language media corporations also follow similar patterns to English language and other Western media corporations, focusing intently on the same chosen conflicts, but their coverage of Africa and its conflicts has shown a tendency to be somewhat greater than that of their English counterparts. In 2000, *Le Monde* newspaper devoted 9.3 percent of its international coverage to Africa, compared, for example, to the *New York Times*, which devoted 6.9 percent, although Africa was still the least covered continent in *Le Monde* (behind Asia at 10.2 percent). In the second half of 2005, Radio France International (RFI) devoted 24 percent of its coverage to Africa, which made it the second most covered continent in that period, coming behind only Europe at 27 percent.[7] Coverage of Africa does have a tendency, however, to be focused largely on former French colonial territories, with conflicts in Algeria, Côte d'Ivoire and Chad, for example, given more significant amounts of coverage than most other African conflicts. It should also be noted that the majority of RFI's listeners are African. As seen in Figure 4.1, coverage of the DRC (a French-speaking country) is much greater in the French media than it is in the English media, and is at its greatest in the Western media in Belgium (the DRC's former colonial master). Even so, coverage is far below that of Israel-Palestine.

Regionalism and language do appear to be factors in media coverage of countries and conflicts in general. As Zixue Tai (2000, 351) notes of the media, 'if our earth can be called a "global village", all the villagers are myopic to those who are culturally, geographically and psychologically close.' Japanese and Australian media corporations will generally respond with greater intensity to conflicts occurring in Asia, for example, than media corporations from other continents, while the same can generally be said for North American media corporations concerning conflicts in Latin America. Conflicts in the Middle East and Europe, on the other hand, tend to attract intensive media coverage from much of the rest of the world, regardless of geographical distance or location. Within Africa, just as French media corporations tend to focus more on former colonies of that country, so too do British media corporations on their former colonies. Of the ten most covered African countries

---

7   Study conducted by author, July to December 2005. Coverage was measured counting the number of stories for one world news program per day.

reported on by BBC radio World News in the second half of 2005, seven of them were former British colonies. This was the same for BBC radio's Focus on Africa program, although the countries that were covered differed. Zimbabwe, for example, received comparatively more coverage on the regular BBC World News program (fourth most covered African country) than it did on the Focus on Africa program (thirteenth most covered African country), although the total amount of coverage was not particularly high in either case.

Oddly, this regionalism does not seem to apply as much to the African media, which can be observed following trends quite similar to those of their Western counterparts. While many African newspapers divide their pages according to national, African, and international news, many do not, and even among those that do, a look at overall coverage levels can be revealing. A search of the website of South Africa's *Mail & Guardian* for articles in the Africa and international sections of that paper from 1998 to 2006 revealed 3,750 hits for Iraq, 1,974 for Israel and 1,029 for Afghanistan, as compared to 1,271 for Congo, 1,144 for Sudan, 465 for Angola and 438 for Burundi. An examination of news in Zambia – a country surrounded by eight others (many of which have hosted major conflicts) and that has actively participated in numerous peacekeeping missions – also shows a disproportionate coverage of chosen conflicts at the expense of African ones, despite its location. In 2004, the *Post* newspaper (a privately owned newspaper that is by far the most read in Zambia) devoted more coverage on its international pages to the Middle East (24 percent) than it did to Africa (20 percent), and while it allocated 13 percent of its coverage to the USA, 11.5 percent to Iraq and 9 percent to Israel-Palestine, it devoted a total of only 4 percent to news coverage of all eight of Zambia's neighbouring countries combined.[8]

The Zambian example is also interesting in terms of positioning and news selection for individual events. On the day that the historic peace deal was signed officially ending the conflict in southern Sudan (9 January 2005), the Zambia National Broadcasting Corporation (ZNBC) broadcast two international news stories on its main evening news: Palestinian elections and the mistaken bombing of a house in Iraq by the US military. There was only a belated brief mention of the Sudanese peace deal in the late evening news. On the following two days, the AU held the first summit for its Peace and Security Council, with ten heads of state present, but the Palestinian elections and even US President George W. Bush's nomination for Head of Homeland Security appeared ahead of (or instead of) the summit in Zambian print and broadcast media (including radio). When the AU Peace and Security Council was launched in May 2004 (with eight heads of state present), Zambia's *Post* newspaper (2004) placed the article covering this event last on its international pages, behind three articles on Iraq and two on Israel-Palestine.

This trend is not limited to Zambia, however. In another example, in the 1990s Angolan TV covered with a minor mention the story of a large-scale massacre in that country, while broadcasting as its top story news on the conflict in Bosnia, backed with CNN footage (see Rønning, 2005 164–5). In the lead-up to the historic

---

8   Study conducted by author, January to December 2004. Coverage was measured counting the number of stories on the international pages for each day.

elections in the DRC, Botswana TV was giving considerably more coverage in the short international news segment of its evening news to the conflict between Israel and Lebanon than it was to the situation in the DRC. Nor is this trend limited to Africa: it can also be found in many other developing countries. In terms of the overall quantity of coverage, some Latin American media corporations provide their customers with more news on Europe or the USA than they do on Latin America (see Lozano et al. 2000, 84).

Positioning and Style of Coverage

It is not only the overall quantity of coverage that demonstrates the low levels of importance attached by the media to African conflicts. The positioning of a news item in comparison to the gravity of its content can also be revealing. Stories that would appear to be major events of historic value are unlikely to be treated with an appropriate level of importance relative to other stories if they occur in Africa. Historic elections in the DRC in July 2006, which were the dramatic culmination of a lengthy peace process, were the first democratic elections in that massive country in 45 years, and were the most expensive elections ever held in Africa. Yet on the day they were held, news of the elections failed to reach the top story on any major Western news outlet – broadcast, print or internet.[9] The story generally came in second, third or fourth behind at least one news item on Israeli airstrikes in Lebanon in their ongoing conflict, as well as other stories. On the Australian Broadcasting Corporation's (ABC) news website the top three stories were on the Israel-Lebanon conflict. The *Australian* newspaper put it behind news of the arrest of the actor Mel Gibson on drunk-driving charges. On the Fox News website the DRC elections were the ninth story featured.

When the results of a mortality survey of the conflict in the DRC, revealing a death toll of 3.8 million, were published in a medical journal (Coghlan et al. 2006), the *Weekend Australian* newspaper (2006) responded with a 50-word news brief in the bottom corner of page 11, sandwiched between two celebrity gossip briefs about a former rock star and a supermodel both in trouble with the law. Next to the brief was a 468-word novelty item about a new note being played in the world's slowest concert, and the rest of the page above was dominated with detailed news items about Iraq, Iran, Syria and terrorism-related issues in the UK and USA. When the original report of the same survey was released a year earlier (IRC 2004), the same newspaper responded with a 479-word article on page 9, entitled 'Aussie counts 3.8m dead in Congo', which focused on the personal difficulties faced by the Australian citizens in the survey team. Words informing the readers of the Australian-ness of the survey team and its members appear five times (not counting the title). There is little in the article about the conflict itself (Harris 2004, 9).

The style used to convey the information can also provide an insight into the media's response. For chosen conflicts, the conflict is typically presented by the media

---

9   Checks were conducted of the websites of ABC (Australia), AP, the *Australian*, CNN, *Die Welt*, Fox News, *Le Monde*, the *New York Times*, Reuters (UK), and the *Washington Post*.

in an emotive morality-play style format, with actors categorized in black and white as evil villain and innocent helpless victims, with the position of hero and saviour usually left open pending the arrival of the Western powers as an intervention force. The style of presentation demonizes the villain (see *Newsweek* 1999), sympathizes unquestioningly with the victim, and questions why the heroes in waiting have not yet acted, applying pressure on them to do something about the unacceptable situation of human suffering, although the hero may or may not appear. Coverage relies more on emotive images of suffering refugees in camps, and malnourished children with bloated bellies and tears and flies in their eyes, than it does on objective analysis of the causes, participants and political developments behind the conflicts. Such tendencies are particularly pronounced in television media. This style of coverage has been called the 'something must be done' school of journalism (see McLaughlin 2002, 182–98). News formatted in this emotive manner has also been described as a combination of information and persuasion: 'infosuasion' (see Savarese 2000), and as a combination of information and entertainment: 'infotainment'.

This style of simplistic emotive coverage is usually employed also for conflicts that receive intermediate levels of media attention, such as Darfur and Chechnya. In fact, the media's method of response to intermediate conflicts is essentially the same as that to chosen conflicts, with the only factor preventing the intermediate conflicts from becoming chosen conflicts being that the 'appointed' hero does not arrive to save the day: that is, there is no involvement of large numbers of Western troops (African peacekeepers do not appear to count). For Israel-Palestine, even in terms of the style of coverage, it occupies a somewhat unique position. As a conflict that evokes strong reactions from many actors and many angles, and with strong criticism of bias in coverage of any event (often from both sides), such simplistic infotainment-style coverage of conflict is untenable. The Western media is consequently much more careful about its coverage of this conflict, and generally avoids the morality play format.

One of the problems with the 'something must be done' style of coverage is that very few conflicts (if any) can be accurately simplified in this way. Conflicts are by their nature highly complex; participants are many and varied in terms of motives and conduct; and the evil, the good and the innocent cannot usually be so easily separated and put into clear-cut categories. As Greg McLaughlin reminds us (2002, 167), taking sides or adopting a moral standpoint in this way (as the media usually does with chosen and intermediate conflicts) 'allows for no grey areas, no doubts, no scepticism, no questions. What happens when certain facts fail to fit the moral framework? What then? What happens when the "bad guys" tell the truth? Or when the "good guys" tell lies?' Afghanistan's Northern Alliance (warlords who were responsible for numerous massacres) and the Kosovo Liberation Army (once listed by the USA as a terrorist organization) became 'good guys' from the perspective of the media as allies of intervening Western forces, and dubious pasts and present actions were glossed over or ignored. Similarly, the military activities of the rebel groups in Darfur are largely ignored or glossed over by the media in order to maintain a black and white picture of villain and innocent helpless victim. From the perspective of most of the mainstream Western media, the Western participants in conflict – as the 'home team' – are automatically the 'good guys', although they may occasionally make 'mistakes'.

'Something must be done' style of coverage is in stark contrast to the style of coverage employed for stealth conflicts. On the rare occasion that these conflicts are covered, it is usually in a detached, matter-of-fact style. A ten-second news brief with few images and no interviews or analysis may inform us that a massacre occurred during a rebel attack on a train in Angola, and a tiny news brief tucked away in the corner of page eleven of the newspaper may inform us that it has been found that four million people have died in the DRC, but there will be little detail, little explanation, and little coverage designed to evoke an emotional response. Whereas emotive terms such as 'slaughter' or 'murder' may be used to describe what has happened to the victims of conflict for chosen or intermediate conflicts, more neutral terms such as 'dead' or 'lives lost' are likely to be used for the victims of stealth conflicts. Furthermore, the use of terms such as 'chaos' and 'tribal clashes' to describe the nature of the conflict in question suggests that the conflict cannot be understood, and that there is nothing anyone can do about it.

Entertainment Media

At a different level, the Western entertainment media industry has similarly shown itself to be nation- and ethnocentric. Hollywood movies that deal with conflict focus almost invariably on US involvement in conflict. In the USA, military movies over the past decades have focused on Cold War issues, the Vietnam War, conflicts in the Middle East and more recently the spectre of anti-Western terrorism. The US military usually cooperates with the making of such movies if it is expected to improve public understanding of the military and to be beneficial for recruiting (Eitelberg and Little 1995, 43–4). African conflicts (real or fictional) very rarely appear as a backdrop in Western movies. There must almost always be a connection to the country making the movie or the dominant racial group in that country. *Black Hawk Down* was about the conflict in Somalia, but it was entirely a US military story. *Tears of the Sun* was set in Nigeria, but again was essentially a US military story. *The Interpreter* and *Blood Diamond* both were stories set in or about Africa, with Africans as leading characters, but in each case, those Africans were white and were played by famous Western actors. The British movie on the Rwandan genocide, *Shooting Dogs*, is essentially the story of white missionaries caught up in the genocide, and *The Last King of Scotland*, although focusing on Idi Amin, is more the story of a white doctor and his relationship with the dictator. *Hotel Rwanda* is at least led by black African characters, although they are played by Hollywood actors.

Similar can be said of regular television programming. In 2006, the *Oprah Winfrey Show*, for example, aired a program focusing on threats facing the world. It featured Queen Rania of Jordan and a number of experts as guests. The entire program, however, was centred on terrorism, Iraq, Iran and Israel-Palestine. Two of the three experts featured were terrorism experts, and all three discussed only the issue of terrorism and the Middle East. Although the program claimed to discuss threats to the world, it covered only those threats seen from a US, or at best Western perspective.[10] The Christian television channel, Trinity Broadcasting Network, has a US base, but broadcasts its message across the globe using a large satellite network. Despite its apparently global message and global audience, television hosts on the program regularly display their pride in rallying around the US flag (see Zahn 2006), and, particularly since the invasion and occupation of Iraq, broadcast programs and hold prayer sessions saluting and/or asking protection for 'our troops' (see TBN 2005).

Internal Dynamics

Decision-making within the media needs to be viewed through the process known as 'gatekeeping'. In a world overflowing with massive amounts of information, the difficulty in media decisions is not necessarily in finding adequate information, but perhaps more in filtering, selecting and making sense of it. 'Gatekeepers' attempt to do this at each step of news production, deciding which options and information to 'let through the gate'. Gatekeeping happens when an editor or a producer decides to send a reporter to a particular country to cover a particular event, or to open a bureau and station a reporter in a particular city, country or region. Reporters gatekeep when they decide which story to explore, who to talk to, and what information or images to include in and exclude from their reports. Editors and producers again become gatekeepers when they decide which stories to include and exclude in the presentation of the news, and the length and order in which they are printed or broadcast.

Media gatekeepers may be guided by many considerations: at times they may feel the need to raise an issue that they think is important, or more likely they aim to give their consumers what they think they want, considering primarily what is likely to sell more newspapers or raise the ratings. Usually, decisions are made on 'gut instinct' developed through years of experience in what sells and what doesn't, without confirming with their consumers each time. Some of the 'rules' that may affect the selection or rejection of a conflict include the following: proximity, recency, prominence, novelty and emotive appeal (see Moeller 1999, 17). The BBC's Nik Gowing (1996, 81) reflects on the media's coverage of conflict 'as supermarket war video ... Editorially we can pick and choose – just like walking down the shelves of breakfast cereal'. Some decisions are automatic, and such factors do not even need to be considered or weighed; if the home country is involved in a foreign conflict or intervention, or is likely to be involved, for example, coverage will be high.

Shrinking Foreign Presence

At the end of the Cold War, gatekeeping appeared to become all the more crucial in international news, as media corporations began shedding their foreign newsgathering capabilities. In an era of rapid globalization marked by an expansion of the reach of information, it is ironic that media corporations have been closing down foreign

---

10 Admittedly, the *Oprah Winfrey Show* does, from time to time, deal with stories in connection with specific conflicts elsewhere (albeit usually from a human drama perspective at an individual level), and the eastern DRC has been the subject of such a story.

bureaux, reducing the numbers of foreign correspondents and the quantity of foreign news produced. This situation is closely linked to the diminishing response by the media to foreign conflict. Melinda Robins (2003, 30) laments that 'the steamroller of economic and cultural globalization and the proliferation of media outlets in a digital age could have meant an increase in foreign news coverage, but the reverse has been true.' To obtain information for foreign stories, media corporations rely instead on 'stringers' (often local freelancers) or on 'parachute journalism', by which reporters based elsewhere fly in, do a story, and fly out again, without the time, background knowledge or connections in the country to provide a substantive picture or analysis of the situation. With the numbers of permanently stationed reporters decreasing, those that remain are becoming less specialized, and are expected to cover increasingly larger areas of the globe and to be more mobile. Despite this reduction, however, news corporations maintain the capacity to mobilize disproportionately large groups of correspondents for conflicts deemed worthy of saturation coverage, with their gathering en masse to cover a chosen conflict. At their peak, chosen conflicts may host thousands of foreign reporters.

This is in stark contrast to the network of coverage for Africa and its conflicts. Although some French-language media corporations do maintain a focus on Africa to a degree, few other Western print or broadcast corporations maintain a significant presence in Africa at all, and even the largest maintain permanent bureaux only in Cairo (which is inevitably focused on the Middle East rather than Africa), Johannesburg and possibly one or two in countries on the east and/or west coast, 'skimming over the rest of the continent' (Robins 2003, 30). Al Jazeera, presenting its line-up of new bureaux in 2006, announced that with just five bureaux in Africa (including Cairo), it would have the greatest presence in that continent of any global broadcaster (AME Info 2006). CNN has four bureaux in the space of just several hundred kilometres in the Middle East – in Beirut, Jerusalem, Amman and Cairo, compared to just three in all of sub-Saharan Africa (Lagos, Nairobi and Johannesburg). The ABC (Australia) has the most extensive network of foreign correspondents and bureaux of any Australian media corporation; this includes two bureaux in the Middle East (Jerusalem and Amman) but just one in Africa (Johannesburg), which is expected not only to cover Africa, but oddly, to assist also in coverage of the Middle East, as if the Middle East needed more than two bureaux where all of Africa could do with less than one. The *Yomiuri* newspaper has ten bureaux in Europe and four in the Middle East, yet just one in Africa (Johannesburg). Having correspondents in place is no guarantee of coverage either. The few Japanese correspondents that are stationed in Africa complain that no matter how many stories they write, most are not selected for inclusion in the final product of the news (anonymous, interviews with the author, Nairobi, March 2005; Pretoria, February 2008).

To augment their supply of foreign news, media corporations also rely on global news agencies. These agencies maintain far more bureaux than the broadcast and print corporations (some with more than 100 foreign bureaux). But the financial difficulties experienced by the 'big four'[11] global news agencies that have traditionally

---

11 Traditionally, the big four were: AFP, AP, Reuters and United Press International (UPI).

dominated the international news market also serve to demonstrate the fall in the demand for foreign news by media corporations, particularly the print industry. UPI went into decline and has virtually disappeared from the international news scene, while Reuters evolved into an agency focusing on business information services, from which the vast majority of its profits are now generated (although it does retain its international newsgathering services). The other two agencies remained largely as they were, with AP retaining non-profit cooperative status, and AFP heavily reliant on indirect subsidies from the French government. It would appear that the consumers of international news have reduced their consumption such that international newsgathering is no longer a profitable business. News agencies admit that they have become increasingly forced to think more like newspapers, and thus gather and provide the news that their customers want (see Moeller 1999, 31).

So why has the expenditure of print and broadcast media corporations on international newsgathering decreased? A number of reasons can be raised. The end of the Cold War brought with it the perception among media corporations that foreign news had lost its political relevance, and the terrorist attacks and Western militarism appear to have only temporarily restored this perceived relevance. This situation coincided with increasingly stiff competition for the news market. The effect of the greater competition meant less revenue for each media corporation and consequently a smaller budget, and with the end of the Cold War and a perceived fading relevance for the rest of the world, the expensive practice of foreign newsgathering became an easy target for cost cutting. The luxury of stationing numerous reporters around the globe thus became unsustainable for many media corporations. The rapid spread of the Internet has also affected how people access news in the Western world, making it difficult for traditional news providers to attract customers. With competition from television and internet news sources, newspapers were suffering a general decline in sales; the overall 'pie', over which competitors could fight for a share, was also getting smaller. Partly due to such economic realities, the provision of news to the public was being seen less as a social duty and more as a business decision, with news being a marketable commodity. As Jeffrey Abramson (1990, 263) notes, 'Whether we are talking about television or newspapers, journalism is a business – big business – and that inevitably means accommodating news values to the needs of commercial success.'

Focus on Packaging, Presentation and Speed of News

Overall budget cuts aside, there have also been notable changes in the allocation of the remaining budget for foreign coverage. Media competition also means vying with other corporations in terms of getting information to customers with greater speed, and CNN's slogan, 'be the first to know', is indicative of this, almost to the point that the speed of the arrival of information is perceived as being more important than the quality or usefulness of the information. Keeping up with the development of information and communication technology has been the key in the speed of delivery. For broadcast media, this means that expensive camera equipment and equipment for receiving and transmitting satellite signals, among other devices, need to be purchased and maintained. As technology improves and the devices emerge with the ability to send better quality images from smaller packages, equipment needs to be replaced and updated. This kind of expenditure makes an already tight budget for foreign newsgathering even tighter, hence the need to make do with fewer foreign correspondents in fewer locations.

Competition not only means beating the others in speed of delivery, but also in terms of making news the most attractive and gripping, with a view to attracting and keeping as many consumers as possible. As such, the packaging and presentation of news has taken on greater importance: again, often at the expense of foreign newsgathering. Increased expenditure for packaging and presenting may include the extensive use of colour in newspapers, and the acquisition and maintenance of new and improved studio news production technologies. But the attachment of greater importance to packaging and presentation does not only have the effect of reducing the overall budget available for foreign newsgathering, it also affects the selection of conflicts for coverage. One strategy used in attracting and keeping customers is concentrating intently on just one or two conflicts, keeping a clear focus on a particular ongoing story, so that readers will feel compelled to 'tune in again tomorrow' to find out what has happened in that particular conflict. To attempt to give broader coverage to a greater number of different conflicts would disrupt the storyline and possibly confuse and discourage the viewer from becoming attached.

The media's prioritizing of the packaging and presentation of news also affects the style of coverage, as news increasingly blends with infotainment that is designed to hook rather than educate the consumer. Conflict news that focuses on individual human drama stories, sensational events, and a general emotive – rather than objective or analytical – focus, is symptomatic of this, as is the media's obsession with 'fresh', and preferably live news. One of the draw cards used to grab the attention of viewers is the fact that the event has just happened, or that it is happening right now. The longer the time is between the event and the report, the less value the report has. Thus, despite having all the latest technological devices allowing reporters to beam crystal clear images in real time to the other side of the planet, it will mean very little if the news crew and their satellite uplink devices cannot reach the scene of the incident in good time. With a thinning of foreign correspondents, more of the world loses its news value, and conflict that is distant from a media bureau, is situated in a location with poor infrastructure, or is otherwise difficult to access, is unlikely to be covered at all. In theory, advances in technology do mean that information can be transmitted from anywhere to anywhere on the planet in real time, but in practice such technology has ironically contributed to a situation in which less of the planet is seen.

This trend is more obvious in television media. While print media can make do with written information (and an occasional photograph), for television news corporations, news without moving images is simply not news and will not be aired. It was seen of South Africa under apartheid, for example, that 'When the cameras were forced out, the amount of television news about South Africa plummeted' (Neuman, Just and Crigler 1992, 116). Conversely, however, ease of access to visual media can mean a disproportionately greater emphasis on that particular story in television news media than in the newspaper media. Although video filmed by local stringers with narrated voiceovers can be used as a substitute, images of a conflict-affected area with a familiar and trusted reporter on the scene have greater value, and thus the ability to get one's own reporters on the scene with a camera in a timely fashion can have a considerable impact on whether or not a story is covered. With a bureau and camera crew permanently based in Jerusalem, for example, the decision by a media corporation to cover a violent or political event in Israel-Palestine is an easy one: excess costs are virtually nonexistent and there is a high probability that sensational and live images can be easily captured.

If word arrives that a school has been bombed in rural southern Sudan, on the other hand, a news crew must first fly from Cairo or Nairobi to Khartoum, then charter a smaller plane or go overland to reach the site; this could mean an expensive trip measured in days rather than hours. Most media corporations simply choose to ignore such inconvenient incidents. On the rare occasion that a media corporation does choose to cover such a remote incident, the reporter almost invariably devotes a significant amount of the news report detailing how difficult it has been for their crew to reach the site, as if the reporter's trip is part of the story. Steven Livingston (1996, 74–9) saw the location and access in this sense as critical factors in the media's decision to provide extensive coverage of conflict and famine in Somalia, yet at the same time almost none at all for southern Sudan, which was also suffering from conflict and famine in the early 1990s. Reporters seeking information on Somalia were able to hitch rides on UN planes from their bases in Nairobi, quickly record some images of humanitarian suffering and be back in Nairobi on the same day. The reliance on live coverage affects the quality (as well as the selection) of news coverage. In order to ensure that the news program can get its news live and on demand, reporters in the field need to stay close to the satellite dish near the pool at the hotel, instead of chasing down a story – a practice called 'palm tree journalism' (Strobel 1997, 75). As Brian McNair (2005, 40) points out, 'Satellite phones and other mobile newsgathering technologies have allowed correspondents on the scene to be constantly present on air, but often with nothing of substance to say.'

Oddly, these trends also affect government-funded media corporations that are supposed to be free from commercial concerns, and that have been 'needed to cover the complex stories that their commercial rivals ducked' (*Weekend Australian* 2005). The UK's BBC, Japan's Nippon Housou Kyokai (NHK) and Australia's ABC, for example, should in theory be able to avoid the shift towards infotainment and sensationalism, providing more global, objective and proportionate coverage than commercial media corporations. To a large extent, however, they have not (see also C. Shaw 2003, 63–4). Although the BBC provides proportionately more coverage of African conflicts than CNN, for example, it is still relatively little. NHK ignores Africa almost as much as its commercial counterparts do in its main news programs. The sad reality is that a non-commercial broadcaster cannot be free of commercial-type pressures because it 'must pay attention to its audience share if it is to maintain political and public support for its licence fee funding. Journalism here, as elsewhere, is a business, manufacturing and selling a product' (McNair 2005, 29).

Issues of Danger and Access in Reporting

One reason sometimes given for the failure to cover some stealth conflicts is the danger involved in getting a story. There certainly is some truth in this assertion; conflict is by its nature violent and unpredictable, and any conflict environment is potentially hazardous for a journalist. Journalists have been actively targeted in places such as Algeria, Iraq and Colombia, and warlords in any conflict situation can appear highly unpredictable. Yet, in reality, potential danger to journalists appears to have little bearing on the choice to cover a conflict; if gatekeepers decide, for other reasons, that a conflict is particularly newsworthy, danger ceases to be an obstacle and the conflict will be covered despite the risks to the lives of the journalists. Furthermore, despite tight foreign newsgathering budgets, media corporations continue to bear the astronomical costs associated with protecting their journalists in such situations, at the expense of reporting in other countries. The high number of journalists killed in chosen conflict zones reflects not only the high number of journalists in the field, but also the risks and costs that media corporations and the reporters themselves are willing to bear for a popular story. More journalists were killed during the initial NATO attack on Afghanistan, for example, than were American or British soldiers (McNair 2005, 42). Post-invasion Iraq is probably the most dangerous conflict in the world for Western reporters to operate from, given the deliberate targeting and high levels of violence, yet Western reporters do operate from Iraq, and coverage is consistently high. Roughly half of journalists killed covering conflicts throughout the world in 2004 were killed in Iraq. For four years straight (since the invasion) it has been the deadliest place in the world for reporters. Danger as a reason for not covering any particular conflict is as such altogether unconvincing.

Political restrictions in access to the conflict zone can also be an obstacle to coverage. Governments or other parties to a conflict may restrict access to a particular region that is in a state of conflict. The Sudanese government has restricted access by journalists to the Darfur region of that country, as has the government in Myanmar to its country, and militants in the Niger Delta refuse entry to journalists into areas under their control. Rwandan forces and the rebel groups in Zaire during the overthrow of President Mobutu were also particularly skilful in their control of access by the media (Pottier 2002, 53–9). Certain countries may exclude certain media corporations from entry into their territories, as in the case of Zimbabwe with the BBC. Yet this is hardly an insurmountable obstacle. For all of the Sudanese government's attempts to control the media, the Darfur conflict receives considerable amounts of media coverage (even if many of the images may not be coming from Darfur itself), and the BBC still manages to cover Zimbabwe, staging occasional clandestine operations into Zimbabwe (which add to the sensationalism of the report) despite a government ban. The level of comfort or discomfort for the journalist stationed in a particular area may also be an issue contributing to the access factor in covering a conflict. In any case, obstacles of danger and access do not prevent journalists from gathering information from the surrounding safer and/or more accessible areas. Any conflict can be covered in one way or another if there is interest and willingness.

A media corporation that is determined to report on a particular story can find any number of ways to overcome the issues of cost, danger and access. And even if Western print and broadcast media corporations choose not to put their own staff at risk, or pay large amounts of money to chase down a story themselves, that should in no way prevent a story from reaching the Western media – particularly the newspapers. The major news agencies continue to gather material from over one hundred foreign newsgathering bureaux, and there are news agencies that focus on developing countries, such as Inter Press Agency (IPS) and Afrol, which focuses solely on Africa. Even the UN agencies provide a certain quantity of print news. A look at the website of All Africa shows how much news is available on that continent from various sources. Although Western print and broadcast media corporations are increasingly failing to gather news from most of the world themselves, there is certainly no lack of available news about the world; these corporations simply choose not to use what is already available. Cost, danger and access are considerations to a degree, but other factors are at work here in the choice of the news that is included in the final product, and how newsworthy a conflict or incident is perceived to be, is at the centre of this decision.

The Close-to-Home Factor

As editors make their decisions on covering conflict, the question of how close to home a conflict is, is not merely a matter of geographical proximity. Nationalism/ patriotism also feature prominently in this process, as editors consider the effect the conflict may have on the home economy, potential security threats, relationships with allies and even the country's honour and reputation. What is best for 'our' country is a constant theme in many newspaper editorials concerning foreign issues. This is particularly prominent when 'our' country is a party to the conflict or involved in some prominent way. As Steven Livingston (1997, 14) points out, from August 1992 'media coverage of Somalia skyrocketed, not because conditions had worsened, but because Americans were there'. Media corporations almost invariably focus the vast majority of attention on the conflict from the home perspective, and many 'rally around the flag', abandoning any pretence of journalistic objectivity. The presentation of news on Fox and CBS in the USA is particularly indicative of this trend, although this phenomenon appears to be present to a degree in many, if not most, media corporations. Such corporations appear to have become steadfast cheerleaders for the US government and military through their involvement in conflicts, showing, for example, the flag flying on the news and asking God to bless America. David Puttnam (2003, 51) notes that during the Iraqi invasion, Fox's 'shamelessly biased coverage seemed to use patriotism as the opiate that lulled the audience into assent and compliance'. This tendency may reflect a business decision, based on the notion that patriotism sells, but it may also reflect the personal feelings of the decision makers in the corporation.

Nationalism/patriotism aside, the home angle of foreign news is also related to a reliance on local sources of information for foreign news, which is often determined by matters of cost, ease of newsgathering and perceived credibility of sources. For foreign stories, although there may be some reporting from the field, a large proportion of coverage is conducted from the home capital city, with sources for information and interviews coming from a small pool of local policymakers, policy analysts and other journalists (one study found that as many as one-third of stories by prominent US news media corporations used journalists as their sources) (Bishop 2001). This compounds the phenomenon of viewing foreign events through a distinctly local lens. Part of the attraction of local sources is that they can be accessed quickly, cheaply and conveniently. This is particularly relevant given today's limited foreign newsgathering budgets and the obsession with real time news and response. Familiarity and the fact that the sources belong to locally known and trusted institutions also are necessary in the interests of maintaining credibility – credibility that they often gain 'by appearing many times, not because of the quality or depth of information they supply' (26).

Nor is 'home' limited to the interests of the people within the borders of the country in which the media corporation is based. It is connected also with other forms of identity, be they racial, religious, linguistic, social or other. 'White' victims of conflict, for example, are treated with considerably greater importance by the Western media than those of other races, because Western media corporations believe that their predominantly white customers will be able to identify most with them. Another of the contributing factors to this situation is that Western media corporations themselves are largely dominated by white people. Non-whites made up approximately 30 percent of the US population in 2001, but less than 12 percent of the newsrooms in that country (Mellinger 2003, 131). Ethnic minorities are almost completely absent from French media (RFI 2005), and the former BBC Director-General publicly admitted in 2001 that the BBC was 'hideously white', with 98 percent of the management structure being white (BBC Scotland 2001). Such decisions based on identity are made not necessarily only in the interests of satisfying the customer, but may well also reflect the editor's own prejudices. Similarly, for media corporations, victims of conflict that speak the same language as their consumers – those who can be interviewed without the need for voiceovers or subtitles – are also seen as important in the process of identification, reducing attributional distance. Phillip Knightley (2003b, 511) tells us of notorious stories of reporters who, upon arriving at refugee camps, shout at refugees, 'Is there anyone here who's been raped and speaks English?'

Examples of race as a factor in media decisions can be seen in the Philippines and Zimbabwe in 2000. Conflict in the Philippines was the second most covered conflict on CNN in 2000 because of the white hostages that had been captured by rebels, not because of the scale, or any significant military or political developments in that conflict. The relative prominence of Zimbabwe in Western media coverage compared to other African conflicts that are of an incomparably greater scale can be explained both from national interest and racial perspectives. Under President Mugabe, Zimbabwe threatens the reputation of Western governments with his anti-Western rhetoric. Such coverage also makes for a good morality play format, with Mugabe the villain. At the same time, because the violence in 2000 was directed against white farmers, the media corporations felt their audiences could identify with their plight. These two examples are notable because their coverage cannot be explained by physical proximity, the threat of refugee flows, or other forms of national interest for the home country, unlike conflicts in Bosnia or Kosovo. Race can clearly be identified as a factor in the media coverage of these conflicts.

Simplification

But making media-coverage judgements based on national, racial, religious, ethnic and other identity-based factors in the parties to conflict is not only a question of the media corporations harnessing their customers' sense of feeling for 'people like us'. Such factors can also boost the newsworthiness of a conflict because they help simplify the conflict into easily identifiable sides for the benefit of the spectators – not unlike the function of different coloured jerseys for different football teams. Perceptions that a conflict is between Christians and Muslims, or between Arabs and blacks, for example, help the coverage of a conflict by making that conflict instantly 'understandable', whether these categorizations accurately reflect the nature of the conflict or not. On the other hand, if a conflict in Africa is black on black, without a perceivable major religious or other easily identifiable characteristic, then it lacks the ingredients for ease of identification and subsequently fails to attract or sustain value in terms of newsworthiness for predominantly white Western media corporations.

Furthermore, if observers perceive the presence of an element of genocide, with one easily distinguishable group apparently intent on exterminating the other, the combination of the ability to identify the parties to the conflict and the sensationalism of genocide can give a conflict a high level of newsworthiness. Darfur is one such example, having acquired newsworthiness largely because it has been characterized as an Arab-versus-black conflict, with Arab as clear-cut villain and black as victim, and because some have associated that conflict with the spectre of genocide. The attention value of the notion of genocide has undoubtedly been assisted by the sense of guilt over the failure to respond to the genocide in Rwanda. Rwanda had much greater difficulty being noticed by the media. As Edward Giradet (1996, 57) points out, 'It is doubtful that the media would have reported on Rwanda had it "just" been a case of Rwandans killing Rwandans', as both the parties were black and not so easily distinguished from each other. Similar large-scale killings in Burundi one year earlier had been almost completely ignored by the media. In Rwanda it took a combination of the concept of genocide and the convenient fact that Western reporters, who had just covered the first post-apartheid elections in South Africa, could pass by on their way back, to convince most editors (who like the policymakers had until then 'refused to budge') to finally cover the story. The inconvenient barriers of distance and access were temporarily overcome by the coincidental positioning of reporters in the area at the time.

In this sense, whether or not media corporations are able to simplify a conflict to make it readily 'understandable', can be an important factor in determining whether or not a conflict is covered. While the media does take great liberties (most notably with regard to African conflicts) in categorizing and simplifying the causes and nature of conflicts, the sheer complexity of most conflicts makes it extremely difficult for journalists themselves to understand, let alone explain to their customers, what is going on in conflict situations. The fact that the one-size-fits-all frame of the Cold War used to explain conflicts has disappeared (and that the new 'war on terror' frame seems to fit very few conflicts), together with the reliance on unspecialized reporters and in-and-out 'parachute journalism', serves to compound this situation. If the media cannot manage to simplify a complex conflict, and easily identify and separate its participants (preferably into 'good guys' and 'bad guys'), and there are no other compelling reasons for it to be newsworthy in the West (such as important national interests, white victims, the spectre of genocide), that conflict is likely to be simply ignored and to remain a stealth conflict in the eyes of the media.

The task of grasping the complexities of the conflict in the DRC, for example, along with its many and varied parties (and their many and varied motives and actions), and the underlying economic and political causes and effects, is difficult enough for anyone, but even assuming a journalist has acquired an adequate understanding of the situation, attempting to convey this information in a 30- or 60-second news item on CNN would be an exercise in futility. As such, more often than not, media corporations simply do not attempt to cover such conflicts, pretending instead that they do not exist, or that they are of little interest or importance, however grand in scale they may be. On the rare occasion that they do attempt to cover them, terms such as 'chaos', 'anarchy' and 'tribal killings' are employed in place of explanation, indicating that the media corporations have not understood the conflict; that they have failed to fit the parties to the conflict into the simplified morality play roles of villain and victim; and that nothing can be done. Having come to such a conclusion, dwelling on the subject would be uncomfortable, and the coverage ends there.

Media Convergence

The various factors presented above can help provide some ideas as to why certain conflicts are covered and others are not, but they do not necessarily explain the high levels of assimilation or 'media convergence': why so many media corporations from so many countries end up making the same choices in their selection of conflicts for coverage. This is particularly a point of concern when the coverage of certain conflicts by the media corporations of certain countries appears to be not only out of proportion with the scale of the conflict (as is usually the case with any media corporation), but even out of proportion with any notion of national interest, racial or religious connection, or geographical proximity: factors that would otherwise be thought to play a large role in conflict selection by the media. Extensive coverage in the Japanese media of conflicts that are 'distant' in many ways, such as those in Kosovo or in Israel-Palestine, is a case in point. One explanation for this phenomenon is the practice of 'pack journalism' (Strobel 1996, 62), by which media corporations rush to latch on to a story that one major media corporation has 'sniffed out' as being newsworthy. Media corporations closely monitor their rivals, and once a number of media corporations take up a particular story, it snowballs into a critical mass of media attention, with the bandwagon effect serving to raise the position of that conflict on the overall media agenda, such that those choosing not to cover it are in danger of being left behind by their competitors.

Another key factor behind this phenomenon is the concentration of ownership of the media. A continuous process of mergers and buy-outs of and among media corporations over the past two or three decades has seen the number of major media corporations shrink, and ownership of much of the world's media become highly concentrated in the hands of a small number of powerful, mostly US-based corporations. Global media tycoon Rupert Murdoch, for example, has 175 editors working for him in a wide variety of media corporations across the world (*Sydney Morning Herald* 2006). The same applies to the media companies within countries. The former Italian Prime Minister, Silvia Berlusconi, controls approximately 90 percent of the media in Italy (BBC World Service 2005a), while in Turkey two conglomerates control 60 percent of the media (and five corporations control 80 percent) (Algan 2003, 186). Concentration of ownership means, to a large extent, a concentration of power over the selection of editors themselves, as well as editorial policy and the selection of topics for coverage (Herman and Chomsky 1994, 3–14). This contributes to an accelerated, more powerful and global bandwagon effect in the selection (and exclusion) of conflicts for coverage.

These factors don't necessarily explain, however, why even many African-owned media corporations cover less of Africa and more of what the Western media corporations are covering. This media assimilation can in part be explained by the fact that many media corporations lacking newsgathering capacity buy their news from news agencies offering set packages of news or from other Western media corporations, simply print the story as is, or translate it into their own language. In relying on news sources produced from a Western perspective, these media corporations also get on the bandwagon, ending up with less coverage of conflict in their immediate surroundings, and more coverage of distant conflicts. This is particularly the case in the media corporations of developing countries, which, in the vast majority of cases, simply cannot afford to station reporters outside their borders for any length of time. Even for some national broadcast corporations, television cameras leave the country only when the head of state does.

Foreign news in Zambia's *The Post*, or ZNBC, for example, comes almost exclusively from external sources. News that appears in Zambian newspapers on neighbouring Angola or the DRC, is not gathered by Zambian journalists, but is bought from a Western or Chinese news agency or from the BBC. Botswana TV broadcasts BBC news from the close of regular programming in the late evening until the opening of regular programming late in the following morning. Most African television stations rely on a large dose of one or more of the following sources (usually subsidized) for their international news coverage: BBC, Canal France International (CFI), Deutsche Welle (DW), Voice of America (VOA), and, recently, China Central Television (CCTV). In the 1990s, the international coverage of the biggest and most prominent Afrikaans language newspaper in South Africa, *Beeld*, was based almost entirely on its own and Western news agency stories, although it maintained full-time foreign correspondents only in London and Washington D.C. (whom it shared with two other newspapers).[12] Even in the wealthy Japanese media industry, a large amount of foreign news that is printed in the newspapers is simply news translated from other, English-language sources. In this way, much of the world's foreign news is not only assimilated, but is assimilated in a way in which the peculiarities and prejudices of the Western media dominate the flow of information. Furthermore, many governments of countries in conflict may restrict information provided on the happenings there, and even in non-conflict countries, governments

---

12 It maintained part-time correspondents or stringers in nine other cities, four of whom were in Europe and two of whom were in Africa (see De Beer 2000, 260, 274).

may contribute to the weakness of private media corporations (often viewing them as a threat to their political power) (see Rønning 2005).

The Rise of the Internet

On top of all of these developments in the internal dynamics of the news media, the Internet has also served to transform journalism. Brian McNair (2005, 40) calls it 'possibly the most important leap in communications technology since the invention of print more than half a millennium ago'. It has, in many ways, changed the way people in the West access news (although this revolution has not reached most of those in the developing world). As early as 2000, surveys showed that 15 percent of Americans were getting online news everyday, and that half of adults under 30 years old were getting online news at least once a week (Eveland, Marton and Seo 2004, 83). By 2006, one in three Americans was getting news online three or more days per week (Jurkowitz 2006). News outlets are mushrooming, with any number of internet websites that can be accessed from computers and mobile phones now providing large quantities of updated news or links to news. News automatically appears on the screen as users access their e-mails on Yahoo!, MSN Hotmail, America Online (AOL) or other internet e-mail service providers. Traditional newspaper and television media corporations have gone online, providing news, features and archives, most of which are freely available. Search engines allow the Internet user to freely search (in just a fraction of a second) for news and information from any number of news outlets just by inputting the keywords of their choice.

There is also a mushrooming of 'journalists' – some with a considerably large readership – who operate primarily through the Internet (outside the traditional print and broadcast media), including webloggers, or bloggers, whose websites range from those providing a public diary account of bloggers' individual lives and thoughts on news items, to those providing professional quality news material and investigative journalism. Advances in technology have given rise to do-it-yourself journalism, whereby anyone with an increasingly inexpensive video camera (or even without) and an internet connection can become a reporter, as was seen by the information distributed on the Internet from Baghdad by a weblogger during the invasion of Iraq in 2003. Communication from end user to end user has also increased online, such that the boundary between the journalist, as gatherer and provider of news, and the public, becomes blurred and the journalist in the traditional sense of the word becomes almost irrelevant in some ways.

But what implications does this internet revolution have for the phenomenon of stealth conflicts? Potentially, the ramifications are highly significant; through the Internet, professional or even amateur journalists living in conflict zones could sidestep the commercial constraints of traditional media providers by providing news and images on their own websites, or providing their news to other popular bloggers or online websites. Theoretically, geographic location, cost, access, availability of images, and other traditional impediments to the flow of news should no longer matter. In reality, however, it is not that simple and the effect can be described as limited at best. Internet news has not escaped commercial realities. With online advertising becoming the big business that facilitates online news, the number of 'clicks' or 'hits' on a website has a great effect on which news provider survives and which doesn't, and it has rapidly become a 'numbers game', not unlike the rule of newspaper circulation numbers and television ratings (Macht 2001, 128–31). Thus, the same old problems of sensationalism, oversimplification, exclusion, the home angle, and ensuring that the target audience (predominantly Western, white and affluent) can identify with the conflict at hand, still apply.

Furthermore, despite the rapid growth of the Internet, it is still said to be in its 'adolescence', and even in the West it remains a supplementary news source. The vast majority of those who access internet news do so together with another news source (television, newspaper, radio), with only 4 percent of Americans in 2006 relying on the Internet alone as their source of news on a normal day (Jurkowitz 2006). The vast majority of news consumers still rely on traditional media channels for their news, and although the circulation of newspapers and the share of television news have declined amid heavy competition, and look to face further challenges, both are still surviving as industries, and appear set to continue doing so, even if they must continue to adapt to a new media environment. In any case, it is the mainstream television and newspaper media corporations that dominate the online news. A Google Zeitgeist study found that the news sites on the Internet that were most commonly accessed in 2001 were those offered by CNN, BBC and the *New York Times*. The data presented above have already shown how similar the Internet news sites are to their traditional counterparts in terms of coverage of chosen and stealth conflicts. Even most of the more popular news blogs cover primarily domestic political issues, and although the material may provide a fresh perspective in a fresh format, it is, more often than not, along similar lines to the traditional media in terms of topics. Furthermore, the Internet still has little meaning for the vast majority of the world's population outside the West who are not yet connected.

Of equal importance is the nature of the Internet as a news source. Unlike the use of the traditional media, which is largely a passive experience for the user as he/she sees, hears, reads, or at least glances over the news as it is presented, the Internet requires active user participation. Despite the apparent ability to access any amount of information about any subject, it can generally be said that the only information that the user can access is that which he/she actively seeks out, either by selecting a particular website or by using a search engine. That thousands of up-to-date articles from any number of African newspapers sorted by country and by theme can be read at leisure in any order by someone on the other side of the globe in their home without even leaving their chair, with just a few clicks of a mouse, is indeed a revolution in terms of the flow of information, but it means little if that person does not already have the initial interest in doing so, and is thus inspired to access, for example, the All Africa website and make use of it. If the websites of the mainstream Western news media corporations are accessed instead, as is usually the case, the user is likely to be no better off, in terms of breadth of global perspective, than if he/she had read a newspaper or watched the evening news. Informative websites on the situation in the DRC, and interventions there, may be freely and instantly accessible, but unless one has the knowledge and interest to access, for example, the MONUC website or the Friends of the Congo website, it is as if the information does not exist for that person. As already noted, the problem is not that information does not exist: it does and it is easily accessible; it is whether that information is accessed or not.

This applies also to the nature of access to information within a particular website. The main page of a news website may present many headlines, but usually it provides only a very short introduction for a small number of the articles. In order to access the information, the user must click on the links, and while this may give users greater freedom to determine their own news agendas in accordance with their own perception of the importance of particular world events, it also increases the selectivity of the news experience. News that the user may not necessarily see as interesting from looking at the title is less likely to be clicked on, and therefore the news remains unread, whereas in the traditional media that news would at least be likely to get a glance as the reader turns the pages of the newspaper or watches the evening news, which may further a broader learning experience over a wider range of topics (see Althaus and Tewksbury 2002; Schoenbach 2007; Eveland, Marton and Seo 2004). This type of selectivity is also creeping into the television news experience, with technology increasingly allowing users to pick and choose which programs, and which parts of programs, they want to watch.

External Influences

Media corporations do not mirror reality in their coverage of conflict; they select only very small portions of it, expressing the 'importance' of each conflict they happen to select by the quantity and depth of coverage they provide and by how they choose to frame it and its participants. This process of selection and framing is determined, to a degree, by the internal dynamics discussed above, including commercial realities and the perceived importance of the home connection. Yet despite the media's independent stance and theoretical ability to freely report on the world as it sees fit, other actors (namely policymakers, the public and academia) also play a significant role in the media's decision-making process.

Policymaker Influence

Both wittingly and unwittingly, policymakers (primarily those of the country in which a particular media corporation is based) have a major influence on the media's response to conflict. Although much has been made of the so-called CNN effect, or the media's influence on policy regarding response to conflict, the effect is certainly mutual, and the influence of the policy agenda on the media agenda in fact appears to be considerably stronger than the reverse situation, particularly concerning selection of conflicts for some form of response. A number of studies have shown how closely the media agenda appears to mirror the agenda of the domestic policymakers, and that media corporations 'index' their agendas and coverage (both in content and tone) according to the range of domestic political debate (see Bennett 1990; Hallin 1986; Mermin 1999). Such studies show that in the USA, for example, 'the news media have rarely moved beyond the confines of "official" Washington policy debates' (Robinson 2001, 527; see also Zaller and Chui 1996), such that 'what carries a story is not necessarily its truth or importance, but whether it is driven by dominant officials within institutional decision-making arenas' (Bennett, Lawrence and Livingston 2007, 29). Some even refer to the media in the USA as a 'semi-independent press', and assert that only this indexing can explain the fact that in a supposedly free press system, 'the thousands of organizations making up the mainstream press generally end up running much the same news every day, with much the same emphasis' (55; see also 46–71). This is hardly surprising, given that a large proportion of sources even for foreign affairs stories are domestic policymakers. The utility of policymakers as a convenient first point of gathering of foreign affairs news, the desire by the media to connect foreign events to local concerns, nationalism/patriotism, and the closeness of policymakers and the media corporations developed in the process of their coverage of domestic affairs, give policymakers a pronounced influence over the media's response to conflict.

The conflict in Somalia in the early 1990s was a key example used by those asserting that the media was able to move policymakers to intervene in conflict situations, but a more detailed examination of this case revealed that conversely, the policymakers had led the media in its response. The majority of humanitarian operations by the USA in Somalia were carried out before the media coverage began in earnest; the extensive media coverage followed, and was in fact a response to these operations. Interestingly, the Office of Foreign Disaster Assistance (OFDA) within the United States Agency for International Development is credited with raising the alarm on the crisis in Somalia; it alerted the media as part of its attempt to attract the attention of other branches of government in order to convince them to commit resources in response to the conflict (see Livingston and Eachus 1995; Mermin 1997). The media, detecting interest within sectors of the policymaking arena, picked up on the story and began to cover it, responding with greater attention as policy decisions were made.

Similar trends can be seen in the response to the conflict in Darfur. The conflict there escalated throughout 2003 but was largely unnoticed by both the media and policymakers in its first year: it was a typical stealth conflict. Interest was sparked in late March 2004, however, when the UN Humanitarian Coordinator for Sudan began to compare the conflict there to the genocide in Rwanda, just weeks before the tenth anniversary of that genocide. In April 2004, on that anniversary, US President Bush gave a statement on the situation in Darfur, lamenting that the conflict there had 'opened a new chapter of tragedy' in Sudan, and condemning the 'brutalization of Darfur' (CNN 2004). He also tied the conflict to Sudan's conflict in the south, calling it 'one of the worst humanitarian tragedies of our time'. These powerful and alarming statements were clearly not prompted by media pressure: at the time CNN had not touched on the subject at all, and the *New York Times* had published a total of only 11 references to the conflict (3 articles, 4 op-ed articles, 3 briefs and 1 letter).[13]

News coverage of the Darfur conflict began to grow slowly following this statement, with 12 references by CNN and 38 by the *New York Times* over the next 2 months and 22 days, at which point UN Secretary-General Kofi Annan and US

---

13 References to CNN and the *New York Times* coverage here were measured from website archive hits using Darfur as a keyword.

Secretary of State Colin Powell visited Darfur in a show of concern. An increase in coverage followed (57 references by CNN and 118 by the *New York Times* over the following 2 months and 22 days), and during the following months Powell announced the US position that genocide was taking place in Darfur, and an arms embargo was declared. Coverage decreased as the West backed away from its strong stance, and remained moderate throughout 2005, increasing only again in 2006 as the USA proposed sending a UN peacekeeping force to Darfur. In each case heavy media coverage followed, rather than preceded, statements and actions by policymakers. Domestic policy interest in foreign conflicts appears to be a powerful influence on the media.

In many ways, policymaker influence on the media is not by design: it is simply a consequence of the close relationship between the two, a relationship in which the media constantly monitors domestic policymakers. But there are also many ways in which policymakers do set out to actively influence the media, usually in an effort to influence other actors (typically either the general public or other elites). The reality during the conflict over Kosovo of a husband (spokesman for the US State Department) and wife (chief reporter for CNN on the conflict) occupying these respective positions obviously constitutes a clear conflict of interest, which may or may not have been a deliberate attempt at influence by either (or both) of the parties. The positioning of a US military psychological operations (psyops) specialist at CNN headquarters during the same conflict (Cockburn and St. Clair 2000), may well have contained some clear intent at influence on the part of the policymakers. Policymakers may also launch public relations campaigns, hiring public relations firms to encourage the media to move in a certain direction. Following the invasion of Kuwait by Iraq, for example, the Kuwaiti government hired a US public relations firm (Hill and Knowlton) to campaign for a US military response against Iraq, developing and sending media kits to numerous media corporations. They also fabricated the story of Iraqi soldiers tossing babies out of incubators in a Kuwaiti hospital during the invasion. The 15-year-old Kuwaiti girl brought to tell the story before the US Congress turned out to be the daughter of the Kuwaiti Ambassador to the USA (see Knightley 2003b, 486–8). Even the government of Uganda hired a US public relations firm in 2005 to improve its image (BBC World Service 2005b).

The example of Somalia above already shows how a certain sector of the policy arena may use the media to attract the attention of other, more powerful sectors in order to promote a particular response to a conflict. The holding of press conferences, the release of documents and reports and anonymous leaks of information by policymakers to the press can also serve the same purpose, and help to put a policymaker's perspective on the issue in the media. Where issues or incidents in conflicts have occurred that are inconvenient or uncomfortable for policymakers (atrocities committed by their own forces or by allies, for example), there are also a number of ways to influence the media to ignore, drop or downplay the news. The government may inundate the media with a large volume of other unrelated information or a sensational story, at an opportune moment, to drive the other story out of the headlines. They may also set flak machines of complaint calls and letters in motion to 'discipline' or 'correct' the media's choice of story or manner of coverage (see Herman and Chomsky 1994, 23, 26–8).

At the newsgathering level, policymakers may also identify reporters who are hostile, or who do not toe the government lines and viewpoints, actively taking measures to restrict their access to policymakers and information. Privileged access to government sources and information thus becomes limited to a small group of reporters who can be expected to swallow and amplify the government line. Aeron Davis (2003, 683), writing on the media-policy relations in the UK, tells us:

> In a sense, journalists operating in political elite circles, have, to a degree, become 'captured' by those they report on. It is not a matter of conspiracy or journalists writing under direct pressure from their sources. Instead, journalists are highly reliant on regular source contacts within Westminster, get most of their feedback on what they write from such sources, and are regularly subject to source threats (loss of access) and rewards (generous information/interview supply).

Government influence on the media is considerably more sophisticated in societies with strong press freedoms than those without. Some countries even sponsor trips by foreign journalists to their country to encourage positive media attention on the issues facing their country. In an article focusing on Israel and the Middle East written by the associate editor of a newspaper in Australia, for example, its author acknowledged the partial sponsorship of his trip from Australia to Israel by the Israel Foreign Ministry (Stewart 2006).

When Western countries are themselves parties to conflict, their militaries employ another broad range of tactics in the conflict zone to prevent information that is disadvantageous to their purposes from reaching the media, and to encourage advantageous information to flow through the media (see Dadge 2004). They set up luxurious press centres, dishing out copious quantities of statistics, information and sensational images of sanitized explosions (but not the deaths) to the media – enough to satisfy an unquestioning and patriotic media to a large extent. Reporters are strongly encouraged to join the military as 'embeds' (even being given honorary military ranks), and independent journalism is discouraged (usually successfully) in the strongest of terms; allegations abound of such 'unilateral' journalists being deliberately targeted in attacks by Western militaries (Knightley 2003a). When US forces occupying Iraq besieged the town of Fallujah in April 2004, Al Jazeera television covered the attacks, showing the large number of resulting civilian casualties, which sparked widespread outrage, and the attacks were called off. When the US forces returned in November of the same year, Al Jazeera had already been expelled from Iraq, and no media organization (except for those embedded and controlled) or even humanitarian organization was permitted to enter the town during the assault. The assault, in which the entire population was ordered to leave, and all that remained were treated as targets, thus went ahead unwitnessed and uninhibited by media coverage, and the town fell.

But such heavy-handed tactics are usually not necessary: 'self censorship' can be seen functioning quite effectively in much of the Western media response to conflict. This may be because of a media system that encourages nationalism/patriotism on the part of the editors and reporters (on their own part and/or on behalf of their customers), and because of media closeness to domestic policymakers and other elites in domestic society. In any case, mainstream media coverage of foreign events and conflicts is by and large based on the fundamental assumption that 'our' country and its allies are the 'good guys' and their enemies are the 'bad guys'. This position takes on greater clarity when a long-term enemy has been identified: in the past, communism, now, terrorism. Any evidence to the contrary is generally ignored or downplayed (or seen as an isolated exception by a misguided individual or group), even without the direct intervention by policymakers, due to a process of selection of key editors and other decision makers, and the internalization of the media's broad political stance and perceived purpose in society by the gatekeepers at various levels within a particular media corporation. Unlike the propaganda system of a totalitarian state, Western media corporations 'permit – indeed, encourage – spirited debate, criticism, and dissent, as long as these remain faithfully within the system of presuppositions and principles that constitute an elite consensus, a system so powerful as to be internalized largely without awareness' (Herman and Chomsky 1994, 302).

There are countless examples of how the Western media's focus on particular conflicts and incidents, and its neglect of others, appear to be in accordance with support of home government positions and ideologies. Media coverage in the West, for example, brushed over the gassing of Kurds in Iraq when Iraq was an ally of the West, but expressed outrage over their oppression when Iraq became an enemy. Similarly, the Western media has consistently ignored the oppression of Turkish Kurds and the conflict in that country; Turkey remains a key ally in a strategic location and a model Islamic country from the Western perspective (S. Cohen 2001, 173). When a US battleship in Iranian waters shot down an Iranian civilian passenger jet on a regular flight path in daylight, the media downplayed it as an unfortunate mistake, but when Soviet forces shot down a South Korean civilian passenger jet that had strayed into DPRK airspace at night, it sparked outrage in the media and was treated as a deliberate, evil act befitting an 'Evil Empire' (see Entman 1991). Support for policy positions at home also partially explains why Western media basically ignored the invasions and occupations of Zaire/DRC by key Western allies in Africa – Uganda and Rwanda. After the Gulf War, both the *Washington Post* and the *New York Times* provided charts detailing the losses in the conflict on both the US and Iraqi sides, but although US losses were presented in terms of numbers of people killed and injured, the only Iraqi losses that were provided were numbers of tanks, artillery and other non-human losses (see FAIR 1991).

At a different level, debates by policymakers through the UN Educational, Scientific and Cultural Organization (UNESCO) over the global flow of information in the decade of 1976 to 1985 also led to some novel attempts to influence the media. Developing countries 'contended that news transmission across national borders is imbalanced and that information about the developing world conveyed by the western news agencies is insufficient and distorted, and therefore cannot meet the needs of the developing countries' (Wu 2003, 11–2). They thus struggled to formulate a policy towards a New World Information and Communication Order (NWICO), seeking to correct this imbalance with a series of policy- and practical-level measures. Key Western countries and journalists rejected the NWICO proposals, seeing them as attempts to meddle in the media's choices and coverage, contrary to the principles of freedom of the press. The debates lost their momentum as the USA and UK withdrew from UNESCO, although a number of the recommendations (though not at a policy level) have had some moderate success, such as the development of regional news agencies, starved of capital as they are (see Sosale 2003).

Public Influence

As the consumers of the products of the media corporations, it can be expected that the general public will have considerable influence over the media. This is particularly the case in the current environment in which more news media corporations are competing for a shrinking market; there would appear to be an increasing tendency for the media to gear its products towards producing what it thinks the people want to know, rather than what the media thinks they should know. One simple conclusion would be that foreign news is decreasing because the general public appears to be becoming less interested in foreign affairs (unless it directly affects them or their country), which suggests a large influence by the general public over the media agenda. In reality, however, it is not quite so simple. Although editors and other gatekeepers may think they are working to satisfy the desires of the general public in their provision of the news, much editorial work is in reality based on gut instinct, rather than on opinion polls or long-term analysis.

Some observers see the 'giving the customers what they want' claim as a myth:

> The corporate media, in their relentless pursuit of profit and market share, are rarely, if ever, passive servants of public demand, but are often actively utilizing their resources to create new audience demand. To that end, the media often opt for what has been commercially successful in the past or the line or path whose marketability has been already tested with competitors (Tai and Chang 2002, 255).

In some cases what the customers want may be determined by those who shout the loudest, rather than necessarily what the majority want. One BBC editor (G. Smith 2007) wrote of a decision to cover a particular event that he felt might have been of questionable news value, because of a large volume of e-mails from the audience (as well as because other major media corporations were covering it: the bandwagon effect). Editors also reason, on behalf of their audiences, that people tire easily of the same sad images of seemingly never-ending suffering: that 'compassion fatigue' is to blame for lack of coverage of certain conflicts, particularly in Africa. But this argument does not hold water when we consider that the same media corporations can continue to cover (for years on end) sad images of seemingly never-ending suffering in Israel-Palestine and Iraq apparently without tiring their viewers. Stanley Cohen (2001, 290) suggests that 'media fatigue' may be a more appropriate term. Other factors are clearly behind these decisions.

Is it true that the general public are no longer interested in foreign news? The evidence appears to be mixed. A Pew Center survey in 1999 found that only 15 percent of Americans were following international news 'very closely', a figure that grew to 21 percent two years later after the terrorist bombings in that country (Stacks 2003–04, 12). A number of other public opinion polls also found what was thought to be declining US public interest in foreign news, at least prior to the

September 11 bombings (Moisy 1996, 10–11). Other studies, on the other hand, show considerably higher levels of interest. A Global Market Insite survey of 8 (primarily Western) countries found that 33 percent of those surveyed thought it was 'extremely important' to keep up with news taking place in other parts of the world, while 53 percent thought it was 'somewhat important', compared to just 14 percent who thought it was either 'somewhat unimportant' or 'not at all important' (GMI 2004). If the results of this survey were followed, it would appear that the news corporations are misreading the desires of the public. To some degree, however, such surveys must be treated with suspicion, because saying that one thinks keeping up with foreign news is extremely important may not necessarily be translated into the action of buying a newspaper and reading the international news section, or clicking on the international links on internet news sites.

Another question concerns whether the media is listening to the public in terms of the type of news they want. A study comparing AP surveys of news editors on what they viewed as important stories and Pew Research Center audience polls (in the USA), found similarities of opinion in the types of stories both editors and audiences prefer, but also that editors failed to choose particular events that most interested their audiences, concluding that 'the media may not be successful in covering specific events that fascinate readers, but they are doing a good job in publishing the types of stories that readers seek' (Tai and Chang 2002, 263). According to the same study (262), 'It appears that what the audiences want most are stories of natural or human-made disasters, unusual weather fluctuations, wars and terrorism involving Americans, and perhaps a dose of titillation and trivia. These are essentially the determinants in international news coverage and flow.' It would appear that media coverage of foreign conflict based on sensationalism and the home connection is closely related to what the majority of its customers want: it is grounded in commercial realities.

The economic success of such sensationalist news presentation hinges not on integrity, but on the ability to always shock, or to always grab the attention of those who may just as easily be distracted by sensational coverage of news on another channel, or on another medium. In an environment of live coverage and instant and disposable news, the success of such news media corporations may also be, like its news, here today, gone tomorrow. The demand for more solid, objective and analytical news that can be trusted to remain that way over the long term does exist – most notably in the older and educated demographic – even though it may appear to hold just a 'little slice' of the market. Much of this audience has 'migrated away', as seen by the increase of 82 percent in ten years of the circulation of the *Economist* magazine, for example (Stacks 2003–04, 17). As Susan Moeller (1999, 321) reminds us, 'one hundred years ago the tabloids of *Hearst* and *Pulitzer* battled each other while papers such as the *New York Times* and the *New York Tribune* somberly reported world events. Which have survived? Not the two which catered to the lowest common denominator.' Despite the apparent boom in infotainment news in recent years, the more serious and objective news may well make a comeback, particularly in Western societies whose age pyramids are becoming increasingly top-heavy.

NGOs involved in advocacy direct much of their attention at the media, but this is primarily as a means to influence other actors – usually policymakers (to encourage action) and/or the general public (to encourage donations or pressure on the policymakers). Nevertheless, rallies, demonstrations, press conferences and publicity stunts organized by advocacy NGOs towards a particular conflict (such as Darfur) or towards a particular aspect of conflict (such as landmines or blood diamonds) can influence the media to adjust the position of that conflict or issue on its agenda, with a resulting increase in coverage. NGOs work on articles for magazines and newspapers, and even contribute to the entertainment media industry. Attempts by Global Witness, Amnesty International and other NGOs to direct attention to the issue of blood diamonds, for example, saw a targeting of media of choice of the affluent readership and 'the heartland of diamond advertising', such as *Vanity Fair*, *Esquire* and *National Geographic* (Smillie and Minear 2004, 178). NGO efforts also appear to have been a contributing factor in the production of the movie, *Blood Diamond*.

NGOs involved in humanitarian aid also attempt to influence other actors through the media, drawing attention to conflict-related humanitarian suffering and at the same time enhancing their fundraising efforts and reputation. The fact that NGOs on the ground are a prime source of information for the media in conflict zones also gives these NGOs influence. The sight of a reporter interviewing an aid worker (usually one from the media corporation's home country) in a refugee camp is a common feature in the media's conflict coverage, and many of the statistics used by the media on deaths, displaced persons and the numbers of those in need of humanitarian aid, come from aid agencies. Nor is it uncommon for such NGOs to be accused of inflating such figures to attract more donor funding for their activities (Smillie and Minear 2004, 204).

Diasporas and other interest groups have a stake in media coverage of particular conflicts, particularly when their interests are threatened. They are usually concerned with the manner in which the media treats the cause of those they represent in relation to the opposing parties. When they believe that the groups they represent have been unfairly treated by what they perceive as biased or inaccurate media coverage, they may organize flak campaigns of complaint letters, telephone calls or e-mails, to 'correct' the substance or manner of coverage. Representatives of the group may also volunteer themselves to go on the media record as guests on news discussion programs, disputing what has been reported. Actions by groups in the West representing the interests of the parties to the conflict in Israel-Palestine are a prime example of such aggressive attempts at media influence by interest groups. The existence of such powerful interest groups contributes to making that conflict such a hot issue in the media, and journalists and editors frequently complain of the difficulties of broadcasting or printing news on this subject because of the pressure applied by such interest groups. Although it would appear that the flak campaigns from the Israeli lobby side are far stronger than those on the Palestinian lobby side (one CNN executive reported receiving on some occasions 6,000 e-mails in a single day complaining about a story) (Mearscheimer and Walt 2006), the same news can often spark vehement complaints of bias from both sides at the same time.

Corporations also are able to influence the media – because the owners of the media are corporations, and because it is corporations who fund much of the media's activities in the form of advertising. As owners of the media, corporations are able to hire editors and other key personnel, and do so usually with a view to ensuring that their own ideologies are reflected, and/or their business interests are protected and promoted. Even if editors are given complete autonomy in the editorial decision-making process of the news, the owner has, more often than not, selected a like-minded editor to take up the position. The editor then decides the tone, mood and content of media products produced, which are internalized by the editor's employees: it is a 'guided market system' (Herman and Chomsky 1994, xii). But editors are not necessarily given complete editorial autonomy. Rupert Murdoch's media empire is particularly representative of corporative influence over the media: 'his views are the company's views. ... No one else has his global reach, nor his ability to breathe in and have all his media outlets exhale in time. When Murdoch decided to back the war in Iraq, 175 of his editors did the same' (*Sydney Morning Herald* 2006). This 'evolution of a corporate culture that gives an overriding primacy to "marketing" rather than "editorial"' has been referred to as 'Murdochization' (Sonwalker 2002, 827), and although Murdoch stands at the forefront of this evolution, it is a spreading marketing trend that goes far beyond his personal influence. The ability of corporations to influence policymakers and public opinion through the media has become an important business tool in many parts of the world (see also Papathanassopoulos 2001).

Studies have also found a long-term trend of influence by the corporate owners of the *New York Times*, for example. Daniel Chomsky (1999, 580) tells us that 'When examples of publisher intervention become known they are viewed as dramatic departures from the norm. But the internal record demonstrates that the publisher's influence at the *Times* has been systematic, persistent and decisive.' It has been observed that a publisher can achieve this and still maintain a 'discrete presence' (596). Sometimes the influence of corporate ownership over the media is in direct relation to a conflict situation. It has been alleged, for example, that some foreign mining companies who played a role in partially financing the rebellion against President Mobutu in Zaire in 1996, together with their subsidiaries 'had easy access to the media' in terms of the coverage (or lack thereof) of the crisis, particularly in the case of companies such as UK-based Lonrho, which also owned newspapers in a number of countries (Otunnu 2004, 52). Of course there was little sympathy in the West for Mobutu, and little interest in the issue in general, which made the projection of influence on the media less challenging. The ease of access by corporations to the media in many such cases is made possible because of interlocking directorates: the boards of major media companies share board members with other major corporations in many fields, including banks, investment companies, oil, mining and pharmaceutical companies (see FAIR).

Even corporations that are not connected to the media by direct ownership or interlocking directorates, can influence the media through advertising. As Edward Herman and Noam Chomsky (1994, 16) point out, the mass media aims to attract 'audiences with buying power, not audiences per se; it is affluent audiences that spark advertiser interest today. ... The power of advertisers over television programming stems from the simple fact that they buy and pay for the programs – they are the "patrons" who provide the media subsidy.' It has been observed, for example, that in Brazil, television content and advertising tend to target specifically those 'who consume at middle-class levels', who are 'disproportionately white in a society that is largely Afro-Brazilian or mixed race' (Straubhaar and La Pastina 2003, 162). Specific corporations may even make their advertising contingent on certain conditions regarding, for example, coverage on certain issues, and may threaten to withdraw advertising if their demands are not met. At a more general level, in order to protect and promote the 'buying mood', advertisers will want to avoid serious and disturbing complexities – a situation which may well affect coverage of conflict situations (Herman and Chomsky 1994, 17).

Academic Influence

Academia also has the power to influence the media in a number of ways (although its power over the media is generally weaker than that of the other major actors). When reporting on conflicts, journalists usually have little background knowledge on the conflict, its causes and its participants – particularly in today's world of parachute journalism. They thus often turn for information and analysis to academics, or specialists in the field or in the region in question, who are seen as authoritative voices on those subjects and thus give credibility to media reports. Experts also gain further credibility through familiarity with their audience. Such experts may be interviewed on television or radio, and write columns or op-ed pieces in the newspapers and other periodicals. Specialists that prove to be popular may be called upon again, becoming regular almost 'in house' contributors to the media. Some may even cross over to the media on a more permanent basis. Since the September 11 terrorist attacks, 'experts' on terrorism have shown themselves to be in high demand in the West by media corporations, who often have difficulty explaining to their audience why their country is under attack and under threat.

On the other hand, while this position as a source responsible for explaining what is happening in the world, why it is happening, and what is likely to happen next, may give academics some influence over the media, in many cases the academic is called upon to give perceived credibility to a position that has been decided upon in advance. That is, the media's 'angle' on a conflict is predetermined by commercial factors – what is likely to sell – and the academic's job is simply to fit into and support this angle, rather than give an objective viewpoint that may conflict with the way the news is being presented. The ability to support what the media perceives as sellable news angles may well be a factor in the media's selection of academics. Hugh Roberts (2003, 251), an analyst specializing in North Africa, recalled being interviewed on the BBC regarding the Algerian army's overthrowing of the Algerian President in 1991:

> It was put to me that Algeria was a second Iran. I said that it was nothing of the kind and (having anticipated this question) gave several reasons why the analogy broke down. The question and my answer were cut from the broadcast interview, and an alarmist prognosis

that better fitted the filmed clichés of thousands of bearded Arabs massing in the streets was substituted for informed analysis.

The ability to influence the media in this manner may be somewhat limited.

Another way in which some prominent academics can influence the media, is by providing a clear frame of reference that media corporations can latch onto, assisting them to simplify and explain conflicts and global political trends that may otherwise be inexplicable. The 'Clash of Civilizations' theory, proposed by Samuel Huntington (1996), is a prime example. It became highly popular in the Western media, particularly following the September 11 terrorist attacks, largely because it provided the West with a 'grand scenario' of a threat (Islamic extremism) that could replace the Cold War theme, where individual villains (such as Saddam Hussein) that emerged from time to time could not (see Seib 2003–04, 73). It has also been argued that the attraction of this theory among the media 'is its attempt to analyze international relations without discussing actual politics – especially the issue of Palestine in particular and of Arab nationalism in general' (Abrahamian 2003, 529). Although such academic influences are somewhat rare, when one does take hold, its influence can be considerable.

Finally, the media may also report on the results of specific studies conducted on conflicts, which may affect the media's coverage or its view on conflicts. Mortality studies are one prominent example. Mortality studies conducted in Iraq after the invasion and occupation revealed death tolls many times higher than those admitted by the occupying forces. The results of such studies prompted, to a degree, media questioning and coverage on the state of affairs in that country, and a renewed interest in the seriousness of the conflict. Similar mortality studies conducted in the DRC revealing that that conflict had become the deadliest conflict in the world in more than half a century also sparked some limited media attention, and those statistics are used by the media on the rare occasion that the conflict is mentioned, but the studies do not appear to have contributed significantly to a rearranging of the media agenda in recognition of the conflict's seriousness.

Chapter 5

The Public

The public, in this context, refers to a complex group of diverse actors (namely the general public, NGOs, interest groups and corporations) that play sometimes-conflicting roles in responding to foreign conflict. Some of these actors are able to take direct action in response to conflict, while others work by speaking and/or applying pressure through policymakers, the media or other actors comprising the public. For some of these actors, foreign conflict is a distant affair with very little relevance to their agendas, while for others it represents a large part of their reason for existence. Still, the similarities among the agendas of many sections of the public and those of the other groups of actors (policymakers and the media, for example) are striking. Examples abound of concentrated attention towards the same chosen conflicts, and marginalization of the same stealth conflicts. Given the diversity of the actors that constitute the public, it is necessary to look separately at each. This chapter examines the responses to conflict of each of these sub-groups of actors making up the public arena, in terms of awareness, advocacy, funding and action. It looks at the internal dynamics of each in determining its responses, as well as influences among the sub-groups. Finally, it discusses the various external influences (by policymakers, the media and academia) affecting them.

Responses to Conflict

The General Public

The general public are able to respond to foreign conflict by speaking about it with the people around them, donating money to humanitarian aid appeals, writing to or phoning media corporations, applying pressure directly on policymakers, or taking to the streets to demand that attention be given to its resolution. Those who feel more strongly may even organize themselves on a more permanent basis, forming NGOs (this will be dealt with below). Regarding the general public, however, before speaking of their response to conflict, it is important to gauge their awareness of foreign conflict: do they even know that the conflict exists? Although governments and any media corporations that deal with international news can have little excuse for not knowing about the existence of foreign conflict (to a degree this forms part of their duties), the general public is not held by any binding social or moral obligation to know about distant suffering, and may well not. Thus, it can be said that simply maintaining the existence of a conflict in one's mind and recognizing its relative importance is perhaps the first response that the general public can offer to distant conflict.

Awareness of foreign affairs and conflicts that do not directly affect the political interests of the home country appears to be very low among the general public in the West. This can be said particularly in the case of Africa. On the whole, opinion polls conducted by Western companies rarely even mention the continent, which is a statement in itself. Domestic issues in the USA dominate the public opinion polls conducted by US polling organizations such as the Pew Research Centre and Gallup, and the majority of polls that do deal with foreign issues generally focus on Iraq and terrorism, with some polls conducted on crises such as those in Iran, North Korea, Israel-Palestine and Lebanon (see Pew Charitable Trusts).

In Gallup's World Affairs poll (2006), questions are largely based not on the world per se, but on the USA in relation to the world, with questions such as, 'What one country anywhere in the world do you consider to be America's greatest enemy today?' Questions on other countries include a series specifically on Israel-Palestine (a high level of public knowledge is assumed), plus a number of others on countries such as Mexico, Canada, Germany, North Korea, Iraq, UK and Russia. Egypt and Libya (countries with Western political significance) are the only two African countries mentioned. January 2002 was the last time a Pew poll report included the issue of any African conflict (those of Somalia and Sudan) in its title, and this was regarding the use of American force in the world (Pew 2002a).[1] A search of the Pew Research Center website in 2008 found 183 references to Israel, compared to zero references to the DRC or Congo. It is interesting to note that the 29 countries in which Gallup maintains offices worldwide represent all continents but Africa.

Some polls aim to capture a broad variety of opinions from a large number of countries on multiple continents. Pew polls such as 'What the World Thinks in 2002' and 'Views of a Changing World, June 2003' aim to capture opinions from throughout the world and of the world, and include interviewees from a number of African countries. Although the targets of the interviews may be global, the focus of the questions is not particularly global. The foreword to the latter survey tells us that it 'focuses on the global reaction to the war in Iraq, attitudes around the world toward the challenges ahead – such as the US-led war on terrorism, the Israeli-Palestinian situation, Iran, Syria and North Korea – and views of American unilateralism and the future of the transatlantic relationship' (Pew 2003). We are left to assume for whom these issues are 'the' challenges ahead, but it is clear that they are the issues that occupy a high position on the Western policy and media agendas. Surveys ask Africans what they think about political changes in Eastern Europe, American policies and ideas, and the issue of suicide bombing. Surveys by World Public Opinion conducted for the BBC World Service ask Congolese and Zimbabweans (together with people from 33 other countries) whether they think US troops should be withdrawn from Iraq and whether removing former President Saddam Hussein was the right thing to do or not (World Public Opinion 2006). But such polls do not ask what those in the West (or Africans for that matter) think about conflict in the DRC, Angola or elsewhere in Africa, with the rare exception of possible intervention in Darfur.

---

1   The issue of Darfur did, however, appear in a subtitle, as part of a news interest omnibus survey (Pew 2007).

The fact that polling data on Western public opinion regarding the vast majority of the world's largest conflicts simply does not exist, tells us that either significant levels of public opinion regarding such conflicts do not exist, or that polling companies and their clients do not regard the measurement of public opinion on such topics as relevant to the 'world', or both. Each year the *Yomiuri* newspaper of Japan takes a survey on the top international events of the year, with the readers voting for events or issues that stood out in their minds. In 1999, NATO's war with Yugoslavia was ranked 3rd (after the major earthquakes in Turkey and Taiwan) and East Timor's troubled road to independence 5th. Other armed conflicts that appeared on the survey included Chechnya (11th), and India and Pakistan (21st). Although even a shooting incident in a US high school was ranked at 7th place, not a single event in Africa (conflict or otherwise) appeared in the survey's top 30 events (*Yomiuri* 1999).

To obtain some idea of the general public's awareness regarding conflicts, a simple questionnaire survey was conducted in 2003, in which 37 Australian university students taking a course on war and peace were asked to name what they thought were the three deadliest conflicts in the world, and the three deadliest African conflicts since the end of the Cold War, as well as the conflict they thought, in terms of humanitarian suffering, was most in need of a solution.[2] Of the 37, only one person could name the DRC as one of the top three deadliest conflicts in the world (and that was at third, behind Israel-Palestine and Afghanistan). The most common response was that the Israel-Palestine conflict was the deadliest (9), and an astonishing 21 people (more than half) thought that, in terms of humanitarian suffering, that conflict was the most in need of a solution. Only one could name the DRC as the deadliest conflict in Africa (13 did not or could not even name a single African conflict). While the sample size is small, it serves as an example of how distorted the general public's view on the state of conflict is – particularly as those surveyed could be expected to have an above-average interest in (and knowledge of) the subject (see also Philo 2002).

Even in Africa, consciousness is very strangely skewed: awareness of smaller conflicts in distant places is often far greater than that of greater conflicts in neighbouring countries. In a similar survey conducted of 50 university students in Zambia in March 2008 (just two months after the latest death toll figures for the DRC were released), 18 thought that Iraq was the world's deadliest conflict since the end of the Cold War, compared to 5 who thought the DRC (Zambia's northern neighbour) was the deadliest.[3] When interviewed on BBC radio in 2004, an Angolan writer/poet, asked what situation in the world had troubled him most, responded that it was Palestine, because it had great problems that were ignored by the world (BBC World Service 2004a).

In the rare cases in which large numbers of people do become aware of a particular foreign conflict to the extent that they share a sense of indignation towards the acts of violence, and/or sympathy towards the victims, there are a number of ways in which they can respond. Making a donation to aid organizations involved in alleviating suffering (or even directly contributing funding to a peacekeeping operation, as was

---

2   Survey conducted by Yasmin Hawkins, May 2003.
3   Survey conducted by Thomas Mabwe, March 2008.

seen in Darfur) is probably the most common form of tangible response. People may give money in response to specific appeals for the alleviation of conflict suffering, or simply offer an earmarked unilateral donation to an appropriate organization. Looking at the amount of such private donations in response to specific conflicts reveals patterns in giving that reflect levels of awareness of those conflicts among the general public. As can be expected, private donations for chosen conflicts are high, while those for stealth conflicts are disproportionately low – sometimes to the point of being virtually nonexistent.

According to statistics compiled by OCHA, following the NATO attacks on Afghanistan, that country attracted 132 million US dollars in private contributions for humanitarian aid in 2002.[4] As Darfur became a high-profile conflict in 2004, Sudan attracted 84 million US dollars (although this also represents donations for the conflict in southern Sudan). South-eastern Europe during and after NATO's attacks over Kosovo attracted 57 million US dollars in 1999, while Iraq following the US-UK invasion attracted 38 million US dollars in 2003. Occupied Palestine received 27 million US dollars from private donors in 2003. In contrast, the greatest amount of private aid that the conflict in the DRC could attract in a single year was 1.8 million US dollars, in 2003. In 1999, the DRC received 0.3 million US dollars while even East Timor was able to receive 1.9 million US dollars. The greatest amount of private aid for Sierra Leone in a single year this decade was roughly 5 million US dollars (in 2000), while for Liberia it was 3 (in 2004). Private aid for Burundi failed to reach 1 million US dollars in any year this decade until 2007. High-profile conflicts mean high levels of public awareness and high levels of private donations. None of these conflicts can, however, compare with the levels of giving in response to the Indian Ocean Tsunami; private donations to OCHA's appeal reached 378 million US dollars, while those outside the appeal totalled an incredible 3,770 million US dollars.

There are a number of other ways that the general public can demonstrate a response to conflict. Writing to or calling the media or one's political representative as an individual, or contributing to an online blog are also forms of response, but unless this is done on a large scale, they may not be particularly effective ones; the effect is likely to be determined by the number of letters, calls or other forms of response generated, rather than by the persuasiveness of a single response. Such responses are usually most effective when they are coordinated by an NGO or other organization. People may even offer prayers specifically in response to conflicts and the suffering they produce. In 2004, examples were seen of worshippers in churches in England choosing to offer Christmas prayers specifically for those suffering in Iraq and Darfur and the victims of the Beslan school siege in Russia (BBC World Service 2004c).

The general public may also join large-scale petitions or demonstrations in response to foreign conflict (or potential conflict). These are often in the form of anti-war rallies such as those usually seen in the West when a Western country decides to

---

4   The source of the OCHA figures provided here is the FTS, and includes all information provided to OCHA by donors and appealing agencies. The figures include only those identified as 'Private (individuals and organizations)'.

instigate a conflict or participate in an ongoing conflict. The most extreme example of this was the large-scale vocal opposition to the imminent invasion of Iraq in 2003: on 15 February 2003 the 'largest anti-war demonstration in the history of the world took place', involving as many as 25 million people in a series of coordinated rallies all around the world (Stearns 2005, 174–5). Such actions are much more rare in the case of a conflict that does not directly concern one's own country. A prominent example of this is the recent series of rallies and petitions demanding action in response to the conflict in Darfur (most notably in 2006). This is the first time since the post-Rwandan genocide refugee crisis in eastern Zaire – a decade ago – that significant public opinion has risen in this way in response to any African conflict.

NGOs

NGOs that deal with foreign conflict situations are many and varied in size, form and priorities. Although they can be divided broadly into advocacy and humanitarian aid NGOs, some conduct both types of activities to a degree. Some are small 'one-man' NGOs that may be established specifically for (and direct their activities towards) one conflict area, while others are international institutions that have projects in tens of countries – and more spending power than some countries' national aid agencies. Furthermore, within the countries at conflict, there may be hundreds of local NGOs working to alleviate conflict-related suffering in their immediate environments. Although the number and variety of NGOs in areas affected by conflict can make generalization pertaining to their response somewhat difficult, it can also be said that 'most NGO emergency assistance in reality is delivered by six or seven major NGOs, or families of NGOs' (Smillie and Minear 2004, 195).

In terms of overall trends in the volume of humanitarian assistance by NGOs, some striking similarities can be seen between the response to certain conflict situations by policymakers and the media and the response by NGOs. Most notably, NGO involvement and funding have a tendency to reach very high levels in response to chosen emergencies with strong Western involvement, such as those in Bosnia, Kosovo, East Timor and Afghanistan – levels that are usually quite disproportionate to the relative scale of the humanitarian emergency. Large numbers of NGOs, each with budgets much larger than those available for any other emergency, arrive and conduct large-scale humanitarian projects in these conflict and post-conflict areas. The same could be said for post-invasion Iraq up until the point that security became a major constraint. High levels of NGO response can also be seen in cases in which, although there may not be direct Western involvement (in the form of military intervention), there is moderate Western political interest and strong media interest, such as in eastern Zaire following the Rwandan genocide and, more recently, Darfur. Moderate levels of NGO response were also observed in areas that traditionally had moderate Western political interest, even in the absence of media interest, such as southern Sudan. Other conflicts will always attract the presence of some humanitarian aid NGOs to a degree, but not in any way at a level resembling that for chosen conflicts.

But even chosen emergencies do not remain that way for very long, and NGOs – particularly those that focus primarily on emergency relief – often quickly scale down operations and move on to the next chosen emergency as the peak of the emergency passes, leaving behind little in the way of long-term peacebuilding projects that are often crucial for ensuring that fighting does not break out again. In this environment, it has been observed that many international NGOs have become 'little more than ambulance chasers' (Smillie and Minear 2004, 194). The refugee crisis in the aftermath of the Rwandan genocide brought more than 200 international NGOs to Goma in eastern Zaire for humanitarian operations in the refugee camps. Ironically, very few NGOs were going into Kigali and Rwanda itself, despite the suffering that had taken place within Rwanda. Romeo Dallaire (2003, 479) observed that 'Even as millions in humanitarian aid flowed into Goma we could not get a few thousand dollars to help in Kigali'. Equally ironically, the same camps were being used by the perpetrators of the genocide to regroup and rearm, with a view to returning to Rwanda to 'finish the job'. When Rwanda attacked the camps, sending the militias fleeing more deeply into Zaire and the bulk of the refugees returning to Rwanda, the crisis was, in effect, declared to be over and the NGOs wound up their operations, despite the fact that the conflict continued and expanded, engulfing all of Zaire until President Mobutu was toppled in the following year.

The Goma emergency was to be the last major concentration of intense high-funded NGO activity in Africa until the Darfur crisis rose to prominence in 2004. During Sierra Leone's 'brief CNN moment', the conflict there did attract some moderate levels of NGO presence, and Angola and Sudan maintained moderate presence throughout their conflicts, but most other conflicts in Africa managed to attract only a very minimal presence of international NGOs. The DRC is most notable in this regard: despite a conflict involving several countries and resulting in millions of deaths, it failed to attract even moderate levels of NGO activity. It was not until 2002, for example, that some major NGOs began projects in the DRC, responding initially not to the suffering from the ongoing conflict there, but to that from the volcanic eruptions in Goma (see CARE 2002, 7). NGOs usually give a much higher priority to humanitarian emergencies caused by natural disasters than to those caused by conflict. One major Japanese NGO, which has not responded to an emergency in Africa since the floods of Mozambique in 2000, sent an emergency response team to New Orleans in the USA to assist in the aftermath of hurricane damage there in 2006. NGO presence has also been lacking in many other conflict-related emergencies, including Burundi, Uganda and Somalia (since the Western withdrawal in the early 1990s).

Funding allocations by NGOs can give an idea of priorities. A look at the budget for the emergency appeals of the International Committee of the Red Cross (ICRC) for 2006 and 2007, for example, shows us that the high-profile crisis in Lebanon in 2006 attracted more than three times the amount of funding for the DRC, which was the tenth highest funded appeal (ICRC 2006, 3). In the budget for 2007, the allocation for the DRC increased slightly, but it still amounted to less than half that for Israel (occupied and autonomous territories). In both years Sudan was the most funded emergency. Similar trends can be seen with other NGOs. There are, however, a number of exceptions to this trend. MSF devoted the vast majority of its budget in 2004 to crises in Africa, the top three recipients being Sudan, DRC and Angola (MSF 2004, 25). Less than one week after the Indian Ocean Tsunami, MSF estimated that they had received sufficient donations to cover their activities there, and appealed to donors to instead donate for other pressing emergencies in Sudan, the DRC and Somalia (Bennhold 2005). Similarly, the IRC not only maintains humanitarian aid projects in the DRC, but has also contributed greatly to awareness of the conflict by conducting a series of mortality surveys, revealing the globally unparalleled levels of death and humanitarian suffering caused by conflict in that country.

The activities of advocacy NGOs in response to conflict also reveal some interesting trends. The major targets of intense conflict-related advocacy NGOs in recent years have been Iraq and Darfur. These conflicts have generated so much public attention, that some advocacy groups have been established specifically to take up their causes. The Save Darfur Coalition, for example, was launched in July 2004 as the conflict there rose to prominence. Similarly, Human Rights Watch (2005, 5), in its annual report covering the year 2004, chose to focus on the conflict in Darfur and the torture of detainees by US forces at the Abu Ghraib prison in Iraq as the two human rights challenges that 'pose fundamental threats to human rights', giving an individual chapter to each of the two issues. Despite the relatively low number of victims of human rights abuse in Abu Ghraib prison (compared to other conflicts and countries), that issue has been given such prominence because it is 'emblematic of a powerful government flouting a most basic prohibition'.

Human Rights Watch systematically investigates human rights abuses in 70 countries throughout the world, and on the whole its work appears to reflect a universally focused approach, exposing human rights abuse wherever it happens. But in the introductory chapter of its annual report the key priority areas it chooses to focus on appear to reflect a largely Western set of perspectives. In the annual report covering 1999 (Human Rights Watch 2000), East Timor and Kosovo were dealt with in individual sections in the introduction under 'Military Interventions'. In the annual report covering 2001 (2002), the Western fight against terrorism was the key theme of concern, with the 'Middle East and North Africa', the 'Global Coalition' (against terrorism) and 'Afghanistan' being given separate sections in the introduction. The Western fight against terrorism again dominated the following year's report (2003), with even a section devoted to a possible US strike on Iraq.

It is only in the report covering 2003 (the introduction of which is still dominated largely by Iraq and terrorism) (2004), that the issue of human rights from conflicts in Africa is given some prominence, with a section entitled 'Africa on its Own: Regional Intervention and Human Rights'. Allocated a section within this part of the introduction, conflict in the DRC rose, for the first time, to the front of the Human Rights Watch annual report (although it was still not particularly prominent, and it came at a time when the conflict was officially being declared over), despite levels of human rights abuse incomparable to anywhere else in the world. For each of the other years from 1998, discussion of the human rights abuse in that country remained within its regular section in the chapter on Africa. This is not to say by any means that that organization has ignored the conflict; on the contrary, it has closely monitored and reported on the human rights abuse in the DRC over the years. It would appear, however, that the conflict has not been given the comparative prominence that its scale has warranted. The International Crisis Group is an advocacy group that examines conflict from the perspective of regional and global security, and, like

Human Rights Watch, has a largely global reach. It has given comparatively greater prominence to the conflict in the DRC, stressing the magnitude of the problem and the regional implications in its many reports, and has included the DRC in some of its targeted campaigns.

Some NGOs also serve as mediators in resolving foreign conflicts, involving themselves directly in informal peace processes. The St. Egidio Community, a Catholic movement, played a significant role in the peace process in Mozambique, and has also been active in peace efforts in Serbia and Algeria. The Centre for Humanitarian Dialogue, that actively attempts mediation in conflicts in Africa and Asia, and the Transnational Foundation for Peace and Future Research, which has worked for a number of years with government and civil society groups towards peace in Burundi, are other examples. This type of work often requires a considerable degree of secrecy for it to be effective, and decisions on where to attempt it depend on a number of factors, including the 'ripeness' of the situation, how high-profile it is and which other actors are involved at the policy level. In many cases, it can be said that the conflicts that are otherwise neglected by policymakers and the media, are the most viable candidates for this type of intervention by neutral mediators from civil society.

Interest Groups

Interest groups are established to protect and promote specific groups (national, ethnic, religious or other) by generating political power and exerting it over other actors; they are primarily advocacy groups that are well positioned to target influential groups to their own advantage. These groups often work directly through policymakers by developing strategic contacts and partnerships with them, and may apply pressure by making large donations to political parties and candidates (or by strategically withholding such donations). They also work through the media and the general public, organizing flak campaigns of complaints against what they perceive as biased or unfair media coverage. Flak campaigns may also be directed at policymakers involved in decisions that appear to threaten their interests. They may also denounce (or, depending on their strength, even attempt to prevent the publication of) academic studies that are potentially damaging to their positions or interests.

Unlike NGOs or the general public, who may respond to conflict, wherever it occurs, on the basis of preventing the suffering of innocent victims, interest groups generally respond only to conflicts that affect their particular interests. The Israel lobby in Western countries, for example, is unlikely to respond to conflict in Angola or Burundi (although it has become engaged in the issue of Darfur, largely because conflict there has been associated with the notion of genocide and because the group apparently responsible has been identified as Arab). Similarly, African-American lobby groups in the USA are unlikely to respond to conflict in Sri Lanka or Kashmir. Given that the response of interest groups to conflict is predetermined in this manner, it is more useful to examine the relative strength of interest groups in responding to conflict, rather than the individual responses of the groups, when considering their overall response to conflict. Key questions to ask in this sense may be whether an interest group exists that can represent in some way the interests of the parties to a particular conflict; and if so, how powerful and influential is that group in encouraging a response from other actors.

Given that the response of interest groups to conflict can be considered largely in terms of the influence they exert over policymakers and the media, much of the response of these groups to conflict has already been examined in Chapters 3 and 4, under the sections dealing with the public influence over policymakers and the media, and unnecessary duplication will be avoided here. Suffice it to emphasize here that there is a vast gap in reach and power amongst the various Western interest groups focusing on foreign interests affected by conflict, and that the level of reach and power is in no way proportionate to the severity of the conflict. In many Western countries, the Israel lobby is probably the most powerful interest group in relation to policy and media response to foreign conflict, and its political, economic and media clout far exceeds that of most other interest groups targeting other conflicts (see Mearsheimer and Walt 2006).

Well-organized, well-funded, powerful interest groups representing the interests of those involved in the world's most major conflicts (namely those in Africa) are largely absent, on the other hand. While there are a number of interest groups founded on racial identities, such as those composed of Western citizens of African origin, that lobby for response to conflicts and issues on the African continent, the limited power that they do have must either be dispersed across the entire continent, or, as is often the case, be focused instead on one or two particular conflicts or issues, such as South Africa under apartheid or the conflict in Liberia. The same can perhaps be said of religion-based lobby groups, such as the Christian ones that chose to focus their attention on the protection of Christians in southern Sudan during the course of the conflict there. And while there may be in the West sizeable diasporas of citizens originally from countries experiencing conflict – often consisting of refugees from conflicts or political oppression, their ability to respond to conflict by influencing policy, media or public agendas in the countries in which they have found themselves is usually highly limited. Although some evidence of effective lobbying by interest groups has been seen in select cases, it can be said that Western interest groups focusing on specific African conflicts have not, on the whole, reached a significant level of power that enables an effective response to conflict.

Corporations

In many ways it can be said that certain sections of the corporate world have been responsive to conflicts, even to those in Africa that appear to be neglected by other actors. This is not necessarily a positive statement, however. The exploitation of extractable natural resources and their export onto the global market has made the continuation of many conflicts in the world possible: nowhere more so than in Africa. Weapons are sometimes exchanged directly for these resources; often the very existence of rebel groups and warlords depends on their ability to control these resources. Needless to say, the weapons themselves are supplied either by foreign arms companies or by foreign governments.

Although the phenomenon of blood or conflict diamonds has become popularly known, there is a multitude of other resources that are inextricably linked with conflict situations, including gold, silver, coltan, copper, timber, cocoa, coffee and even wildlife, and in each case it is the corporations that maintain the link. In Liberia, the Oriental Timber Company not only facilitated the trade in timber for arms: on some occasions it even used its own trucks on its own logging roads to transport arms and troops throughout Liberia (see Pugh, Cooper and Goodhand 2004, 108–9). Mining companies have also made their trucks and planes available for use by armed forces in other conflict situations (see BBC News 2005). In Zaire, powerful Western mining companies helped finance Laurent Kabila's push to topple President Mobutu in exchange for mining contracts when his rebel forces were still 1,000 kilometres from Kinshasa (Otunnu 2004, 51–4). In these ways, foreign corporations form the critical link between parties to a conflict and the global market on which they depend, facilitating large-scale global shadow markets.

The chain of exploitation of natural resources from extraction to the point of final sale is often long and complicated, with the resource changing hands several times as it is transported and processed (see Pugh, Cooper and Goodhand 2004, 28–9) and the major Western firm selling the product that is the reason for the initial extraction of the resource may or may not be fully aware that that resource is contributing to the perpetuation of conflict in Africa. It must be said, however, that the exploitation of such resources is highly profitable, and it would go against the business interests of these corporations to cease their involvement in such business, or to use their leverage to reduce the violence related to resource exploitation. In most cases, it can be said that corporations dealing in such resources 'have been willing to "do business" with combatants as long as their access to these valuable raw materials is not denied' (Laremont 2002, 12). One possible exception is the apparent commitment shown by major diamond corporations to stop the movement of blood diamonds, and their cooperation with the Kimberley process, which aims to ensure that the origin of all diamonds can be verified and certified.

Corporations also lobby their politicians and contribute to their election campaigns to encourage support for their business interests, which may also have a bearing on conflict situations in Africa, as seen, for example, through the oil lobbies in the USA pressuring their government to pursue a conciliatory approach toward the government in Sudan to allow them access to oilfields there, and in the ties between the Western mining companies bankrolling advancing rebel forces in the DRC and key Western policymakers. Often the absence of other interested parties in such cases gives these corporations considerable lobbying power. In other cases, the corporations enjoy such close relations with key policymakers that the process appears to be one of collaboration, rather than lobbying. A notable example is the allocation by the occupying US government, following its invasion of Iraq, of lucrative reconstruction contracts to US firms in which key US policymakers had themselves held key positions.

Western-based private security firms (a more politically acceptable term for what are essentially mercenaries) are also seen as having an increasingly significant (albeit controversial) role in conflicts in Africa. The security firm Executive Outcomes appeared to be instrumental in rescuing President Valentine Strasser's government in Sierra Leone from rebels in 1995, and such firms have also played a critical role in stopping rebel advances in Angola. They usually play more modest roles, such as supplying arms, and protecting mines and key government installations from rebel attack in conflict areas such as that in the DRC. Governments may pay for such work in cash or in mining contracts. The growth in private security firms in Africa since the end of the Cold War can be linked to 'globalisation, the failure of African countries to achieve sustainable development, concomitant with the general weakening of the African state and Western peacekeeping disengagement from Africa after the Somali debacle' (Cilliers 1999, 1). These firms are most active where there are easily extractable natural resources available to ensure lucrative payment for services rendered.

Internal Dynamics

The General Public

Individuals, busy living their own lives, constitute the general public, their prime concern being with the 'world' immediately surrounding them, and with the issues that have a tangible and direct impact on them and the individuals that they care about. The majority of these individuals 'operate in a world outside the rarefied realm of public discourse. It is a personal world, with an equally pressing set of career and family demands, economic and health problems, personal dreams and aspirations' (Neuman, Just and Crigler 1992, 4). In general, there is little room for awareness about, and much less for engagement in, some form of action in response to foreign conflicts. Still, the human capacity for absorbing and processing information is remarkable; the lack of awareness concerning foreign conflicts cannot simply be explained by the fact that people are busy with their own lives. Access to information is also a major constraining factor. Unlike other actors, the members of the general public do not have their own independent sources of information, instead relying on the media, policymakers and NGOs to inform them about the existence of foreign conflicts and their seriousness, and to advise them on who can do what in response. This is a fundamental weakness in the ability of the general public to be aware of and respond to foreign conflicts.

But even if the members of the general public are provided with information on all foreign conflicts (and setting aside the influence of other actors in determining which conflicts should be deemed important), it does not necessarily follow that they will respond in a manner that is proportionate to the level of humanitarian suffering. As has already been discussed in Chapter 2, individual consciousness regarding foreign conflict is affected by a wide variety of factors, such that even in the absence of policy perspectives, saturation media coverage and NGO campaigns, the scale of a conflict is unlikely to be a major determining factor in the response to a particular conflict. Individuals' perspectives of foreign conflict are certainly likely to be greatly influenced by the presence of human suffering (although not so much by the quantity of it), but this occurs within a certain context. Identity plays a large role, with the ability of the individual to identify with victims of conflict, in racial, national, ethnic, religious, linguistic and/or socioeconomic terms, making a considerable difference in the levels of sympathy and outrage felt towards a particular conflict.

Geographic proximity, the perceived simplicity of the conflict ('good guys' versus 'bad guys'), how innocent the apparent victims are seen to be, and if a particular group as a whole is threatened (genocide), are also among the factors influencing individuals' views of which conflicts demand their attention. A sense of being able to do something about the suffering, as opposed to a sense of helplessness, can also be a deciding factor in whether one chooses to shut off emotional responses to a conflict or to stand up and respond in some way. The results of some of these factors could be seen in the contrast between the failure of Western publics to react substantively to the suffering caused by the genocide in Rwanda, and the outpouring of support for the alleviation of suffering in the refugee camps in neighbouring countries following the genocide. The former situation appeared confusing and chaotic with no apparent innocents, while the latter situation appeared to be a simple case of innocent people dying from cholera and starvation (see S. Cohen 2001, 290–1). The sense of guilt at having failed to react to that genocide would greatly contribute to a strong public reaction to any future hint of a perception of genocide (as seen in Kosovo and Darfur). There is also undoubtedly a bandwagon effect among members of the general public, whereby individuals are influenced by their own peers in forming opinions about the gravity of particular conflicts.

NGOs

NGOs that respond to conflict, through advocacy or aid, are founded by members of the general public who feel compelled to do something about conflict and conflict-related suffering, and the spark for the establishment of an NGO can usually be found in a specific conflict. Save the Children was established because of the suffering of World War I, CARE from World War II, World Vision from the Korean War, and MSF from the Nigerian Civil War. Stopping conflict and alleviating human suffering caused by such conflicts (and other humanitarian disasters) remains the overarching reason for being for such NGOs and guides their activities. No NGO, however, has the capacity to respond to all the needs of all the humanitarian emergencies. Funding is always limited, most of it is earmarked, and the level of funding that is potentially and actually available is almost always dependent on the specific emergency in question. Selectivity inevitably becomes an issue, and decisions must be made on which emergency to respond to, and to what degree.

Funding is undoubtedly one of the most critical issues in NGOs' decision-making processes. NGOs that respond to conflict must source for funding either from the general public or from the actors in the policy arena: national governments or international organizations. In many cases the funding from the general public (usually in the form of donations) is in response to a specific conflict or emergency and is earmarked as such. Most of it cannot be used freely by NGOs according to their assessment of which emergency is most in need, although they may try to encourage awareness among potential donors, and to influence the agenda of the general public through campaigns. Funding from policymakers is even more restrictive in this sense (this will be dealt with below in the section on policymaker influence). In any case, because the long-term financial situation of NGOs is so precarious, NGOs are forced to scramble for resources when and where they are available (see Cooley and Ron 2002). When humanitarian aid from private donors and from contracts with government and international organizations becomes available in large quantities (usually in response to a chosen conflict), active participation in the 'scramble' by NGOs with a view to securing as much aid money as possible from that emergency is crucial to offset overhead costs of the organization and even to help fund lesser responses to other less high-profile emergencies. The funding factor means a greater response to chosen conflicts by NGOs and a lesser response to stealth conflicts. Furthermore, this selective and short-term funding environment encourages short-term intensive responses by NGOs, often allowing little room for long-term peacebuilding and local capacity building (see Goodhand 2006, 144–6).

But it is not only the short-term scramble for funds aimed at securing organizational survival that determines NGO choices in responding to conflict. As with any other organization, the securing of long-term survival and realizing of prosperity and growth are also important goals. The issues of reputation and fame thus also become factors in NGO choices. Being noticed, recognized and remembered by other actors, as an organization capable of responding effectively to an emergency, as an organization that can be entrusted with large amounts of donor money, is important for NGOs in this sense. This encourages NGOs to prioritize accordingly, committing resources to and working in places where the levels of external visibility are high, in response to chosen and other relatively high-profile conflicts, and conversely, not 'wasting' resources in responses to unseen conflicts where their contribution will not be noticed. On the other hand, NGOs may over time develop long-term relations with donors and more stable channels of funding in response to certain conflicts that allow a more stable response, as seen in the maintenance of NGO activity in southern Sudan and Angola over the years, even as their visibility levels remained low (Olsen, Cartensen and Høyen 2002, 11).

Security in and access to conflict zones are sometimes also factors in determining the areas of NGO activity. However much NGOs may wish to provide humanitarian assistance to a needy population, if danger makes such operations unacceptably risky, or the relevant authorities do not grant access, NGOs will be unable to respond to that conflict. Despite the high-profile nature of the conflict in Iraq, for example, and the high levels of funding potentially available there, humanitarian activities by NGOs that flocked to Iraq in the aftermath of the invasion began to decrease as the security situation worsened and their activities and personnel came to be deliberately and heavily targeted. NGOs withdrew and, as a result, humanitarian aid by them in response to that conflict has not reached the levels of that in other chosen conflicts. Restrictions in Darfur by the government of Sudan have also prevented access by NGOs to much of the vulnerable population, although this has not necessarily prevented a high level of response, with NGOs operating instead from neighbouring Chad and other areas where access is possible. A strong willingness or incentive to respond can often overcome obstacles of access.

Institutional identity can also influence the activities and priorities of NGOs. This can often be seen for NGOs that are founded on religious principles. NGOs with a Christian background, for example, may see it as their mission to protect Christians that are being persecuted, and thus focus their activities to that end. The same can apply for NGOs with an Islamic background, who seek to protect persecuted Muslims. The heavy Christian NGO presence in southern Sudan contrasting with the heavy Islamic NGO presence in northern Sudan during the conflict there is indicative of this (Lavergne and Weissman 2004, 159), as is the heavy Islamic NGO presence in Palestine. This situation is often, however, closely related to funding opportunities. As Abdel-Rahman Ghandour (2004, 339) notes, 'Many Islamic NGOs are involved in programs for which it is easy to raise funds, such as Palestine, but do very little in other regions with large Muslim populations.' To a degree there may also be some regionalism, determined by considerations of geographical proximity, racial, ethnic or regional solidarity, and/or a sense of 'turf': a conflict being close to home can be a factor. Asian NGOs, for example, may choose to focus the bulk of their attention on emergencies in Asia, and European NGOs may focus more attention on emergencies in and around Europe.

Interest Groups

Generally speaking, interest groups based on race, religion, ethnic or national identity, respond only to conflict that affects their particular group. Thus, the strength of response to a particular conflict is not so much a question of choice of conflict, but of the strength of a particular organization: its ability to influence other actors. This ability depends on a number of factors: strong leadership, coordination and unity, access to government institutions or media corporations (positioning), and the ability to form mutually beneficial relationships with such institutions. It also depends on the assimilation of the members into the host society and the maintenance of strong emotional (and possibly political and financial) ties with the homeland (see Haney and Vanderbush 1999). All of these factors are reasons behind the unrivalled strength of the Israel lobby in the policy and media arenas of the USA and other Western countries. These lobbies have access to considerable wealth, which they draw from in providing extensive campaign funding for political candidates and parties sympathetic to their cause. The lobby is also able to draw upon the cooperation of Jewish politicians and associated staff within government (Mearsheimer and Walt 2006). It is well positioned in ownership and on boards of major media corporations as well. This lobby also draws strength from a number of other factors, such as sympathy related to the holocaust suffered by the Jews during World War II, and Christian sympathy and support related to the Biblical significance of Israel.

Turned around, the reasons behind the strength of the Israel lobby are also the reasons behind the weakness of the African lobbies in the West. For historical reasons dating back to the era of slavery, Western citizens of African descent are more likely than other groups to occupy lower socioeconomic groups in society, and have been largely politically marginalized. Furthermore, with much of the African-American population coming from a background of slavery, the connection with the 'homeland' is weak (many do not know which part of Africa they have come from). There may be some general sympathies towards Africa but, particularly in the absence of media attention, the connection is weak, and such sympathies are usually too broad and weak for any effective mobilization in response to specific conflicts. On another note, citizens of African origin, in the USA for example, have been hesitant to rise in vocal opposition to the actions of African leaders involved in repression and/or conflict because 'there has been a sense, rightly or wrongly, that a measure of their self-esteem as a black race in America is somehow tied to the success or failure of independent black governments running their own shows' (Berkeley 2001, 90). Finally, for those who have arrived from Africa in more recent years from areas of conflict, as refugees perhaps, in many cases sufficient time has not passed to enable a high enough level of assimilation into the community and the reaching of a position of political influence in their host communities. Many may simply have a hard enough time, on an individual level, trying to make a stable livelihood in their new environment, or supporting loved ones still suffering in the conflict area.

Corporations

Corporations are motivated by the pursuit of profits. While it can generally be said that peace fosters long-term economic development and conflict destroys it, this does not necessarily mean that corporations and authorities will therefore strive to achieve peace in order to enhance their mutual prosperity, particularly when the business in question concerns the extraction of natural resources – a major component of the interest of Western corporations in Africa. From the perspective of corporations, who have little incentive to be concerned about the long-term economic development of a state from which they are extracting natural resources, as long as the extraction of the resources is not interrupted, the existence of conflict may mean little more than a possible change of the authority with whom the corporations are doing business. Parties to conflict are generally less interested in long-term economic development and more in short-term control and power, measured relative to the control and power of their rivals. For the local authority, whether government, rebel or warlord, natural resources serve as a key source of revenue to maintain power and/or to continue to engage in conflict, and thus, the authority in charge at the time is equally content to allow business to continue in partnership with foreign corporations that they feel will serve their interests and help further their cause, at least in the short-term.

In order to facilitate the extraction of the maximum amount of resources at the lowest possible cost, corporations make deals with governments, rebel groups and warlords. Such deals are often highly advantageous to the corporations, with little benefit for the host government or citizens: a situation that is usually only possible because of corrupt practices, by which corporations pay off individual representatives of authorities to accept deals that would be otherwise unacceptably disadvantageous. The World Bank estimates, for example, that government representatives of the DRC have signed away as much as 75 percent of its copper and cobalt reserves in dubious deals with foreign corporations that would bring little, if any, share of the profits to the state (Le Carré and Stearns 2006). Similarly, in Nigeria, deals for the extraction of oil resources are perceived to have greatly benefited the foreign oil companies and some government officials, but the host communities themselves appear to have been left with little but the pollution from the extraction process; the opulence of the oil company facilities is in stark contrast to the abject poverty on the other side of the fence. This is a key source of escalating violence in the Niger Delta region in that country.

But profits are not only dependent on the raw ability to extract the maximum quantity and quality of resources at the minimum cost. In some cases, damage to reputation from the perspective of consumers who question the business practices of corporations can adversely affect profits, necessitating adjustments in corporate strategies. As a number of advocacy groups in the West conducted campaigns aimed at raising public awareness of the issue of blood diamonds and encouraging boycotts, for example, the diamond industry found itself in a position where bad publicity would harm sales and profits. It responded by showing active cooperation in the process to identify and certify the origin of diamonds and to curb the trade in diamonds associated with conflict (known as the Kimberley Process), at the same time stepping up its regular marketing strategies for diamonds. While some question whether the diamond industry was ever threatened by the NGO campaigns, given the marketing and advertising clout that the industry enjoys (see Campbell 2004, 208–9), it was able to largely defuse whatever threat there was by showing its concern and cooperation in the process to stop the trade in such diamonds.

In any case, the emergence of public pressure able to force, to a degree, a change in the behaviour of the diamond industry is a rare example of such influence; although the corporate world is being increasingly forced by consumer pressure to adjust production and products to meet environmental concerns, it remains largely impervious to pressure over activities in areas of conflict where the consumers can see little connection between their own lives and the issue at hand. In the case of diamonds, this influence was undoubtedly only possible because of the glamorous image attached to the stones, and the obvious irony that what are supposed to be symbols of love have been procured and brought to the West through a process that causes death and suffering at the source. Terms such as 'blood timber', 'blood copper' or 'blood coltan', on the other hand, simply do not have the same impact as 'blood diamonds', and cannot hope to elicit a similar level of response to that for diamonds. Some innovative attempts have been made, however, to mobilize consumer action for less high-profile issues, such as the 'gorilla-friendly' mobile phone campaign by wildlife conservation groups and the 'no blood on my mobile phone' campaign by Belgian NGOs against coltan from the DRC (see Wardell Armstrong 2003, 8–9), and the 'hot chocolate' campaign by Global Witness (2007) to raise awareness about the link between cocoa and conflict in Côte D'Ivoire. While personal reliance in the West on mobile phones, and sympathy for the endangered gorilla, did facilitate some limited rise in concern, and some response was achieved (most notably from mobile phone companies), public awareness of the issue and the broader traction of the campaigns remain low.

External Influences

The general public are quite susceptible to the influence of other actors (most notably the media, but also policymakers), considering their reliance on them for information on foreign conflicts. The ability of NGOs to do their work is also dependent on the responses of other actors, particularly in the area of funding, making considerable room for influence here also. Although interest groups and corporations are generally able to fund their own activities independently and move according to their own interests to a certain extent, they have limitations, and do enter into mutually beneficial partnerships with other actors to protect or further their interests, meaning that they are also influenced (although to a lesser extent) by other actors outside the public sphere.

Policymaker Influence

As already seen, the general public have the power to influence policymakers through the expression of public opinion and other forms of pressure, particularly in liberal democracies. But the policymakers do not passively accept this influence as is. Conversely, they will often take steps to lead, mould or manipulate public opinion in such a way that it will come to support, or at least shift to a position closer to, the policies preferred by the government of the day. Policymakers can influence public opinion by making statements or releasing information that may raise the perceived importance of a particular issue that they are determined to address or act on. Where public disinterest or opposition is anticipated, policymakers may take steps to 'prepare' the general public for a course of action that they have decided upon. This was seen, for example, in the manner in which France took steps to mould public support for its participation in the Gulf War (La Balme 2000, 271–2). The success of such influence often depends on how well policymakers are able to articulate and present the issue to the public (see Shiraev 2000, 302; Chanley 1999, 41). Effective leadership at the highest levels of the policy arena is key to overcoming public scepticism and turning 'public opinion from its traditional "charity starts at home" attitude to a support of humanitarian efforts overseas' (Rotberg and Weiss 1996, 180). Once some form of action in response to a foreign conflict has become imminent (particularly one involving the military), patriotism also serves as a tool to influence public opinion, in the form of a 'rally around the flag' effect, but the effectiveness of this phenomenon also depends on how well policymakers handle and present events (see Baker and O'Neal 2001).

In the converse situation, where policymakers are determined to avoid responding substantively to foreign conflict, but where the general public are applying pressure for a response of some form, policymakers may attempt to influence public opinion using a number of different tactics. One such tactic is to downplay the crisis. During the genocide in Rwanda, for example, Western policymakers determined to avoid responding to that crisis, presented the situation to their publics as a conflict between two military forces, and refused to use the word 'genocide', in an attempt to give the impression that it was not a one-sided affair and that nothing could be done to stop it. Or policymakers may release important information or statements on other, unrelated domestic or foreign issues, through legitimate channels or through leaks to the press, to divert the public's attention from the conflict in question (see Herman and Chomsky 1994, 23). They may also release public statements expressing concern or outrage at a particular conflict, or take token steps (such as allocating minimal amounts of humanitarian aid) to provide the appearance of having made a substantive response, thereby releasing some pressure being applied by a public unhappy that their own government appears to be doing little about a conflict that they are concerned about. In any case, the strength of public opinion in response to most foreign conflicts (particularly those in Africa) is rarely sufficient to force a response by policymakers.

In the attempt by policymakers to influence the general public either to support a response to conflict or to oppose it, public opinion polls are a tool that they frequently employ. Since the actual individual preferences of the general public are largely unknown, polls are usually the only way that members of the general public can know how the majority of their peers are thinking on a particular issue. By presenting opinion polls with results showing support for their own positions, policymakers are able not only to counter claims by vocal members of the public opposing their positions, but to convince other members of the public that their positions are supported by the majority of their peers. Polls conducted on behalf of policymakers are often designed in such a way as to elicit a certain response. As already seen in Chapter 3, many Western governments have refused to engage in military interventions, citing the lack of public support, for example, despite evidence suggesting the opposite in most polls. Thus, while public opinion can certainly be a constraint for policymakers in making decisions independently, it can also be a tool that can be manipulated by them (see Shapiro and Jacobs 2000).

Policymakers also have an increasingly powerful influence on NGOs. Although NGOs involved in the provision of humanitarian aid once were largely able to take initiatives unilaterally in responding to conflict, because the majority of their funding came from private donations, most have now come to rely to a large degree on government and international agency funding for their activities. For some NGOs, official sources account for 80 percent or more of their income. This means that via their choices in the allocation of government funding to NGOs for certain emergencies and not for others, policymakers are able to influence where and when NGOs are active. But this goes beyond the simple allocation of funding for specific emergencies. Because NGOs are largely dependent on official funding sources to cover even their headquarters and other administrative overhead costs, they simply cannot afford not to follow their government sponsors into humanitarian activities of the government's choice, regardless of ethical concerns or questions of priorities that the NGOs may hold (see Rieff 2004, 296; Goodhand 2006, 89–91; Smillie and Minear 2004, 192–3).

By following their own independent agendas, NGOs risk not being able to cover overhead costs, losing their market share of aid money, as well as the opportunity to promote their activities and organization amidst the concentration of attention on a chosen conflict. They may also be 'punished' by government sponsors for not participating in the aid effort, with funding for other crises being withheld. Furthermore, NGOs may be forced to refrain from criticizing policy choices and failures (essentially biting the hand that feeds them), or risk losing aid contracts, as a number of prominent NGOs discovered in responding to conflicts in Iraq, Afghanistan and Israel-Palestine (see Smillie and Minear 2004, 143). In terms of the selection of conflicts for response, NGO agendas have thus become increasingly aligned with those of their government sponsors; chosen conflicts receive massive responses and stealth conflicts, very little at all. In the case of conflicts in which those government sponsors are involved, key policymakers from those countries often see NGOs not as independent entities with their own agendas, but as 'force multipliers', that are part of the 'combat team' and of a 'military-humanitarian coalition' (Calas and Salignon 2004, 82–3). The influence of policymakers on NGOs is also apparent in cases where access is restricted: Japanese NGOs in Myanmar, for example, have had greater access to that country than their US or European counterparts, because of the relatively conciliatory stance of the Japanese government towards the regime there. Many NGOs carry considerable 'political baggage' relating to the governments of their base country, sometimes only by association (see Smillie and Minear 2004, 142).

With their own funding for their activities, interest groups and corporations enjoy a much greater level of independence from policymakers than do NGOs. But this does not mean that policymakers are without influence over these groups. To a degree, there is a mutual influence between policymakers and these actors in the public sector. Politicians rely on election campaign contributions from both interest groups and corporations, and, in return, interest groups and corporations rely on politicians to support their interests through legal, diplomatic, and sometimes financial means. In the case of interest groups, policymakers encourage and support the activities of those groups that are able to promise financial rewards to their political campaigns (see Haney and Vanderbush 1999, 345). The facilitation of this process by policymakers means that those interest groups that are financially well off are more likely to have a greater political clout.

In the case of corporations, policymakers can pass laws that regulate where and how they do business, and in extreme cases can put sanction regimes in place to prevent business activities and the remittance of funds to groups in conflict zones. UN Security Council sanctions affect corporations in conflict areas, and even laws passed in individual countries (or states within countries) can prevent corporations from conducting business in areas of conflict. US-based oil and other multinational companies, for example, have taken to the courts to fight against state legal restrictions preventing them from doing business in Sudan, as have other companies to fight laws preventing business activity in Myanmar. US-based oil companies are unhappy that such restrictions made by US policymakers are allowing other oil companies from Canada, China and Malaysia, among others, to sign lucrative oil extraction contracts with the Sudanese government in their place. Sometimes, companies may find ways around these restrictions. The UK private security firm, Sandline, was implicated in a scandal, for example, that involved supplying arms to the government of Sierra Leone against the provisions of UN Security Council sanctions. On the other hand, policymakers may actively support the activities of domestic corporations in other countries, negotiating deals at the policy level and opening doors that corporations might not be able to open themselves.

Media Influence

The media has a major influence on the general public. First and foremost, this is because the media is the prime (if not the only) source of information the general public has on foreign conflicts. How the general public responds to conflict is often contingent on what information media corporations present to them, how much of it they present, and in what way they package it. Even the influence of other actors, such as policymakers, is almost always mediated by the mass media. Numerous studies in agenda-setting have demonstrated strong links between the media agenda and the agenda of the general public, with public awareness and prioritization of issues (issue salience) appearing to match, to a large degree, the rise and fall of issues in the mass media. The media appears to 'prime' the general public to view certain issues with more importance than others, although their individual opinions on those issues may show considerable variety. Bernard Cohen's oft-cited statement (1963, 13) that the press 'may not be successful much of the time in telling people what to think, but it is stunningly successful in telling its readers what to think about', still would appear to ring true today. Studies in which members of the general public are asked such questions as, 'What is the most important problem facing this nation?' and the results then compared to the level of attention that the media gives to such problems, have found a substantial level of influence by the media on the public agenda (see McCombs and Shaw 1972; Rogers and Dearing 1994). Although such studies often focus on domestic issues, a number of studies have also demonstrated the media influence on foreign affairs issues (see Soroka 2003; Wanta and Hu 1993).

This agenda-setting effect is not entirely straightforward, however. The effectiveness of the media in influencing the general public may to a great deal depend upon the individuals in question.

> Television coverage is particularly effective in shaping the judgements of citizens with limited political resources and skills. Those who rarely get caught up in the world of politics find network news presentations particularly compelling. Partisans, activists, close observers of the political scene, on the other hand, are less apt to be swept away (Iyengar and Kinder 1987, 60).

Furthermore, examples have also been raised of situations in which there appeared to be a considerable gap between the media agenda and the agenda of the general public. In the USA in the late 1980s and early 1990s, for example, the media's heavy coverage of apartheid in South Africa did not appear to correspond with a comparable level of interest by the general public, and conversely, high levels of public concern about domestic drug abuse and crime were not matched by high media coverage (Neuman, Just and Crigler 1992, 111).

In many ways, the media effect on the general public is stronger on the issue of foreign conflicts and foreign affairs than it is on domestic affairs, because the general public is more reliant on the media for information about these issues. The general public may not need the media to tell them that there are problems with drug abuse and crime in their neighbourhoods: they see, hear and feel these problems around them. On the other hand, the general public may remain completely oblivious to the existence of a foreign conflict that has no perceivable impact on their daily lives, unless the media informs them and stresses the gravity of the situation in terms of humanitarian loss and the threat to international peace and security. Without media prompting, the individual members of the general public are unlikely to know that they were unable to purchase a Play Station 2 game console for their children for Christmas because of a shortage of coltan in the international market, that is related to conflict in the DRC, or that the diamonds in the rings they have bought may have been extracted at the cost of human lives in conflict in Angola or Sierra Leone.

The media effect on general public consciousness of foreign conflict is also more pronounced because of the high levels of selectivity that the media practises in its coverage. By covering a select conflict at concentrated levels on a daily basis, they have the power to increase public awareness on that conflict considerably. On the other hand, with twenty or thirty conflicts ongoing throughout the world, but only one or two being given significant media coverage at any given time, coverage is so selective that the general public, without other sources of information, may well not know about the very existence of most of the world's conflicts. In this sense, it is perhaps the omission of information about foreign conflicts that is most powerful; if provided with information about a foreign conflict, the general public is at least able to make a choice as to whether or not to attach importance to it, but without that information, there is simply no choice to make. As Everett Rogers and James Dearing (1994, 89) point out, 'one of the strongest pieces of evidence of the media's agenda-setting influence may consist of the fact that issues and events that are completely ignored by the mass media do not register on the public agendas.' It is not at all surprising that in 1999 not a single event or issue in Africa appeared in the top 30 foreign events or issues that stood out in the minds of the readers of the Japanese newspaper *Yomiuri*, when one considers that the same newspaper devotes less than two percent of its small international news section to the continent. Even conflicts that have been 'chosen' by the media may fall away into obscurity when media corporations perceive 'compassion fatigue' among their audience: real or imagined.

It is not only in the sheer quantity (or lack thereof), or even in the positioning of news items and articles that the media is able to influence the general public. The choices made in the packaging and framing of the information provided by the media in its coverage of foreign conflicts is also critical. Coverage presented in the 'something must be done' style of journalism is specifically designed to evoke an emotional response from readers, viewers and listeners. By presenting a conflict in a morality-play format, the media aims to elicit feelings among the general public of outrage towards the perceived perpetrators, and sympathy towards the perceived victims, and hope that strong nations will step in to contain or eliminate the perpetrators and rescue the victims. The key assumption is that something can be done about the conflict. On the other hand, when the media uses a matter-of-fact style to portray a conflict as one in which both parties appear to bear responsibility for the violence, in which there appears to be no clear innocent victim, and/or as a tribal or ethnic clash that no one can do anything about, a sense of powerlessness sets in among the general public, leading to disinterest and apathy, and there is less likely to be a vigorous response.

The Internet is a tool that potentially has a great impact in alleviating the reliance of the general public on the highly selective and Western-centric mainstream media for their information about the outside world, allowing them access to a more comprehensive picture. But as we have already seen in Chapter 4, the actual utility of the Internet so far in countering the influence of the mainstream media has been limited for a number of reasons, particularly in terms of the view of foreign conflict and foreign affairs in general. Internet news remains largely dominated by news from traditional sources, including newspapers, television news and news agency services. Furthermore, the use of the Internet for accessing news requires active participation in selecting individual stories, unlike television or newspaper news that is fixed in a predetermined package for passive consumption by the consumer. This may allow for greater choice, but unless the interest in a particular story, conflict or country already exists, there is less chance that the consumer will 'discover' or pursue a new news story. In any case, very few people rely on the Internet alone as a news source, and therefore the vast majority continue to take cues about the perceived importance of foreign events from newspapers, television and radio.

The media can also have a considerable impact on NGOs. The media can be instrumental, for example, in fuelling general public response to a conflict, which often determines the effectiveness of NGO fundraising for a particular emergency.[5] The general public can hardly donate to a cause they know nothing or little about, and although NGOs can and do run their own fundraising campaigns (including targeted mailing, adverts, charity events and donation box placement), the presence or absence of media coverage about a conflict or other emergency, and how the media chooses to frame its coverage, can make a huge difference in the success of NGO fundraising campaigns. Because of the level of general public concern media corporations raise in their coverage, they may even come to serve as temporary intermediaries between private donors and the NGOs. Having seen news broadcasts about the suffering caused by a particular conflict, private individuals may phone in to the program asking what can they do to help, which may even prompt the media corporation to set up a donation hotline on behalf of NGOs and/or other aid organizations. The media is a crucial factor as well in the work of advocacy NGOs, particularly those that rely on general public support. Media attention (or the lack thereof) can determine the success of petitions, demonstrations and boycotts, and can also influence the prominence of views of advocacy groups in the agendas of their target audience.

In the case of NGOs that are involved in humanitarian aid, media coverage may not only be influential in determining the success of a fundraising campaign, it may even be instrumental in determining whether or not a fundraising campaign happens at all in response to a conflict or other emergency. This is particularly relevant considering the all-or-nothing approach of the media towards foreign conflict. The influence of the media in the choice of emergency for response in this sense can be seen in the words of an NGO director: 'You know instinctively what will sell and what won't. ... You can't raise private donor money for Angola; you need sustained media attention' (quoted in Smillie and Minear 2004, 180–181). In the case of a conflict that 'won't sell' (no media coverage), sufficient money cannot be raised to

---

5   Although the role of government and international organization funding appears to be overtaking that of private donations as the source of income for many NGOs, private donations still make up an important part of NGO income; some refuse to accept government funding at all and others, such as World Vision, continue to rely on their independent (and successful) fundraising mechanisms.

even begin humanitarian activities. The media has a hand in the very establishment of many NGOs, with the founders often being inspired by media portrayals of conflict situations. The founder of Amnesty International, for example, was inspired to set up that organization after reading a newspaper article about jailed prisoners of conscience in Portugal.

Interest groups and corporations too may be affected by media coverage of conflicts in which they have an interest, although given that their interests are already predetermined by other factors, it is unlikely to affect which conflicts or countries they choose to focus their attention on (unlike other public actors). Instead, the media's coverage can affect the public image of those that interest groups represent. Interest groups may be buoyed by coverage that supports their cause, or be forced to adopt mitigating strategies when coverage is not in their favour. The power of the media in this sense can perhaps best be seen in the mitigating strategies that interest groups pursue to counter disadvantageous media coverage. The resources the Israel lobby, for example, bring to bear on media corporations critical of Israeli actions (in the form of flak campaigns and advertising choices, among others responses) demonstrate how threatened interest groups feel by what they perceive as a hostile media that is damaging to the reputation of the group they represent.

Corporations may also be affected because of coverage that portrays their roles and activities in a negative light. Media coverage that focuses on the role that a particular corporation allegedly plays in fuelling conflict (in the exploitation of natural resources or business deals with parties to conflict, for example) can adversely affect shareholder and customer image, which can be highly damaging to the reputation and financial stability of that corporation. Corporations thus may be forced to take some form of action in response to such unwanted media attention to mitigate its effects. The issue of blood diamonds is a case in point, where the diamond industry was forced to cooperate with and contribute to the movement to regulate the trade in illicit diamonds, not only because of the advocacy groups that had taken up the case, but also because of the media attention (particularly from those media corporations that targeted potential shareholders and customers) that was amplifying the advocacy activities of these groups.

Academic Influence

Academics influence the general public primarily because they write the history books that are used to teach those in schools, colleges and universities, and they directly teach university undergraduate and graduate students in such subjects as history, international politics, and security studies. They are thus largely responsible for moulding the perspectives of students, in terms of which issues in the world around them are to be considered important and how such issues should be viewed. This influence may be manifested in decisions regarding the courses that are taught, which geographical regions, issues and events are covered (and in what quantities), and from which perspectives the world is viewed. Outside schools and universities, academics' recordings of history are also found in books on the shelves in family homes and in public libraries, and their analyses of conflict, international politics and current affairs are sold as well in the bookstores in forms that are accessible to the general public, rather than simply for their trained peers. Similarly, academics write op-ed pieces in newspapers and columns in current affairs magazines, and appear on television and radio programs as experts and specialists to give their views on certain topics. Although the media filters this expression of academic opinion, the general public consumes the final product, and these members of the general public may come to know and trust the opinions of guests from academia who regularly appear in these arenas. This means that what academics choose to write (or perhaps more importantly, what not to write) affects the awareness of the general public on the state of conflict in the world.

Academics may also influence NGOs, by producing and supplying information and analyses on countries and conflict situations. NGOs may hire consultants and experts from academia for needs assessments, evaluations, and information on security. This type of interaction can lead to mutual influence. In conducting its mortality surveys which measured the scale of the conflict in the DRC, for example, the IRC teamed up with the Burnet Institute in Australia (IRC 2004). Just as interest groups may be influenced by media presentation of events affecting their particular group, they may also be influenced by historical writings and/or academic interpretations of such events. Academic interpretation of events that is seen as detrimental to interest groups may be met with strong criticism or even attempts to block publication, depending on the power and placement of the interest group and its members. Corporations also enter into relationships of mutual influence with sections of academia, purchasing information and analyses pertaining to business opportunities, as well as to short- and long-term trends in the stability and security of the areas in which they operate, to guide their investments and activities. This type of analysis is particularly critical in parts of the world that are experiencing (or are likely to experience) conflict, and in which their activities may be targeted by parties to the conflict.

Chapter 6

Academia

Academia includes academics in universities, in research institutes and think tanks, as well as specialists and experts who may be independently working as consultants and advisers. It refers here particularly to those in the field of international relations, politics and security, and historians. Its response to conflict involves gathering, recording and analyzing information pertaining to the background, causes, progress, external responses and peace processes of conflicts, from political, military, economic, and/or social perspectives. Academic response also includes efforts to make other actors – including policymakers, the media and the general public – aware of the existence and nature of conflicts, through teaching, through the production of journals, books and other academic materials, and through policy advice. Academics propose strategies as well: to the parties to conflict, and to those potentially in a position to deal in some way with conflict. This chapter focuses on how academia as a whole has responded to conflict in recent years, in terms of theory and thematic research, conflict- and region-specific research, and the recording, analysis and teaching of history. It goes on to explore the internal factors affecting this response: namely, personal perspectives and attachments, and career and institutional issues. Finally, it discusses how other actors (policymakers, the media and the public) influence academia.

Responses to Conflict

The agendas and priorities of academia in its response to conflict can be seen through the development and application of theory and thematic research relevant to security and conflict, through the quantity and content of academic materials such as journals and books, and through the study and teaching of history. Looking at the overall quantity and content of academic activity in this field, a distinct and pronounced Western-centric slant can be observed, and analysis and discussion of the security issues, together with the political, military, economic and social implications of the world's largest conflicts, most notably those in Africa, are largely absent from mainstream academia.

Theory and Thematic Research

The study of the relations among nations around the globe has been traditionally examined by academics through the lens of International Relations (IR) theory. Although IR is usually presented as a universal theory, it is based on 'great power' experiences originating in the West, and remains Western-centric. Incredibly, Africa and much of the rest of the world have been (and remain) absent from such 'universal' theorizing. As Craig Murphy (2001, ix) laments, 'More than one out of ten people are African. More than one out of four nations are African. Yet, I would warrant that fewer than one in a hundred university lectures on International Relations (IR) given in Europe or North America even mention the continent.' Many key thinkers in IR have even rejected outright the contribution of Africa and the developing world to IR. Hans Morgenthau, for example, made the assertion in 1973 (369) that prior to World War II, Africa was a 'politically empty space'. Limited to such a myopic view of international relations and politics, traditional IR fails to explain much of the African political experience throughout its history to date (see also Engel and Olsen 2005).

The unquestioning use of the 'state' as the fundamental unit for analysis in international relations is a prime example. Recent conflict and history in Africa have convincingly shown that, when analyzing international relations, there are many other key actors that simply cannot be ignored, such as armed nationalist movements, regional strongmen (warlords), international financial institutions and extractive corporations (see Dunn 2001). Political systems have evolved differently in Africa, and the so-called state does not hold the same relevance or weight that it would appear to hold in Europe. One of the key reasons for this situation is that states in Africa in their current form are mostly the result of artificially imposed line-drawing by the colonial powers to serve their own interests, and in most cases this has meant that the state is incongruous with the nations that pre-dated colonialism (see Malaquias 2001). Because of this reality and the influence of a wide variety of powerful actors, the line between domestic and international is also considerably blurred. Yet instead of rethinking the viability of IR theories to take into account this African experience of politics and conflict, mainstream academia has, on the whole, responded by simply ignoring the lessons, or dismissing them as exceptions. As Tandeka Nkiwane (2001, 284) points out, in the liberal perspective of IR, 'African examples and perspectives are regarded as primarily of nuisance value'. African examples have been largely excluded (as anomalies) from the democratic peace theory (the notion that democratic countries rarely fight each other) (286–7).

Academic activity is again considerably limited on some of the defining features of conflicts that, although being the greatest in scale in the world, appear to have little relevance for the West. Research on the issue of warlordism, for example, is particularly deficient in mainstream academic work, despite the role it is increasingly playing in most of the world's largest conflicts. So-called state failure is another area that is somewhat under-researched. The *Peace Research Abstracts Journal*, which provides indexed abstracts of a large number of academic studies, and claims to be 'the definitive source of literature concerning peace studies and international relations', published only 5 abstracts indexed under the term 'warlord' in the four years from 2000 to 2003, 5 under 'militia', and 10 under 'failed states' and 'state collapse'. The Penguin *Dictionary of International Relations*, which was updated to include events of 1999, does not even include the term 'warlord' (Evans and Newnham 1998).

Recent theoretical development and thematic research have instead been responsive to issues affecting the security of Western countries. The conflict in

Bosnia, considered with great concern in the West, gave birth to the term 'ethnic cleansing', for example, and unlike 'warlord' or 'warlordism', the term has taken root. The Penguin *Dictionary of International Relations* recognizes the term with an entry, as it is considered by the authors as one of the issues that indicates 'developments and shifts of understanding which have greatly affected the subject since the end of the Cold War' (Evans and Newnham 1998, viii). When Western countries attempted to justify their attack on Yugoslavia over Kosovo in 1999 through the concept of 'humanitarian intervention', this sparked a wave of academic work including books, journal articles and workshops on the subject. From 2000 to 2003 the *Peace Research Abstracts Journal* recorded 79 entries under 'humanitarian intervention'. Similarly, the terrorist attacks on the USA in 2001 sparked a flurry of academic activity on the subject of terrorism. In the same journal in 2002 and 2003, there were 152 entries under 'terrorism'. Even 'apartheid' was the subject of 41 entries over the same period.

Some academics and academic institutions have inflated the global significance of the September 11 terrorist attacks on the USA to the point that they assert that the event has changed the fundamental nature of conflict throughout the entire world. The National Defense Council Foundation, for example, decided in 2003 to take the extreme measure of discontinuing its World Conflict List that it had maintained for ten years, on the grounds that 'conflict has become asymmetrical. ... Terrorist organizations disregard boundaries, hence solely counting state to state conflicts, or internal state conflicts leaves the total count incomplete/inaccurate'. Similarly, in the book *How Governments Work* (a basic reference work aimed at a general, rather than academic, audience), the two pages it devotes to 'International Security' focus almost entirely on the issue of terrorism directed against the West. In the opening line, it claims that the September 11 attacks on the USA 'changed the network of international security worldwide' (New Earth Media 2006, 24–5). Even the 18 photos featured in the photo gallery on the page provide a similar impression: more than half are related to terrorism. The alleged rise in high-profile terrorist acts against Western targets can hardly be considered significant enough at a global level to discount the significance of the rest of the world's conflicts, most of which are far more deadly and destructive. Such a Western-centric view largely ignores the fact that many of the world's major conflicts have since continued for the most part unaffected by those attacks and by terrorism targeted at the West in general (although many parties to conflict have tried to take advantage of the intense focus on terrorism in the West – some successfully – by accusing their opponents of being terrorists in order to garner Western sympathy and support).

Some of the theory and practice behind the counting of the human costs of conflict through the death tolls can also serve to marginalize (albeit often inadvertently) some of the world's deadliest conflicts. The extensive use of report-based methodologies in measuring the scale of conflict is a key example, given that few reports on casualties in African conflicts emerge, and that nonviolent deaths (which are not counted under this methodology) account for the vast majority of conflict-related deaths. Death tolls found through more in-depth epidemiological surveys in some cases can reach (or exceed) one hundred times the tolls found through report-based methodologies. Thus, report-based methodologies seriously undermine the perception of the scale in many of the world's major conflicts, both in absolute terms and relative to other conflicts that are more closely observed and have greater access to humanitarian aid: death tolls from low-profile conflicts are seriously undercounted. This serves to further reinforce the gap between stealth and chosen conflicts. The updated Human Security Guide (2006, 24) does, however, promise to focus on the nonviolent deaths resulting from conflict – the hidden costs of war – in its next report, which could result in some major (and welcome) changes from the previous report's conclusions.

Research on Conflicts and Regions

Theory and thematic slants aside, the volume and content of academic works in the form of journals and books, and the programs of research institutes, similarly reveal a distinct slant towards what other actors see as important (chosen) conflicts and away from the stealth conflicts that they marginalize. Most major journals on issues of international security, conflict and peace tend to focus heavily on issues that are perceived as important for Western countries, and neglect those that are not. If the number (according to the region covered) of articles in such journals is any indication, it would appear that, incredibly, there is much more academic activity on the conflict in Israel-Palestine than there is on all of the conflicts on the entire African continent: sometimes double or more. In the five years from 1999 to 2003, the *Journal of Peace Research* carried 13.5 articles specifically devoted to Israel-Palestine, compared to just 6.5 on Africa or conflicts in Africa.[1] In the same period, *Foreign Affairs* carried 10 articles on Israel-Palestine and 6 on Africa (42 were on the Middle East). For the journal *Survival*, there were 8 on Israel-Palestine, but only 4 on Africa. During those five years, *International Security* carried only 2 articles focusing on Africa or African conflicts. In each of those journals, Africa was by far the least covered continent in terms of article numbers; in fact, with the exception of the *Journal of Peace Research*, the number of articles for that continent was less than one-tenth that of the most covered continent.

The number of journal articles on specific conflicts in Africa (within these limited numbers of articles) is also revealing. The conflict in the DRC, for all of its unparalleled magnitude and its relevance in a multitude of ways for the academic study of conflict, security and international relations (given the direct military involvement of so many foreign countries and the interrelations among states, rebel groups, militias, warlords and foreign mining and investment companies), has barely made an appearance at all in the major Western journals in this field. The same can be said for many of the other major yet otherwise marginalized conflicts, including those in Angola and Burundi. In the four years from 2000 to 2003, the *Peace Research Abstracts Journal* recorded just 32 entries for Congo (DRC) and Zaire combined, 18 for Sierra Leone and 13 for Angola. The number of academic references for these conflicts pales in comparison to the 388 entries for Israel-Palestine, 175 for Kosovo,

---

1   The number of articles in the journals examined here includes those that contained a specific country, region or continent in the title and/or those in which the content distinctly focused solely on that country, region or continent. In cases where the article focused on the relations between two countries, regions or continents, each was allocated 0.5 of an article.

105 for September 11 (in 2002 and 2003 alone) and 83 for Iraq. The volume of research for many current African conflicts also appears to pale in comparison to that of the ongoing research for many conflicts and issues of the distant past. In the same period, that journal carries 150 entries for World War II, 103 for Nazi Germany, 89 for Vietnam, and even 63 entries for World War I. If the *Peace Research Abstracts Journal* is representative of academic activity, these numbers suggest that twice as much research is being conducted in explaining a war that ended more than eighty years ago, as in explaining the world's deadliest conflict in more than fifty years, which has yet to be completely resolved.

The numbers of books available, dealing with certain countries and regions, can also serve as a general indicator of academic activity, and a cursory look leads to similar conclusions to those seen above. For example, a search in 2003 of a database (Webcat) of books and documents on the DRC (published since 1999) available in all Japanese universities revealed a total of 11 relevant works – in English and French. An identical search for those relating to Kosovo revealed more than 120 works in over five languages. A similar series of searches in the Harvard University Libraries of the books published from 1995 to 2005, found 59 hits for Burundi, 144 for Angola, and 230 for Congo, compared to 306 for Kosovo, 578 for Bosnia, 1,254 for Northern Ireland and 3,660 for Israel.[2] A search of the non-fiction books published since 2000 available on the Amazon bookstore website revealed 13 for Burundi, 30 for Angola, and 86 for Congo, compared to 115 for Bosnia, 418 for Afghanistan, 1,095 for Iraq and 1,750 for Israel. Although these searches are in no way limited to academic work on issues of conflict, peace and security, they provide some idea of the geographical areas of interest in academic studies in the West in particular.

Perhaps more importantly, the content of books and journal articles that do focus specifically on issues of conflict, peace and security, reveals major slants in academic activity and perspectives. Chapters in such books can sometimes be indicative of perceived priorities. In its 1999 yearbook, SIPRI offered individual chapters of analysis on the Middle East, Russia, the Caspian Sea and Europe in its 'Security and Conflict' section, but no chapters were devoted to Africa's major security issue in the DRC (or to anywhere else on the continent). In-depth analysis was also notably absent from its yearbooks of 2000, 2001 and 2002, with the focus being on Europe, although the DRC did appear in an appendix to the 2000 yearbook. *The New Security Agenda: A Global Survey*, a book published in Japan and edited by Paul Stares (1998), discusses new security challenges and how they are perceived in 'key countries and regions'. While its focus is on Asia (with separate chapters on Japan, China, South Korea, the ASEAN region, South Asia and the southwest Pacific), it also presents chapters on each of the world's other regions (North America, Western Europe, the former Soviet Union, the Middle East and Latin America), with the exception of Africa, which is completely left out of this 'global' survey. Ignacio Ramonet's *Wars of the 21st Century: New Threats, New Fears* (2004) presents individual chapters on September 11, the Middle East, globalization, Kosovo, the ecosystem and Iraq; again, nothing on Africa. These may be extreme examples, but they are indicative of

---

2　The search was limited to subject words in English language books published from 1995 to 2005.

a general trend in which the mainstream academic community appears to attach very little academic value to conflicts and security issues that occur in Africa, despite the fact that that continent accounts for the vast majority of the world's conflict-related deaths.

The content of what is actually written can also be revealing. The prioritization of certain conflicts, countries, regions and security-related issues over others in academic analysis (often highly disproportionate to actual conflict scale), and the use of certain examples (and neglect of others) in categorizing issues or proving points, shows a major Western slant in academic response to conflict. Samuel Huntington's *The Clash of Civilizations and the Remaking of World Order* mentions Africa only in passing. In a simplistic conclusion that appears to overlook almost completely the nature of conflicts and clashes on the continent, he stated that despite pervasive and intense tribal identities, Africans were developing a sense of African identity, and 'could cohere into a distinct civilization, with South Africa possibly being its core state' (1996, 47). In his analysis of conflict trends, conflicts within Africa did not appear to be considered with any serious concern. He also noted that 'The bloody clash of tribes in Rwanda has consequences for Uganda, Zaire, and Burundi but not much further' (28). The following wars in Zaire and the DRC would soon prove him very wrong.

Along similar lines, an article by Patricia Youngson in the journal *International Relations* (2001, 39), divides post-Cold War conflicts into three categories:

a) Those that pose a threat to national and international security and will therefore have to be dealt with by the major powers ... [for example, Iraq].
b) Those that do not initially pose a major threat to external stability but which have the potential to escalate regionally and therefore need to be contained ... [for example, Bosnia and Kosovo].
c) Those crises that do not require the deployment of troops from the major powers because they are inter-mural or intra-mural conflicts, locally focused and their nationalinterests are not crucially at stake ... [for example, Sudan and Rwanda].

This reflects an extreme Western-centric view of the world. Such divisions and categorizations of examples can make some sense only if the concept of 'international security' is understood as serving as a substitute term for 'US and European security'. Incredibly, the author goes on to make the assertion that 'An example of the third type of crisis, that which does not pose a threat to other nations, occurred in Rwanda and resulted in mutual massacres, leaving thousands of Tutsis and Hutus dead' (Youngson 2001, 42). Either the author is completely unaware that the Rwandan genocide was one of the major sparks behind the outbreak of two massive conflicts raging across Zaire/DRC directly involving troops from at least eight other nations, or else African nations simply don't count as 'nations'. While this article may represent the highly subjective views of a single author, the fact that such major factual errors could be overlooked in a peer-reviewed journal article shows how widespread in academia is the marginalization of African conflicts.

Numerous other examples abound in which Western security interests appear to be used to represent so-called 'international security' interests, with a resulting apparent disregard for conflict scale in analyzing security threats, and the general marginalization of African conflicts. The Penguin *Dictionary of International Relations* contains entries for the Korean War, Arab-Israeli conflict, Vietnam, Afghanistan, the Gulf War, Yugoslavia (including updates detailing the conflicts over Bosnia and Kosovo). Other entries include the 1969 Football War (included to show the many and varied reasons that countries engage in conflict), the 1818 Rush-Bagot Treaty demilitarizing the US-Canadian border, the Antarctica Treaty, and US presidential doctrines from Monroe to Clinton. Numerous regional (and sub-regional) organizations and groupings are also included, but for Africa, only the OAU is included (most notably, ECOWAS does not appear, despite its active interventions in conflicts in West Africa). No African conflicts are included, and the African continent appears relevant only in terms of the struggle against apartheid, with entries under apartheid, African National Congress (ANC), and frontline states (Evans and Newnham 1998). At a level of publication directed more at the general public, the reference book, *How Governments Work*, in its section on International Security names the 'key zones of conflict' as follows: Myanmar (Burma), Chechnya, Colombia, Indonesia, Israel, Iraq, Kosovo, Liberia, Northern Ireland, and Rwanda (New Earth Media 2006, 24). Only two of the ten are African. One wonders how the violence in Northern Ireland that has resulted in fewer than 400 deaths in more than thirty years could possibly be considered a key zone of conflict, and how instead, the world's three most deadly conflicts since the end of the Cold War (DRC, Sudan and Angola) do not appear at all.

Similar Western-centric patterns can be observed in the research programs and academic output of key think tanks and research institutes. In the Brookings Institution's list of regional and country studies (as of 2006), continents, regions and individual countries are listed. Europe, for example, includes separate entries for Balkans, Eastern Europe, Western Europe and Russia/Eurasia. Individual countries covered include China, France, India, Iran, Iraq, Mexico, Pakistan, South Korea, North Korea, Turkey and Australia/New Zealand. Africa, on the other hand, is listed as a single entry, with no regions or countries within the continent given a separate listing. A count of the academic output items listed by that institution (in the form of books, articles, speeches, op-ed articles, and events) reveals 82 items for Africa from 2000 to 2006, compared to 619 for the Middle East. Of those 82 for Africa, only 2 (an op-ed article in 2002 and an event in 2006) focused on the DRC – Darfur was the object of far greater focus. The IISS has eight regional programs, one of which is sub-Saharan Africa, but as of April 2007, no experts on Africa were listed as staff members on their Staff/Expertise homepage (eight experts on Asia are listed, three on the Middle East, and four on terrorism). The Carnegie Endowment for International Peace has specific programs for China and Russia/Eurasia. The Centre for the Study of Civil War at PRIO has specific area projects focusing on Afghanistan, Georgia, Haiti, the Middle East and the Kurdish issue. Africa appears not to be a priority in studies on conflict and security in Western academic institutions.

The same can be said for corporate providers of analysis and intelligence, such as Stratfor, which calls itself 'the world's leading private intelligence service'. As of January 2008, the cumulative number of analysis articles on its members' website for sub-Saharan Africa was less than half of that for Latin America, one-third of that for Europe or East Asia, and less than one-tenth of that for the Middle East/North

Africa. This intelligence service has produced more analysis articles on Israel alone than it has on all of sub-Saharan Africa.

History

Academic marginalization of Africa and the major conflicts on that continent does not end with the analyses of current issues. This marginalization is also being seen in what is (and what is not) being recorded as world history: the chronicle of events and issues that are perceived as having significance for the human race. This marginalization is seen both in the quantity and content of historical records and analysis. A simple look at the shelves in the history section of any bookstore in a Western country can be quite revealing. A shelf count at the major bookstores in Sydney Australia in June 2003, for example, found 3 shelves of books on Africa in the history section of Borders – the same as the number of shelves on Antarctica and the Arctic, while the books on the USA covered 21 shelves and the Middle East, 15 shelves. In that store's military section, roughly half of all books were on World War II. Meanwhile, Dymocks bookstore devoted 1 shelf out of 40 in its history section to Africa, and 16 shelves to Europe. Interestingly, many of the books in the Africa section of these stores were memoirs of white travellers in Africa, rather than historical records. Similarly, a check of the small Times bookstore in the Suntec Shopping Centre in Singapore in January 2006 found 26 books on the Middle East (11 of which focused on Israel-Palestine), but only 1 on Africa: a book on the UK-initiated Commission for Africa.

The content of history books and works is also revealing, with the proportion of paragraphs and pages that books covering overall world history devote to the African continent and its conflicts being highly limited. In Martin Gilbert's *History of the Twentieth Century* (2001), for example, the 70-page chapter covering 1990 to 1999 contains 27 paragraphs on conflict and politics in Israel-Palestine, 15 on Kosovo and 11 on Northern Ireland, but only 1 paragraph each on Zaire and the DRC. Interestingly, the book mentions Angola only with a reference to the visit by Princess Diana of the UK to that country to support de-mining. Similarly, only 5 of 220 pages covering the period of 1750-2000 in Clive Ponting's *World History: A New Perspective* (2001) are devoted to Africa, and concentrate mainly on the issue of colonization. The Penguin *History of the Twentieth Century* (J. Roberts 2000) contains no coverage of events in Africa in the post-Cold War era, with the focus being on Europe, USA, Asia and the Middle East. The conflict in the DRC does not feature at all in either the *Cambridge History of Warfare* (G. Parker 2005) or the *Collins Atlas of Military History* (P. Parker 2004). Both books focus instead on the former Yugoslavia, Chechnya, Afghanistan and Iraq in their recording of post-Cold War conflicts. In a short review of US foreign policy under the Clinton presidency, Stephen Morris (2004) criticizes the handling of conflicts and issues in Somalia, Bosnia, Kosovo, North Korea and of the issue of terrorism, as well as the failure to act in Cambodia and Rwanda. The handling of (or failure to handle) the world's largest conflicts during that period in the DRC, Sudan, and Angola, and of other major conflicts in Liberia, Sierra Leone, Algeria, or Ethiopia-Eritrea, is not mentioned at all.

Numerous examples of such priorities can be found in regular publications chronicling history as well. In 1999 (July/August), *Keesing's Record of World Events* devoted less than a quarter of a page to the details of a major peace agreement in Sierra Leone, and about one-third of a page to the peace agreement in the DRC. In contrast, in the same year (June) it devoted 12 full pages of explicit detail to the peace agreement over Kosovo. In 1999, its issues contained a total of approximately 35 pages of information on Yugoslavia (Kosovo), compared to 5 for the DRC. In 2002, 32 pages on Israel-Palestine overshadowed the 3 pages devoted to the DRC. In the four years from 1999 to 2002, it contained a total of 81 pages on Israel-Palestine, 66 on Yugoslavia, 30 on Afghanistan and only 15 on the DRC.[3] The *World Almanac and Book of Facts 2004*, in its Chronology of the Year's Events section (for 2003), contains 10 references to events in Africa compared to 50 on the Middle East, that are dominated by Iraq and Israel-Palestine. In the *SBS World Guide* (2004), which provides a short recent history and detailed information about every country in the world, the number of pages allocated for the recent history of each country also reveals their perceived importance. In its twelfth edition, it devoted 8.75 pages to the recent history of Israel-Palestine, 7.25 pages to the USA, 6.5 pages to Serbia and Montenegro, 4.75 pages to Pakistan, 4.25 pages each to Bosnia and Iraq. In comparison, it devoted no more than 2.5 pages to any sub-Saharan African country: 2.5 to Rwanda, 2.25 each to Angola and Sudan, 2 to the DRC, and 1.5 each to Sierra Leone and Liberia.

This Western-centric view of history is manifested again in the textbooks of history taught in schools. The syllabus for the study of Modern History in high school in the state of New South Wales, Australia, for example, has in recent years been broadened to include more of the world, but there is still little on Africa. South Africa is included as one of nine options for national studies, and one African (Nelson Mandela) is included among 27 people in the 'Personalities in the Twentieth Century' part of the course (there are two from Israel-Palestine alone: Yasser Arafat and Golda Meir). The 'International Studies in Peace and Conflict' part of the course includes the options of Anglo-Irish relations, Europe, Indochina and Arab-Israeli conflict, but not any African conflicts (although within the option for 'United Nations as Peacekeeper', 4 African conflicts appear as sub-options within a total of 13 conflicts that are designed to show the role of the UN in conflict) (see Board of Studies NSW 2004). The majority of Western university courses and texts that deal with the issue of international relations and security also do so from a Western-centric perspective. This situation contributes to the so-called 'we' problem in international studies: the use of the first person plural to subjectively refer to the policies and actions of the government of one's own country, in what is supposed to be an objective profession (Marks 2002).

Internal Dynamics

In Western countries, where academic activity and influence are strongest, academics in the field of international relations, security and policy have a considerable degree

---

3   Figures compiled by Reiko Okumura.

of freedom (theoretically) to pursue research on whatever theme, topic, country or region they desire. That being the case, one might be tempted to predict that academics studying conflict, for example, would gravitate towards places where the challenges of conflict appear, objectively, to be the greatest in the world. Yet this is usually not the case. Academic priorities and interests appear instead to closely mirror those of the other actors – policymakers, the media and the public, particularly in their regions of origin, or regions in which they are based. There are a number of reasons that can explain this situation, and there is, of course, a considerable amount of influence from these other actors, but these will be dealt with in the following section. This section will look at the internal factors that influence academic decisions to focus on particular topics and regions.

Personal Perspectives and Attachments

Many scholars choose for themselves a particular topic, theme or region early in their careers and specialize in that area for the rest of their academic lives, while others are more flexible, dabbling in a number of areas. In either case, there may be a broad range of factors behind the decision to focus on a particular area. Joseph Lepgold and Miroslav Nincic (2001, 63) tell us that 'Social scientists usually select their research tasks on the basis of simple intellectual curiosity, a sense of what is most challenging, disciplinary agendas, career calculations, and variety of idiosyncratic circumstances'. But intellectual curiosity is not something that occurs in an objective vacuum, and is usually closely connected to one's surrounding environment.

> The choice to study a particular topic is based on the assumption that it is worthy of explanation, and what is worthy of explanation is based not on a neutral standard, but on what is intellectually curious. Topics are considered 'problems' worth explaining not because of some characteristic intrinsic to the issue, but because issues are framed in terms of their problematic relationship to the social context in which scholarly investigation takes place (Marks 2002, 35–6).

So what is the social context or environment that leads to the choosing of research topics? In the case of scholars of international studies, it undoubtedly includes an array of social experiences and interactions, education and access to information about international affairs, in many cases going back as far as childhood. The spark of intellectual curiosity over a particular topic or region may be ignited by high school history classes, by undergraduate courses on international relations, security or policy, by books found in the university library, by an advising professor, mentor, or even a visiting lecturer or guest speaker. Yet, as we have already seen, there has always been, and there remains, a heavy Western focus in each of these areas. Considering, for example, that 'colonialism and imperialism in Africa existed parallel to the development of the canon of IR' (Nkiwane 2001, 280), and that the study of international relations has traditionally been a consistently Western-centric discipline that has rejected the notion that Africa and other developing regions of the world can contribute to its development, such sources of the spark for intellectual curiosity are much more likely to lead up-and-coming academics to lean towards topics, regions and perspectives that are relevant to Western interests. This is compounded by the fact that those headed for academic careers have had, throughout their lives, little access to information or perspectives about other parts of the world that appear not immediately relevant to their own country (see Marks 2002, 26).

How 'close to home' an issue is, is also a major consideration in choosing topics and regions for research, for a number of reasons. The simple geographic proximity of certain conflicts or events in international relations/security to the location of the researcher, can be a spark for interest. Western researchers may feel little motivation (as long as they stay primarily in Western countries) to study the issue of warlords, an issue with little apparent bearing on their own lives. They may perceive terrorism against Western targets or the issue of weapons of mass destruction, on the other hand, as having considerable bearing on their own personal security, which can motivate them to study such topics. Furthermore, as with other actors, other forms of 'proximity', or forms of identity, can also be powerful motivators. A link between particular foreign events and one's nation, race, religion, ethnic group, language, culture or socioeconomic status, for example, can be reason enough to interest an individual academic in pursuing research in that area.

Among these forms of identity, nationalism/patriotism appears to have particular relevance, although Michael Billig (1995, 37) warns us that because of its deep effect on contemporary ways of thinking, nationalism 'is not easily studied. One cannot step outside the world of nations, nor rid oneself of the assumptions and common-sense habits which come from living within that world. Analysts must expect to be affected by what should be the object of their study.' Among many academics, particularly those who work on practical matters of policy, there would appear to be an almost reflexive sense of nationalism/patriotism – a belief that it is their role as academics to work for the benefit of the particular country that they call home, by contributing to policy development. When academics devote their attention to examining the link between academia and policy (the notion of academic work 'being useful'), it is usually less in the sense of being useful in the formulation of global policies that will make the world in general a better place, and more about being useful in serving the policymakers and policy formation of their own particular country (see Nincic and Lepgold 2000). This is in some ways based on pride and in the fundamental belief that their country is a 'good' country, and that it is their duty to work to protect and promote its interests through their academic activities.

This phenomenon can perhaps serve to explain the marginalization from mainstream academia of the rare academics that are critical of their countries of origin (or the countries in which they are based), and the silence over the issues they raise, however sound their academic methodology and however valid their points (see Herring and Robinson 2003; Laffey 2003). As Stanley Cohen (2001, 164) notes, 'Intellectuals have an especially shameful record of political inhibition against speaking out against their own friendly or idealized societies on the grounds that this would damage a good cause.' Some academics even openly argue that it is their duty to be 'patriotic', a notion that goes against the most basic principles of academic integrity and independence (see Rorty 1994; Kramer 2001). This trend is particularly strong in the West in the post-September 11 political environment. In any case, whether one is critical or supportive of one's country, the important point is that the subject of the vast majority of research of either variety remains 'home'-centric.

This sense of attachment to one's country can be seen as well in academic institutions, with many often explicitly stating their mission as being attached to the interests of the country and/or region in which they are based. The Brookings Institution in the USA, on its 'About Brookings' homepage, for example, states that its mission is to conduct research and provide recommendations aiming to 'Strengthen American democracy; foster the economic and social welfare, security and opportunity of all Americans and secure a more open, safe, prosperous and cooperative international system'. Similarly, as seen on its homepage, Harvard University's International Security Program (ISP) goal is to address 'the most pressing threats to US national interest and international security'. The stated focus of the Foreign and Security Policies program of PRIO is 'on foreign affairs and security policies of the European states (including Russia), and on organizations like the UN, NATO, the EU and the OSCE'. In most cases the priorities of academic institutions dealing with international issues appear to be home first, the rest of the world, second.

Nationalism and other forms of identity are major factors again in the recording of history, for similar reasons. Historians cannot detach themselves from the societies in which they are entrenched, and inevitably conduct their research from a certain subjective perspective, from an attachment to a particular identity that affects how history is written. This results, at best, in the subjective selection of events (relevant to one's affiliation, in terms of identity) to remain in recorded history, and at worst, in the distortion and invention of facts. As Eric Hobsbawm (1997, 69–70) notes:

> History is inevitably so impregnated with ideology and politics that its very subject-matter and objects are from time to time called into question, especially when its findings are thought to lead to undesirable political consequences. ... we historians operate in the grey zone where the investigation of what *is* – even the choice of what *is* – is constantly affected by who we are and what we want to happen or not to happen: this is a fact of our professional existence.

Career and Institutional Issues

Personal perspectives and attachments to certain identities aside, the selection of topics for research is affected by other considerations as well, perhaps most notably concerns over career advancement. The tendency of academics to gravitate towards topics that are already the subject of attention (the bandwagon effect), for example, can be linked to a number of reasons. There is an assumption that if many others are already examining the subject, then it must be worthy of attention; academics believe that opportunities for intellectual support and feedback will be greater; and finally, contributing to a field that attracts attention enhances academic visibility and career advancement: 'novelty is achieved by looking for new, usually smaller questions within broadly traveled approaches and areas' (Lepgold and Nincic 2001, 15). One's academic work is given its value by how it is viewed by one's peers. Academics can easily identify 'hot' topics for research, such as 'democratic peace', 'humanitarian intervention' or 'terrorism', and may get on the bandwagon to further their careers and reputation in such popular fields. At the same time, topics fall out of favour and fashion, and the quantity of academic work on them decreases and shifts to other topics as times change.

Institutional factors also affect academics' research choices. Academic environments, particularly universities, have a tendency to be resistant to change. Leaders in departments are prone to seeking protégés that will take over their work, approaching the same topics and themes and from similar perspectives, and may well resist the introduction of perspectives and topics that clash with their own vision of the field. Funding opportunities are also more abundant for established programs and topics. Furthermore, departments have traditions to uphold, and to begin to tread a new academic path into less popular, less traditional, and/or not-yet-established areas and perspectives, carries with it significant career risks that most are unwilling to take. Institutional factors can affect the funding of a particular program, or of a particular research project, as well as hiring and promotion (see Krasno 2003). On a related note, there is a strong tendency among Western academics and journals to accept primarily work that is within their 'circle': the same country or the Western 'core', with work from the 'periphery' being left out. Susan Strange accused US authors and editors of professional journals of appearing 'to be deaf and blind to anything that is not published in the USA' (quoted in Aydinli and Matthews 2000, 291). A study found that among four key international relations journals in the USA, only 3 percent of contributors came from outside the Western world, and only 12 percent from outside the USA (298).[4] In the same study, a Middle Eastern scholar reported that she had greater success in publishing academic works in the USA when she included the name, as co-author, of her professor from a Western country (299). Foreign authors appear to be able to contribute to comparative politics related to their countries of origin, but are largely excluded from contributing to broader theoretical issues.

Language is also a factor: it creates advantages and disadvantages in the production and audience of academic work, regardless of its inherent academic quality. With English apparently emerging as a worldwide lingua franca in academic circles, native speakers have a distinct advantage over those whose mother tongues are not English. Major conferences, internet sites and databases are dominated by English, the majority of academic journals are in English, and the majority of sources cited in academic works are also in English (see T.W. Smith 2000); this book is no exception. The advantages for those using English as a mother tongue are considerable: 'Some of them will even increasingly enjoy the privilege of addressing an international congress or writing in an international journal in their mother tongue, while realistically expecting to be understood straightaway by anyone who matters, indeed while realistically expecting anyone who matters to address them in that same mother tongue' (Van Parijs 2000, 223). Thus, even within the West, scholars from countries such as the USA, the UK, Canada and Australia have a linguistic advantage in having their work recognized, while colleagues from most other countries are at a disadvantage. On a related note, the failure to examine and

---

4   The four journals were: *International Organization, International Security, International Studies Quarterly* and *World Politics.*

write ancient African history can, to some degree, be explained by the fact that, with some exceptions, there was a lack of written language on that continent, but this excuse does not hold for modern history (see Magyar 2001, 182).

Logistical issues may likewise affect the research of specific conflicts and issues. In terms of ease of information gathering, comfort and risk, some conflicts are easier to research than others. Researching conflict waged by Western powers, for example, is not a difficult task. The 'official line' is broadcast through specially set-up press centres, and information abounds from numerous sources. Other areas, such as Israel or the Balkans, are also relatively easy to access, relatively comfortable to spend time in and generally convenient to conduct research on. Attempting to get to the bottom of conflicts in Africa, on the other hand, may require significant lengths of travel, discomfort and even danger, travelling through inhospitable terrain to reach warlord strongholds where outside attention may not be welcome. Such logistical constraints contribute not only to the marginalization of the study of such conflicts, but also of thematic concepts associated with them, most notably warlordism (see Jones and Cater 2001, 238). In any case, the levels of information available in the first place for such conflicts (from past research) are also highly limited, which also discourages further attention and research, thus maintaining a vicious cycle.

With a strong trend in academia for research to be concentrated on issues close to home (issues that affect the interests of one's country and/or region), there exists a kind of division of labour, with US and European academics focusing on security interests that are perceived to be affecting their countries (primarily in the northern hemisphere), and African security interests, which apparently are not seen as affecting the interests of the West, left primarily to African academics. But the academic playing field is far from even. As with most other human endeavours, the levels of funding have a great effect on the strength of the achievement. Largely because of the availability of funding for academic activity and establishments throughout modern history, and the associated development of academic tradition and infrastructures, the West dominates academic activity. The USA in particular is the 'trend-setter in academic research' (Gibbs 2001, 417), with levels of funding for academic work available in far greater quantities than elsewhere (Reeves 2003).

The funding available for African universities and think tanks, on the other hand, is incomparably low. Africa's colonial masters left behind little in the way of facilities and human resources for secondary and tertiary education. As the independence era was beginning on that continent, no more than 3 percent of the student-age population in black Africa had obtained secondary education, and in the French colonies there were still no universities (Meredith 2005, 151). At independence, Belgium left the Congo with fewer than 20 university graduates. Today, academia in Africa is still able to attract but a fraction of the funding of their Western counterparts. This severely hinders academic activity and contributes to the 'brain drain', with large numbers of African academics leaving Africa for greener pastures in the West. There are currently more African scientists in the USA than there are in Africa, and there are 40,000 African doctoral graduates outside Africa (Felix 2006). Some, such as Abdul Karim Bangura (Voice of America, 2006), argue that the movement of African academics to the more prominent West makes them able to better transmit their research about the continent to the Western world, thereby increasing its position on the academic agenda. On the other hand, African academics in the West are likely to find themselves operating under the same pressures as their Western counterparts (to involve themselves in researching the popular issues of the day because of funding and career concerns), and as already noted above, non-Western academics are, in any case, more likely to be marginalized within Western academic communities.

External Influences

It has already been established that academics are influenced by their surroundings, and to some degree, academic output in the social sciences can never be truly objective. The influence of the surroundings for academics includes not only the world of academia in which they usually operate, but the views, concerns and agendas of external actors as well. Academics listen to the statements and debates of the policymakers, are consumers of the news, and are aware of what appear to be public concerns. This section will discuss the extent of the influence exerted by these external actors on academics in their choice of topics, countries and regions in studying international relations, security and policy.

Policymaker Influence

Academics produce a wide variety of output in the field of international affairs, ranging from abstract theory that appears to have little practical policy application, to works designed to address and solve specific policy concerns (see Lepgold 2000). Policymakers may exert little influence on academics engaged in work at the abstract theory end of the spectrum; most of this type of work is aimed at, and influenced primarily by, peers within a largely exclusive environment. Towards the other policy-oriented end of the spectrum, however, academic work is highly susceptible to policymaker influence, although both actors attempt to influence each other and both are successful, to a degree. David Gibbs (2001, 417) accuses mainstream scholarship in the USA of being 'written from the ideological and normative standpoint of the makers of US foreign policy', and claims that 'political bias is not confined to the history profession, which is if anything more independent of US foreign policy than political science or international relations. Nor is the problem of bias confined to the Cold War era; indeed, it has increased considerably since the fall of the Berlin Wall'. He goes on to state that 'It really should come as no surprise that social science reflects the ideologies of the most powerful nations and social groups. It is after all a truism that the victors write the history (and, it might be added, the social science)' (425). But assuming these statements are valid, to what extent does this reflect policymakers projecting their influence onto academia? One might argue that a nationalistic/patriotic academia that is (for a number of reasons) interested in issues close to home, will offer its services to domestic policymakers in areas perceived to be of interest to them of its own volition, without a direct influence by policymakers.

Evidence of direct policymaker influence, however, can be found in the fact that much policy-oriented academic work can be seen as having demand-driven elements (see Wilson 2000, 126; and Lepgold and Nincic 2001, 55–67). The fact that much of the funding for research on international issues comes from government sources, means considerable influence by policymakers on the topics selected for research, even if they do not attempt to project influence over the results or conclusions of that research. Policymakers may commission specific studies for areas in which they feel the need to enhance their understanding of a subject or region; they may also create positions within government for specialists in certain fields; or they may invite experts to participate in panel discussions with policymakers. In such cases, it is clearly the policymakers that are setting the agenda. While some academic institutions pride themselves on not accepting government funding (to protect their independence), the majority do rely to a large extent on government funding. The US think tank, RAND, for example, is closely linked with the US military, while the United States Institute for Peace is funded by the US Congress, and SIPRI is funded by the Swedish government. In the USA, the military has maintained close links with universities, funding research and providing scholarships for officer-students (see Eitelberg and Little 1995, 39). There are also connections between the Central Intelligence Agency (CIA) in that country and some prominent social scientists (see Gibbs 2001, 426).

Other examples can be found in Australia. After competition among a number of universities in that country, Sydney University was chosen in 2006 to be the host to a multimillion-dollar United States Studies Centre, which is heralded to become the country's leading think tank on political, economic and cultural issues. Its establishment has been possible due to the large financial contributions of government at both the state and national levels (*Daily Telegraph* 2006). On a different note, the head of an inquiry into that country's intelligence services, 'lashed out' at Sydney University over likely cuts in teaching certain Asian languages (namely Indonesian and Thai) that he felt were strategically vital to the intelligence capabilities of Australia, and called for government subsidy initiatives to address the problem (see D. Snow 2004). Both of these examples demonstrate that through government funding, policymakers have a considerable potential to influence the focus and direction of academic activities in institutions.

On a more sinister note, the influence of policymakers may go beyond the desire to make use of academia as a resource to enhance their policies and understanding of the world (as it appears relevant to their interests). In some cases policymaker influence may be geared towards shutting out dissident views and ensuring the dominance of academic output that is favourable to their authority, ideology and policies. Edward Herman and Noam Chomsky (1994, 23) call this 'co-opting of experts': a process that involves 'putting them on the payroll as consultants, funding their research, and organizing think tanks that will hire them directly and help disseminate their messages. In this way bias may be structured, and the supply of experts may be skewed in the direction desired by the government and "the market."'

Although even institutions receiving government funding may claim to be (and may to a large extent be) independent, government funding for research is often attached to specific programs on specific subjects. In situations in which academics or academic institutions work directly with elements of government in such a demand-driven environment, the topics of academic research will almost certainly reflect government priorities and concerns. Nationalism/patriotism aside, accepting to work with or for policymakers, with the influence in terms of research topic selection that this entails, means considerably enhanced funding and employment opportunities, as well as greater access to data, inside information and feedback. Such institutional and job security and privileged access to the subjects of academic attention are great incentives for academics to gain and maintain the favour of the policymakers that they become close to. Research may emerge independently on a relevant subject without a direct government request, but it is likely to be a response to an implied demand, by academics that believe it is their role to contribute to the policymaking of their country. Academics are more likely to take note of speeches, statements and policies made by their own governments than those of others, and this may well become a spark for intellectual curiosity.

The demand for research by policymakers (direct or implied) may be country- or region-specific or thematic. Some Western academics did, for example, take an interest in African politics during the Cold War, but this was 'typically to highlight the Soviet threat to the region', and declined with the end of the Cold War (Clark 2001, 86). The implementation of policies and their perceived success or failure can be seen to affect academic research, as was evident in research of so-called 'low intensity conflicts' after the US involvement in the conflict in Vietnam.

> In the aftermath of the US withdrawal from Indochina, the feeling grew that dealing with low intensity conflicts was unbearably problematic from which no good could come. ... It contained a dangerous tendency to politicise both military and scholarly practice. It killed off a generation of the best and the brightest. ... So it was that the study of insurgency became the orphaned child of strategy (M. Smith 2003, 28–9).

More recently, research on democratic peace theory is popular among, and has been encouraged by, policymakers in the West because it is expected that confirmation of this theory will benefit preferred Western policies. The same can be said of the theory of 'humanitarian intervention' in the aftermath of NATO's attacks on Yugoslavia over Kosovo. Similarly, there is currently a great demand on the part of policymakers for research on the issue of terrorism, given the threats that Western countries perceive to their security in this area.

Policymakers affect the academic world as well through the movement of personnel between the two sectors. It has already been noted above that many academics are brought into the policymaking arena (often at the request of government institutions), which gives academics an opportunity to influence policymakers. But it is not a one-way movement of knowledge and influence. In what is known as the 'revolving door', many retiring policymakers are given places in academic institutions so that the knowledge and experience gained in practical policymaking can be applied to the development of theory and future policy advice. And it is not necessarily a matter of policymakers waiting for retirement before actively contributing to academia: policymakers may move between both worlds at different times during their careers. Even during their time in positions in government, policymakers may contribute works to academic journals, conferences and other focal points for academic exchange.

It is not only policymakers that belong to the executive or bureaucracy that are in a position to influence the work of academia. In some cases, lawmakers are able to project influence as well. Lawmakers may be responsible for the approval of grants to certain academic institutions through parliament or congress. At a more extreme level, some lawmakers even restrict academic freedoms in certain cases. French law, for example, requires that history textbooks portray French involvement in colonialism in a positive light. Similarly, Japanese textbook writers are greatly restricted in how they can portray Japanese history, particularly in relation to the role of that country in its invasion and occupation of much of Asia prior to and during World War II. This applies likewise to more recent history. The publishers of a current affairs text in Japan were instructed in 2006 to remove a section suggesting that Japanese troops were deployed to Iraq while that country was in a state of war: a suggestion that clashed with the official government position that the war in Iraq ended when President Saddam Hussein was toppled, and that would have made Japanese involvement in Iraq appear unconstitutional (Alford 2006).

Media Influence

The media is regarded as the 'first rough draft of history' (see Indo-Asian News Service 2008; and Taylor 2000, 296), and of the analysis of current events, one might add. By focusing on certain conflicts and ignoring others, the media can have a considerable effect on the perception among academics of which conflicts and which events have important historical value and which do not. This is particularly pertinent given the necessarily selective nature of the choice of topics, events and issues for academic review, both in terms of history and in the analysis of current international affairs. As Eric Hobsbawm (1997, 59) reminds us, all historical study 'implies making a selection, a tiny selection, of some things out of the infinity of human activities in the past, and of what affected those activities. But there is no generally accepted criterion for making such a selection'. The media serves to spark the individual academic curiosity of researchers, or to rouse objection to the way something is being viewed or handled by policymakers or even by the media itself.

There are numerous examples of this apparent influence. On the back cover of the book, *Political Issues in the World Today*, edited by Don MacIver (2004), for example, the book is introduced as one that 'analyses the important political issues that dominate the media and demand the attention of political leaders of the modern world'. The media is clearly recognized as one of the key determinants of the perceived academic importance of political issues. Similarly, in the introduction to his book, *Global Outrage*, Peter Stearns (2005, 3) states that the book is

> very much shaped by recent events, which triggered my desire to trace and use a history of a phenomenon in order to understand it better. ... Like many Americans, I watched in considerable awe at the weekly procession of huge protests against imminent American war on Iraq, as they unfolded in many of the world's great cities in February, March, and early April 2003.

It can be assumed that the media is the portal through which Stearns has watched this 'weekly procession' in many of the world's cities, and it can also be assumed that the media's coverage of these events has played some part in stimulating his interest.

Media corporations do not simply report the events of the day each day as they occur. They make their own assumptions about what is historically 'important', both in the past and in the present, and often end up producing their own summarized versions of history. Many media corporations release 'top ten' lists at the end of each year, ranking what they perceive have been the most important world events of that year. The introduction to CNN's top ten world events of 1998, for example, summarizes the events of that year as follows: 'From outright conflict in Kosovo, to the latest tortuous chapter in the Israeli-Palestinian peace process, to the economic upheaval across Asia, Russia and Latin America – 1998 has been a year dominated by violence, diplomacy and economics.' Neither the outbreak of major continental conflict in the DRC, nor any other African event, featured in CNN's top ten events for that year. The top ten stories for Fox News for 2006 included Venezuela's President insulting the US President, the illness of Cuba's President Fidel Castro, and the poisoning of a former KGB agent, but neglected any news from the African continent, including the holding of historic elections in the DRC and Ethiopia's military intervention in Somalia (Fox News 2006).

Writing in Australia's *Sunday Telegraph*, Greg Sheridan (2004) asserts that:

> The war against terror, the supreme effort required to stop the spread of weapons of mass destruction, the new shape of the Middle East, which is going to be so profoundly affected by what happens in Iraq – these are the issues that history will concern itself with when it looks back to this period.

Similarly, on the occasion of the 60th anniversary of D-Day, World War II, *The Weekend Australian* (2004) briefly summarized post-Cold War history as follows:

> 1991 Gulf War over Iraq's invasion of Kuwait marks first major post-Cold War conflict. Later in the decade sees delayed international intervention in ethnic conflicts in Rwanda, Bosnia-Herzegovina, and Kosovo. Sept 11, 2001 Age of terror begins with attacks on twin towers in New York and Pentagon in Washington. United States launches war against Taliban and al-Qa'ida in Afghanistan. March 2003 US and the 'coalition of the willing', including Australia and Britain, launch war to expel Saddam Hussein from power in Iraq, claiming he holds weapons of mass destruction.

The fact that the Western-centric 'histories' and analyses of current events (that completely ignore the world's deadliest security issues) provided in such top ten lists and newspaper summaries appear to be in close alignment with the accounts and analyses that academia eventually produces, may suggest that academia, as a consumer of media products, is taking some cues from these first rough drafts of history and of current events.

Media corporations also influence academia because they are consumers of academic work and thereby provide a platform for enhancing a scholar's academic visibility. In reporting on conflict situations, media corporations interview academics, invite them onto analysis programs and request their contributions in newspaper columns and op-ed pieces. Academics are used to enhance news consumer understanding and to add credibility to the work of the media. While this provides an opportunity for academics to influence the media, conversely it can generally be said that invitations for such contributions are dictated by the demands of the media corporations: the selection of topics for discussion is usually a demand-driven practice. As NATO prepared to go to war against Yugoslavia over Kosovo, for example, the media (on behalf of the general public) wanted to know whether it was legal and what were the political implications. Based on this 'demand', academics were brought on to programs and into the papers to answer these questions. Similarly, after the September 11 attacks in the USA, the media wanted to know who would do such a thing and why. The academics were again called upon to answer such questions. For academic institutions and individual academics alike, such media attention and visibility enhances prestige, credibility, opportunities for funding for future research, and book sales. Thus, the more that academics gear their academic programs to meet the demands of the media, the more they are likely to be noticed, and the more successful they are likely to be. Again, research is encouraged to focus on the popular issues of the day.

The manner in which the conflicts are covered by the media may also influence academic work. The media's tendency to portray African conflicts, for example, in the frame of destructive, tribal and chaotic violence that defies logical explanation, contributes to an impression that academic analysis will fail to unravel the causes and provide any solution. The notion apparently held by some sectors of academia that African conflicts are caused by ancient tribal hatreds in a continent virtually devoid of politics may well be related to such a style of media coverage of conflict there. The less political value academics perceive in a particular conflict, the less likely they are to attach importance to the academic investigation and explanation of that conflict. Similarly, the media's tendency to focus largely on the aspect of humanitarian suffering of conflict, rather than on in-depth explanation of the causes and dynamics, serves to discourage academic analysis. As Jakkie Cilliers (2000, 5) points out, 'condemnation often replaces explanation'.

Public Influence

As with the media, the general public are also consumers of academic work to some degree. A certain proportion of historical works and of books on current affairs is marketable to the general public, and sales of textbooks can also become a source of income for academics. While the media is a powerful vehicle through which academics can enhance their visibility, reputation and the subsequent projection of their messages, it is often sectors of the general public that are the final target for their work. Through the output of the media, the statements and actions of policymakers, and interactions with the public, academics are able to gauge what topics are likely to sell to the general public. This saleability of academic work can give the general public some influence over academia. Other considerations aside, a book containing analysis of the security situation in the Middle East, for example, is far more likely to sell in the West and lead to enhanced academic visibility (given the familiarity and perceived political importance of that part of the world) than is a similar analysis of the security situation in Africa. This fact may encourage greater academic interest in the former region than in the latter.

For academic institutions, financial viability and reputation as leading institutions may well be closely related to sustaining their public visibility, and these considerations can serve as factors guiding the selection of research topics and the determination of academic direction. Student fees, for example, serve as a major source of funding for universities, so attracting a large number of students is an important part of protecting and promoting a university, or a department or course within a university. The popularity of universities, departments and courses is generally related to the reputability and influence of the university and/or that of individual professors, as well as to the relevance to general public interest of the courses and the issues they cover. This can mean emphasis, in courses and course content, on the issues that the consumers of academic teaching see as important in the world that is relevant to them. The pursuit of popularity and relevance by academic institutions in this manner can thus give the general public some influence over which courses are offered, and subsequently over the academic agenda.

NGOs are able to exert some influence over the academic agenda as well. NGOs, and the practice of humanitarian assistance, have become prominent features of outside response to many conflicts, and with the academic value of NGO work increasingly being recognized, it is becoming a target of academic attention. At the very least, NGOs can influence the academic agenda by providing opportunities for academics to conduct fieldwork and interviews at their project sites, and some practitioners may even actively collaborate with academics to produce academic work on conflicts, NGOs and the practice of humanitarian assistance. The NGOs that are involved in humanitarian aid are themselves becoming more sophisticated and are not only able to implement humanitarian projects, but also to gather, process and academically analyze data and issues relevant to this field. Some are capable of independently producing their own books and academic works on such subjects.

Other sectors of the public are also able to project some influence on the academic agenda. Compared to their colleagues in the USA, think tanks in other Western countries have a relatively weak financial base, and therefore are more likely to have their academic agendas set by others (those who provide funding for research), although the majority of US think tanks are by no means exempt from such pressures. Interest groups or even interested wealthy individuals may invest in what they perceive are like-minded institutions: those that will produce work that is likely to protect and promote their interests, or further their point of view. They may fund the establishment of specific projects within such institutions that produce work on a particular region, topic or issue. Conversely, where certain academic work is seen as potentially posing a threat to the interests of a particular interest group, that group may take measures (depending on its organizational strength) to attempt to halt its publication, or at least to prevent or reduce its extensive distribution. This may include legal challenges or other forms of pressure on the publisher. They may respond with vocal criticism challenging the quality and/or accuracy of the study, or attempt to refute and counter its results with academic works of their own.

As consumers of academic products, corporations are also able to influence the academic agenda. As with any business, it is in the supplier's interest to provide the products that the consumer is interested in. Corporations are particularly interested in security and political developments and trends in foreign countries (from short- to long-term) that will affect their business interests and help to guide future investments. It is thus in the interests of academic institutions (particularly private think tanks) to cater for the needs of this lucrative market, supplying information and analysis particularly in areas where Western business interests are concentrated. There is little benefit in producing and providing security and political analysis in parts of the world where big business is generally not likely to be interested, a factor that is undoubtedly related to the relative lack of academic interest in Africa, for example.

Chapter 7

Conclusions:
What Makes Stealth Conflicts?

Perception defines our reality. Where access to information that may enhance our perception is limited, the reality we see becomes distorted and warped. Our view of the state of armed conflict in the world today is one of the most unfortunate victims of such distortion. Despite supposedly unprecedented access to unlimited amounts of information from anywhere in the world, the volume and tone of information that is sought and received on the various conflicts occurring throughout the world is so skewed that the reality is almost unrecognizable. This is primarily due to the highly selective and increasingly assimilated agendas of the various actors that play a role in responding to foreign conflicts: policymakers, the media, the public and academics. One or two of the twenty or thirty conflicts ongoing throughout the world appear to be 'chosen' as the subject of intense scrutiny and selective indignation, very rarely on the basis of scale or the level of humanitarian emergency. Although some of the others make appearances at certain levels at certain times, the majority remain, to all intents and purposes, undetected: absent from the consciousness of these actors. These are stealth conflicts. They are numerous and include the largest and deadliest conflicts in the world.

As a species we hold in high regard how advanced our communications technology has become: how we can have any amount of information about anything beamed to us from anywhere in the world in real time. In many developed countries in particular, we also like to think that our awareness of violence and injustices around the world, together with our willingness and ability to respond, are at an unprecedented level. And yet, in this supposedly technologically omnipotent and morally enlightened era, the deadliest conflict the world has seen in more than fifty years, a conflict directly involving troops from nine countries, spanning a battlefield the size of Western Europe, and resulting in more than five million deaths, has scarcely been noticed at all by the outside world. Relatively speaking, hardly an expression of outrage or indignation has been heard, and little in the way of attentional, political, financial or military resources has been allocated towards its resolution, at least not until much of it was over. The conflict in the DRC has hardly been noticed, and it is unlikely to be remembered by the outside world. Given these circumstances, it can be said that the conflict in the DRC is the greatest stealth conflict of all time.

How ironic it is then to look back in history and find that consciousness in the West of the injustices occurring in the Congo was, relatively speaking, far greater one hundred years ago than it is today. A self-made investigative journalist and lobbyist named Edmund D. Morel established the Congo Reform Association (what would today be called an advocacy NGO) and began a concerted campaign to draw attention and put a stop to the violent exploitation and large-scale atrocities being perpetrated by forces under King Leopold II of Belgium, who colonized the Congo and ran it effectively as a personal fiefdom. The death toll over a period of 20 years was later estimated at roughly 10 million. Morel succeeded in bringing the conflict firmly onto the public, media and policy agendas of several Western countries, inspiring a parliamentary protest resolution in Britain in 1903, and series of talks, meetings and emotive photographic displays on the subject from Europe to the USA to New Zealand. He attracted staunch allies in political and public spheres, and much of his campaign was funded by rich sympathizers, such as the chocolate manufacturer William Cadbury. Mark Twain became a vice-president of the American Congo Reform Association and personally lobbied the US President on the situation on several occasions. Reports of atrocities poured into Western newspapers and numerous books were written on the subject. Interestingly, the actors involved and the webs of influence among and between them are not all that different from how they are today (see Hochschild 1999).

Of course, the overall effectiveness of these campaigns may have been questionable in some ways, and it must also be said that the atrocities that were perpetrated in the Congo, although relatively excessive, were in many ways similar to those perpetrated by other Western powers: by the other European powers in Africa, by Britain in Australia, and by the USA in what became the western USA and the Philippines, for example. As a weak European power, Belgium made an easy target for the more powerful Western countries (Hochschild 1999, 279–83). But the fact remains that the consciousness among the various actors in the powerful West on one of the greatest humanitarian tragedies of the time was far greater then than it is now for the greatest conflict-related humanitarian tragedy of today. This reality casts a large shadow over the real-world value of one hundred years of progress in information gathering and delivery technology (in terms of conflict reporting), and of the willingness and ability of the powerful and supposedly enlightened West to be conscious of and do something about large-scale atrocities and injustice in the 'outside' world.

What should be the greatest scandal of our time in terms of human conflict, because of the level of devastation – incomparable to any other – that it has caused, is doubly scandalous because it is not even recognized as a scandal (let alone the greatest scandal of the past half-century), and may never be. When policymakers, journalists, editors, advocacy-group leaders and academics reflect on the world's recent violent history, Somalia, Bosnia, Rwanda, Kosovo, Israel-Palestine, Afghanistan, Iraq and Darfur are the conflicts most likely to be heard from their lips and seen in their writings. These are the conflicts that will remain on the pages of history. The conflict in the DRC almost never rates a mention on such grim lists. It is also rare for the conflicts in southern Sudan, Angola, Burundi, Liberia or Algeria to appear on such lists, despite the fact that the scale of these conflicts in many cases far outweighs that of those that will be mourned and remembered.

What Are the Factors Determining Attention?

So what are the common factors that make the difference between a chosen conflict and a stealth conflict? It is abundantly clear that both at a global level and within Africa, the size of a conflict and its overall effect on human beings have very little to do with whether or not the conflict is noticed or responded to by the outside world. The preceding chapters of this book have examined this phenomenon and attempted to identify the internal dynamics and external influences that are behind the levels of consciousness and the choices that major actors make in this regard. Given the wide range of considerations and the intricate web of influences within and among these actors, it is necessary to bring together the factors that determine how a conflict is collectively seen and treated by the powerful policymakers, media, public and academia. All conflicts are unique, as is the combination of factors that lead (or fail to lead) to responses by outside actors, so there is no golden rule in this regard, but a number of key common factors can be identified. These have been recurring themes throughout the preceding chapters, and include: national/political interest, geographic proximity and access, ability to identify, ability to sympathize, simplicity, and sensationalism. Many of these factors overlap, and it is a combination of some, and at times even all of these factors, that contributes to the selection or rejection of a particular conflict for attention and response by external actors.

National/Political Interest

In a world so dominated by the ideology of nationalism, national interest is probably the most critical factor in deciding whether or not a foreign conflict should be the object of attention. Strategic military and economic interests are, of course, the initial concerns in this regard. That is, does a foreign conflict or security issue pose a direct or indirect physical or economic threat to one's country or its interests? Many Western countries, for example, have been the victims of, and remain seriously concerned about, direct physical attacks from non-state terrorist groups, and they have linked those attacks with foreign conflicts and security issues. Country-based actors are also highly attentive to foreign conflicts that may indirectly affect their country, its interests, or even its reputation. Conflicts that threaten to disrupt a cheap source of oil, refugees flowing into one's country from a conflict in a neighbouring country, or any other form of physical or economic destabilizing influences, are key causes for concern, as seen, for example, in Western interest in the Middle East, and European concern over conflicts in the Balkans. By extension, these concerns also apply to one's allies, whether bound by treaties, historical friendship, or mutual interests and concerns.

The failure of a conflict to significantly affect the critical national interests of other countries is perhaps the most important contributor to the lack of attention and response. It should be noted that national interests may well be present in the midst of some such conflicts, but the conflict in question does not necessarily affect them to the point of concern. Conflict in the resource-rich eastern DRC, for example, has little significant effect on the national interests of many other countries largely because, thanks to close collaboration among warlords, multinational corporations and allies, they can continue to access these minerals even in the presence of conflict.

It should also be noted, however, that national interests are often subjective, and are not necessarily agreed upon by all parties concerned within a country. Individuals and institutions may well differ greatly in what they perceive as being relevant to and important for the national interest. Separate political concerns can serve to distort what might otherwise be perceived as national interests. The perceived political popularity of a response, whether in terms of the support from voters or from political campaign donors, is likely to be an important consideration that policymakers factor into their decisions. Seemingly unconditional support for Israel among many Western policymakers, for example, is probably less a reflection of national interest in the military and economic sense, and more a reflection of political interest governed by the large political campaign contributions made by Jewish interests to political parties and individual politicians.

While national/political interest is likely to be the absolute prime concern for policymakers at a national level, by no means is this a concern applicable only to those in the policymaking arena. Although certainly under no small amount of influence from their policymakers, the media, the public and academia also remain independently concerned about the effects of foreign conflicts on the national and political interest, and even their effects on countries perceived as allies. Supposedly objective newspaper editors and academics openly use the 'we' word in referring to their countries of origin, and may even see their role in society as contributing to the protection and promotion of their particular country. Individuals making up the general public are raised and trained from a very young age to 'love' their country, and are constantly reminded throughout their lives to continue to do so. Armed with this sense of patriotism, and with such limited information on the world beyond their country's borders, individuals almost inevitably have a tendency to view foreign conflicts from the perspective of how it affects their own country, an effect that is echoed within the particular institution to which they belong.

National interest does not always serve to attract attention to a foreign conflict. In some cases it may conversely help keep attention away from conflicts for which attention would be inconvenient, with powerful countries ignoring or downplaying the presence of a particular conflict on behalf of an ally or cooperative supporter. National sovereignty may no longer be an effective refuge for leaders to do whatever they want within their own territories, but anonymity, in this sense, remains a very effective refuge for leaders who prefer to remain 'off the radar' when engaging in violent or oppressive policies. This is often achieved through friendship with and support for the world's most powerful countries, as Rwanda and Uganda found on the two occasions that they invaded their massive neighbour; as Turkey has found in its conflict with its Kurdish minority; as former President Niyazov found in continuing his oppressive dictatorship in Turkmenistan; and as countless warlords in conflicts across the world have found in running their private and violent fiefdoms.

Speaking out against or refusing to cooperate with the West, on the other hand, is a sure way of attracting attention to one's own conflicts and policies, and to the treatment of citizens under one's rule. It attracts attention largely because it threatens to damage the reputation of Western countries and their leaders, pricks the patriotic pride of Western media and the public, and attracts academic attention for both of these reasons. Such leaders quickly become targets for scrutinization and often demonization. Such a tactic is usually a gamble, aimed at galvanizing domestic opinion against a foreign foe to shore up waning internal legitimacy, but at the risk of attracting unwanted attention, sanctions or worse from that foreign foe. This helps explain, for example, the relatively high levels of foreign attention trained on Zimbabwe under President Mugabe, as opposed to the low levels of attention on Guinea under Western-friendly President Lansana Conté (the latter country is the world's largest producer of bauxite, much of which is mined by US companies).

Geographic Proximity and Access

In many ways, geographic proximity is inseparable from national interest as a factor influencing attention to foreign conflicts. Conflicts that are occurring in relatively close proximity to one's country are likely to be linked to the national interest in some ways, if not because of a direct security threat, perhaps because of the business interests of corporations with ties to both countries or the possibility of an influx of refugees from that conflict. But even when there are negligible effects on national interest, the very fact that there is a disturbance in the area can serve as a cause for attention, if only out of a vague sense of closeness perceived among the general public or other actors. This is especially the case when a disturbance occurs in the vicinity of a country that is powerful in its particular region. Unrest in countries in the south Pacific, for example, tends to attract the attention of actors in Australia (from policymakers to the media and aid organizations), who may see the area as belonging to its own 'backyard', or sphere of influence.

But the issue of geographic proximity is not necessarily limited to the location of one's own country. It is also likely to be related to the location of branches or agents of a particular actor. For example, the proximity of a conflict to the bureaux of media corporations, who seem to place excessive degrees of importance on the speed with which they are able to gather and present news, can be a critical factor in determining whether or not that conflict is responded to. Even in the absence of national or political interest, a clash occurring within a few kilometres of a media bureau in Jerusalem is highly likely to attract the attention of that particular media corporation at the very least. An outbreak of fighting in Brazzaville, Congo, on the other hand, is unlikely to attract the attention of a media corporation whose closest bureau is Johannesburg, South Africa, unless there are other factors that serve as major sparks for interest.

Geographic proximity is also affected by access, which may be impeded by transport infrastructure, security issues, or legal restrictions. The physical distance between Nairobi and Mogadishu is not all that different from that between Nairobi and southern Sudan, but for media corporations with reporters based in Nairobi in the early 1990s, when deciding to cover conflict and famine in the region, the fact that the state of transport infrastructure meant a day trip for the former and a three-day trip for the latter seemed to make the difference in the decision. Dangers for reporters in covering conflict in Algeria, a country on the doorstep of Europe, were undoubtedly a factor in limited coverage there, with reporters being deliberately

targeted. The choice of locations for the work of aid NGOs is also affected by
security threats and legal restrictions on entering a particular area, as it is for the
media and academics pursuing fieldwork. In many cases, countries may ban reporters
or aid workers from entering or operating in their territory, as seen, for example, in
Myanmar and Zimbabwe. It may be a combination of factors. Limited access caused
by dense jungle, poor transport infrastructure, and the threat of being kidnapped,
have been factors in limited response to conflict in Colombia by many actors, despite
relatively high levels of perceived national interest for the USA, linked primarily to
the trade in illicit drugs.

Ability to Identify

The ability of actors (and the individuals that comprise them) to identify with the
participants and/or victims of a conflict appears to be a major determinant in the
levels of attention a conflict attracts. Group identity can, to varying degrees, serve
to facilitate a sense of affinity or solidarity with other members of the same group,
or groups that are closely related in some way. This identity is likely to be based
on one or more perceived racial, national, ethnic, religious, cultural, linguistic,
historic or socioeconomic ties. The very existence of many interest groups is solely
attributable to such ties. The power of national identity can be seen, for example, in
the high levels of attention by various actors (perhaps most notably the media) from
a particular country, to situations in which a small number of individuals from that
same country have been taken hostage, injured or killed (in places like Afghanistan
or Iraq). Racial identity helps to explain comparatively high levels of interest within
Western countries in the plight of white commercial farmers being forced off their
farms in Zimbabwe, just as religious identity helps explain high levels of interest,
among Jews and Muslims alike, in the Israel-Palestine conflict. A combination of
racial, national/ethnic (among the diaspora), cultural and socioeconomic ties help
to explain interest among actors in Australia in the conflict in geographically distant
Kosovo. Similarly, terrorist attacks hitting Western urban centres provoke identity-
based responses in other such urban centres, creating a sense of 'it could have
happened in this city' or 'it could have happened to me'.

Black-on-black violence in Africa, on the other hand, holds little in the way of
ties based on identity for actors in the Western world, thereby failing to spark or
sustain interest. Individuals and institutions concentrated around high-tech urban
environments in predominantly white, wealthy countries in the West may find it
difficult to identify with the plight of poor black people speaking a foreign language
and living a different culture, struggling to make a life for themselves in makeshift
huts in isolated villages, in an arid rural or jungle environment. Religious ties may
serve to provoke a degree of concern in such cases, when fellow Christians or
Muslims are perceived as being threatened, for example. Historical ties may link
actors from former colonial masters with violent events occurring in their colonies,
and a common language (linked with colonialism) may also serve this purpose to a
limited extent. But such ties in isolation are often comparatively weak, and beyond
this point, the only identity-based tie that can be found in many of these cases is the
tie as a fellow human being, and it is clear that this tie usually is quite low on the

priority list of forms of identity, almost certainly below national, racial, ethnic and religious ties. Identifying with the suffering of a fellow human being, regardless of other ties, can and does happen, however, and this leads us to the next factor.

Ability to Sympathize

Another important factor in determining the level of attention and response to a particular conflict is the ability to sympathize with the victims of that conflict. If one of the parties to a conflict can be perceived as being the evil perpetrator of the violence, and the other as being a good, innocent and perhaps helpless victim, outside viewers are likely to take an interest, driven by feelings of sympathy towards the perceived victims, and of indignation towards the perceived aggressor, an aggrieved sense of justice arising. Such perceptions are boosted by images personifying the evil and innocence of the players: leaders like Saddam Hussein and Slobodan Milosevic serve as the individual faces towards which outside actors can direct their indignation (rather than towards a vaguely identified armed force or ethnic group), while sympathy can be directed at images of individual starving, crying babies and their frail and helpless mothers. Genocide is another frame that boosts sympathy, as it embodies what is seen as the ultimate divide between evil and innocence. Even the suggestion of the existence of genocide can constitute a major factor in attracting outside attention, as seen in the response to conflict in Darfur. Sympathy may also be generated by historical experiences. A particular group that is seen as having a history of being mercilessly victimized is likely to be able to generate sympathy in future conflicts as a result of the residual guilt. This sympathy factor is particularly relevant to response choices made by the general public, NGOs and the media, but it certainly applies as well to individuals serving as policymakers and academics.

Conversely, if a clear-cut case of good versus evil cannot be shaped from a situation of conflict, sympathy and attention are unlikely to arise and be sustained. Conflicts that are portrayed as being 'tribal' are particularly affected in this way; they are seen as part of a cycle of retaliatory violence, or ancient bloodletting, for which both parties share a significant portion of the guilt, and for which nothing can be done. Combined with the fact that there is so little information available to begin with on such conflicts and the parties involved, there is little to trigger sympathy. In any case, for the vast majority of conflicts, the evil-versus-innocent-victim scenario is at best a gross oversimplification, and is often a gross misrepresentation of the reality. One or more inside and/or outside actors with an interest in the conflict being seen in such a manner are usually responsible for moulding perception of it to reflect such a scenario, in an effort to generate sympathy and a desired response from the outside world.

Simplicity

This factor is related in many ways to the ability to sympathize. In many modern conflicts, the participants are not limited to two clear-cut sides in different uniforms squaring off against each other on two sides of a fixed battlefield with well-defined grievances and objectives. Particularly in an era in which warlordism is a key defining characteristic of conflict throughout the world, the lines between friend and foe, between combatant and civilian, between ends and means, and even between war and peace, often appear to be blurred, sometimes beyond recognition for the outside observer. By way of an analogy, in most ball sports, the simplicity and understandability of one ball, two teams wearing different colours, and two goalposts at different ends of a clearly marked field, appear to be critical components in ensuring sustained interest. Adding extra balls, teams or goalposts, making it difficult to distinguish teams from each other, or changing the rules mid-game would undoubtedly have a disastrous effect on the ability of the sport to attract and maintain the interest of the spectators, and on the general popularity of the sport. Similarly, the simpler the appearance of the conflict, the easier it is for individuals and institutions to make sense of it, and thereby devote sustained attention to it.

While the vast majority of conflicts in the world are in reality highly complex (few, if any, can claim to fit anything resembling the mould of a simple football match), conflicts that can be made to appear simple and clear-cut, either by actors with an interest in the conflict (such as policymakers) or by actors with an interest in simplifying matters (such as the media), have a much better chance of attracting interest and a response. Dividing the identities of the players into two clearly identifiable sides is a key component of such a simplification process. A conflict seen as pitting Muslims against Christians, blacks against Arabs, or Americans against terrorists, for example, gives a conflict the simplicity it needs to have a broad following. Setting out well-defined objectives is another component: toppling a cruel tyrant or freeing an ethnic group from oppressive rule, for example. While the appearance of some conflicts may be able to be somehow moulded to fit such simple forms (if there is sufficient interest in doing so), this is simply not possible in the case of many others, such as in the DRC, and thus interest and attention are difficult to sustain. This is particularly relevant to media corporations, who typically need to fit news stories into short and easily understandable formats to attract viewers and readers. But even for those actors and individuals who may have a genuine interest in trying to understand the dynamics of a conflict, time constraints and the sheer complexity of the conflict often serve to inhibit this interest.

Sensationalism

How dramatic or sensational the appearance of a conflict is can also be a factor in the levels of attention and response, with the high degree of novelty making a conflict difficult to ignore. Explosions are by their nature sensational. The sequential crashing of commercial airliners into the two towers of what were once the tallest buildings in the world, and their subsequent collapse, in the heart of the world's most powerful country, constituted a visually and conceptually dramatic attack, and was all the more gripping because it was caught on camera from a variety of angles. The sudden, unexpected and explosive nature of an attack in an otherwise peaceful place is part of what gives such terrorist attacks such high levels of attention and response. The air attacks marking the US-UK invasion of Iraq, designed to 'shock and awe', provided ample dramatic images (caught on camera) of massive explosions in Baghdad and thus also served to give that campaign a sensational quality, as did footage from attacks in other Western-led conflicts, including those in which missiles, themselves fitted with cameras, hit buildings and even moving passenger trains. The combination of sudden natural disasters and conflict can also produce a sensational effect.

Conversely, dramatic is hardly a term that can be applied to the slow death of individuals and entire communities from conflict-related starvation and disease, or to the prolonged suffering of those who have fled violence into inhospitable jungles and deserts. This is the phenomenon responsible for the vast majority of conflict-related deaths. Reporters and aid workers do try in some cases to evoke a sense of shock by portraying the harrowing experiences and pitiable appearance of individuals who are victims of such conflicts, and sometimes novelty becomes a major factor in attracting attention, such as in the famous photograph depicting a vulture waiting for a starving and dehydrated young child to die, against the backdrop of conflict-related famine in southern Sudan. But usually it is the ability to sympathize, rather than the sensationalism per se, that attracts the attention in these cases.

The presence or absence of visual images (usually via the media) is often critical in determining whether a conflict, by virtue of its sensational nature, can become the object of attention. The fact that nothing was caught on film perhaps helps to explain the lack of dramatic effect of the 2001 terrorist attack on a train in Angola, for example. In a similar vein, sudden and dramatic moves by Rwanda and Rwandan-backed rebels, at the outbreak of the DRC conflict, could perhaps have had some novel and sensational appeal had Western camera crews captured the critical moments: the hijacking of civilian planes and the initial advance on the capital, for example.

How Do the Factors Determine Attention?

These factors tell us what is commonly held by individual actors as being important in determining their awareness of and response to conflict, but they do not tell us how these actors weigh each of these factors, particularly considering that they may be conflicting. Nor do they tell us how such a determination will be made when the agendas of the major actors differ, who the lead actors or trendsetters will be, how interest will initially be sparked, and how it will spread.

Combining and Comparing Factors

Some choices are clear-cut, when most or even all of the factors match. The September 11 attacks on the USA in 2001, for example, were seen as representing a major threat not only to that country, but also to other Western countries. Reporters, academics and prominent policymakers from many countries were present or within close proximity, could identify and sympathize with the innocent victims of the obviously one-sided attack and feel indignation for the perpetrators, and the attacks were dramatic and gripping in nature. All of the ingredients for attention and response from the perspective of the West were present. The choice of the West to focus on conflict in Kosovo was also a relatively simple one in this sense. Western Europe was potentially going to have to deal with an influx of refugees from the conflict that was occurring on its doorstep. The area was easily accessible, Western actors could identify with the victims who were similar racially, culturally and socioeconomically, and the conflict could be portrayed as a simple case of persecution by evil Serbs against a helpless and innocent Albanian minority.

The choice to ignore other conflicts can also be equally simple if the conditions are all reversed. The conflict in the DRC serves as the prime example. It did not significantly affect the national interests of the West, who still had access to that country's mineral wealth and were out of reach of the vast majority of those displaced by the fighting. If anything, national interests in the West were probably better served by the conflict being played out quietly. It was relatively distant geographically, and not easy for Western actors to access. The fact that it was black-on-black violence made it difficult from the outset for Western actors to identify with, but this was compounded many times over by the sheer complexity of the conflict. With nine national armies involved at one stage, and a much greater number of rebel groups and splinter groups, many with very murky agendas and objectives, it was extremely difficult to comprehend or follow the conflict (or perhaps more accurately, conflicts), let alone single out any particular identifiable group that could be perceived as being collectively worthy of sympathy. Finally, with the exception of the initial attacks, most of the fighting and associated suffering that followed could hardly be portrayed as sensational, even if there had been an inclination to capture it on film. In short, from the perspective of the West, there were really no aspects of the conflict that could serve to generate interest or a response, beyond the obvious fact that so many human lives were being lost. The same can be said of the vast majority of conflicts in Africa.

But other decisions do not fit the formula so neatly. The conflict in Iraq, for example, may be considered important in national interest terms because of its oil wealth, and because it is seen as a conflict related to anti-Western terrorism (albeit arguably as the result of a self-fulfilling prophecy), and nationalism helps Western countries to identify and sympathize with their own troops present there. On the other hand, there is probably no conflict on Earth that is more difficult for Western actors to access given that they are deliberately and persistently targeted in that country, and it is also somewhat futile to attempt to simplify the conflict in any form, or identify specific groups that could be perceived as innocent victims. The complexity of the Israel-Palestine conflict and the difficulty in identifying an innocent and blameless side could be seen as a factor in reducing foreign interest, but the interest remains consistently high.

Significant levels of attention for the conflict in Darfur are even more difficult to pin down. The conflict does not threaten vital Western national interests, although Sudan has been a traditional enemy of the USA, and the West is interested in oil exploitation there. Distance, transport infrastructure and government restrictions make access highly problematic, and it is difficult for the West to identify with any particular group. Under other circumstances it could probably easily have been written off as another tragic yet unintelligible tribal conflict and ignored. Yet the conflict was simplified into a Muslim-versus-black scenario, with the black side seen as innocent and helpless victim. This portrayal was strengthened by allegations of genocide, and it was able to attract attention. It is also not easy to understand Japan's relatively high level of interest in the conflict in Kosovo, considering that there were no significant threats to national interests, and no common characteristics enabling identification with either side. Zambian media and public interest in the Iraq and Israel-Palestine conflicts (above and beyond any of the much larger conflicts in Zambia's neighbouring countries) also seems extremely odd, defying any apparent concern for national interest, geographic proximity, or ability to identify with either side.

Internal priorities specific to each actor will of course be important determinants in how actors weigh the aforementioned factors in setting the level of attention and response that they devote to each conflict. National and political interest will clearly be the highest priority among the factors for policymakers, particularly at a national level, and no other is likely to even come close in terms of priority. Perceived national interest will remain a high priority for the other actors as well, but other factors are likely to take on more importance, and may well exceed national interest. For the media, sensationalism, simplicity and access will undoubtedly be given a high priority. The general public are likely to give priority to identity, sympathy and sensationalism. Identity is by far the greatest priority for interest groups, while sympathy is likely to be the highest priority for aid organizations. Academics in the field of international affairs may place greater importance on national and political interest, as well as identity and perhaps access.

But whatever the internal priorities appear to be for each group of actors, to a considerable degree their agendas are open to the influence of other actors. We have already seen many of the mechanisms by which external influences distort the internal priorities of each actor, to the point that the agendas of the vast majority of actors able to respond to foreign conflict appear to have become increasingly assimilated. But the critical questions remain as to who leads this interactive process, how interest is sparked and how it spreads. The relative strength of each actor is undoubtedly the key determinant in this process, but this is tempered by how interested the actors are in a particular conflict, with weaker yet strongly interested actors able to take a lead in attracting interest and encouraging a response. The bandwagon effect then serves to bring many of the actors together. Sometimes plain luck, in terms of timing or a clear path of influence, can also play a role in determining the attraction of interest and responses to a conflict.

The Role of Strength within Groups of Actors

The relative strength or power of an actor or group of actors appears to determine the direction and concentration of attention and response to foreign conflicts in the vast majority of cases. This is both because of the capacity to respond (in terms of resources) and because of the ability of the strong actors to influence those that are less powerful. Within the policymaker group of actors, it is the interests of the strongest that come to the fore and demand attention, because they are able to give more aid, enact more effective sanctions, deploy stronger military capabilities, and generally project more military, economic and diplomatic power in furthering their interests: they exert a stronger gravitational pull over others. The security interests of the weaker countries are inevitably affected by the stronger ones, whether out of fear (from intimidation), opportunism (a calculation of the benefit and loss associated with supporting or opposing a stronger power), or peer pressure. The clashing security interests of the USA and Soviet Union, for example, demanded attention, without respite, from policymakers across the globe during the Cold War. Both countries threatened for decades to destroy the world with weapons of mass destruction, and there were highly destructive consequences from proxy conflicts in countries as distant from these superpowers as Vietnam, Angola and Mozambique. As the African proverb goes: when elephants fight, grass gets trampled.

Because of the unrivalled strength of the USA since the end of the Cold War, the security interests of that country currently reverberate most strongly throughout the rest of the world. The current focus on terrorism is a case in point, with the policymakers of countries that are otherwise unlikely to be directly affected by anti-Western terrorist attacks nevertheless taking an interest and taking steps to respond to the issue. Similarly, countries with seats on the UN Security Council become the focus of intense lobbying and pressure to vote in a certain way by more powerful countries with an interest in a particular conflict. Australian participation in the invasion of Iraq is difficult to explain in the absence of the gravitational pull of the USA; Australia has since signed a free trade agreement with the USA. It is also difficult to explain the relatively high amounts of Japanese aid to Kosovo in the absence of such high levels of interest among NATO countries; peer pressure was clearly a factor. A gravitational pull from Australia (through diplomatic power) over its interest in East Timor may have helped to attract a certain degree of interest in and response to that conflict from distant Europe. A similar pull exerted by regional powers such as India, Pakistan and Nigeria is felt by weaker countries in their respective regions. Although not endowed with military or economic power, the UN Secretary-General has a certain degree of moral authority that can be used as diplomatic power in attracting interest from other policymakers.

The gravitational pull of the strong policymakers often operates at the expense of the security interests of the weak. Without interest from the strong countries in their security concerns, and without the strength to attract interest, the concerns of policymakers in weak countries are likely to remain off or in a low position on the policy agenda beyond their immediate region. The critical interests of policymakers in the DRC, for example, were severely threatened by the invasion by Rwanda and Uganda, as were those of policymakers in the Republic of Congo when Angola participated in the rebel overthrow of the government, but in the absence of inherent external interest, and without sufficient military, economic or diplomatic strength to exert a gravitational pull on policymakers beyond the region, interest and response from policymakers in the outside world were not forthcoming.

Similar principles apply to the media. Media corporations with greater resources are able to gather more news and present it to a larger and more powerful audience in a shorter time and in a more attractive format than can their competitors. This makes them trendsetters in a very trend-conscious industry; their agendas influence other media corporations that do not have the same capacity for gathering and presenting news. The majority of media corporations outside the West, for example, do not have the budget to gather news from foreign countries, and are forced to rely on the news from those that do, buying articles and footage from their more powerful counterparts. This leaves them highly susceptible to the influence of powerful Western media corporations, who inevitably play a key role in determining the levels of interest, among the media, in foreign conflict. The Zambian media's almost complete reliance on foreign media corporations for foreign news, for example, helps explain the dominance in the Zambian news of conflicts in the Middle East, at the expense of news on conflicts in neighbouring countries. Even in Japan, much of the foreign news that is presented is simply bought and translated from foreign news sources, raising the position in the Japanese news agenda of conflicts that interest powerful US and European media corporations. Furthermore, because Western media corporations dominate the news market, and because weaker media corporations are unable to contribute significant quantities of news to the international news market, the little news that is generated on conflicts beyond key Western interests is typically framed from a Western-centric perspective.

Strength is a key determinant of attention and response to foreign conflict in the public agenda as well. The general public in countries with a high socioeconomic status are likely to have better access to information about conflicts in the outside world than those living in countries with a low socioeconomic status. Because of the greater availability of resources, the measurement of public opinion is concentrated in and about the West, which in itself gives greater power to the general public in powerful Western countries. The vast majority of opinion polling about security issues is conducted in Western countries, and the topics are usually limited to issues that are perceived as being of concern to the West. Even on the rare occasion that such opinion polls are conducted in Africa, for example, the security issues raised are those relevant to the West; surveys may ask Congolese citizens what they think about conflicts involving the USA, but not about conflicts in Africa. In addition, because of their wealth, Western publics are able to devote greater resources and time to addressing foreign conflicts in some way. The same can be said of NGOs, interest groups and even corporations. Greater wealth and influence gives them greater power to respond to conflict and greater influence over other actors. Conversely, with fewer financial resources and connections, weaker NGOs and interest groups (particularly those based outside the West) are generally less able to draw attention to conflicts of concern to them.

Nor is academia free from the distorting influence of strength. Academic institutions with greater long-term access to resources are able to build academic tradition, produce more influential research and present findings to a larger and more powerful audience. Like those in many other professions, academics have a tendency to gravitate towards centres of power, where there are more plentiful funds available for research, where salaries are higher, where there can be a greater market for their academic products, and where there is greater potential ability to influence other actors. As a result, academic work on conflicts and security issues is concentrated in the West, and consequently the subject of that work is also determined based on Western perspectives. Academic work from and about conflict zones that are not of particular interest in Western security circles rarely reaches prominent academic publications and forums, and its distribution and audience is therefore highly limited by comparison.

Thus, because of the high levels of wealth and power generated by and within powerful countries, it can generally be said that it is the actors from the policymaking, media, public and academic arenas based in these countries – who have access to wealth and influence – that lead the agenda-setting process relevant to foreign conflict. That is, they are able to speak the most loudly, and project their own will and perspectives as to which conflicts should be seen as important and which should not.

The Role of Strength amongst Groups of Actors

The principle of strength also applies amongst the groups of actors. With far greater economic, military and diplomatic strength than any of the other actors, the policymakers (particularly the executive branch at a national level) appear to have an unassailable advantage in this regard. This is seen most clearly in military intervention decisions. Whether in a democracy or a dictatorship, other actors seem unable to stop determined policymakers from responding to security issues as they see fit, or to force them to intervene in response to a conflict. The largest anti-war demonstrations in the history of the world could not stop the USA and UK from invading Iraq, and emotive media coverage of massacres in Rwanda and Darfur (albeit belated), even with allegations of genocide, failed to move Western policymakers to intervene militarily. While much has been made of the power of the media to move policymakers since the 1990s, research has since discounted this power, particularly in intervention decisions. Critically, studies have shown that the poster case of media power – the US-led intervention in Somalia in the early 1990s – was in fact more a case of the policymakers leading the media than the other way round.

Intervention decisions are, however, only one example of a response to conflict or security issues, and although its ability to influence other actors may be overstated, the media has indeed become more powerful in recent years. Civil society has similarly gained power in this regard, with an increasing number of groups taking an interest in foreign affairs, and humanitarian aid organizations able to intervene in some conflict situations, regardless of the policies of their home governments. More and more academics studying international affairs are moving in and out of the policymaking arenas. The preceding chapters have shown numerous ways in which other actors are able to influence policymakers in their response to conflict. To some degree it can be said that the policymakers' dominance in foreign affairs is indeed being chipped away as other actors grow in strength.

Furthermore, the strength of a particular actor is not necessarily the sole determinant of attention and response to a conflict. A weaker yet more strongly interested actor can take a lead in drawing attention and response to a foreign conflict, particularly where the stronger actor does not have a clear policy already in place. NGOs have certainly shown the ability to influence stronger organizations to be responsive to conflict and conflict-related issues, as coalitions of NGOs have demonstrated in drives to curb conflict diamonds, landmines and small arms. Similarly, it was an inspired individual who was behind Western moves in response to Belgian atrocities in the Congo a century ago. Corporations can also serve as a leading influence. In the absence of media and public interest in the DRC, for example, mining corporations were able to wield considerable influence in Western responses (or lack thereof) to that conflict. The strategic use of limited resources is what gives interest groups their influence. Even within powerful policymaking institutions, relatively weaker branches sometimes have the power to lead more powerful branches, as the US Office of Foreign Disaster Assistance demonstrated in its efforts to draw attention to the crisis in Somalia.

But does this mean that other actors have taken their place alongside policymakers, or even wrested control from them, in the process of setting the collective agenda with regard to foreign conflict? It would seem that the policymakers are still largely in control of the foreign policy agenda, and generally lead the other actors. They may have more pressure to contend with, but it is usually more a case of resisting or managing that pressure, or responding to pressure with token steps that don't affect overall policy objectives, rather than of following the lead of other actors. The fact that NGOs and academics rely heavily on home governments for the funding of their activities, and that the media is heavily reliant on domestic policymakers for its sources of information and inspiration, also serves to rob these actors of the power to independently raise and pursue agenda items. This is further exacerbated by the trend among most of these actors to align themselves and their activities according to the context of their home country and its policies. Sustained and emotive media pressure can be effective in significantly altering government policies, but only if there is a lack of policy or clashes among policymakers, not if government policy is firm. With the media taking its cues from the policymakers, for example, it can easily pick up on and exploit clashes of opinion within those circles, but it is unlikely to light the spark that initially draws attention to a foreign conflict.

The spark that initially leads to a conflict being noticed may appear to be media pressure or public pressure at first, but often that too is the result of the attention of sectors within the policymaking arena sparking media interest, which in turn sparks the public interest, as seen in Somalia and Darfur. Media and public pressure followed, rather than preceded, statements and initiatives by policymakers in these cases as well. It cannot be denied, however, that once a conflict is sparked and the media, general public and NGOs begin to show a concentrated interest in it, policymakers are usually forced by this pressure to 'do something'. Whether this is a token attempt to show the media and the public that they are indeed doing something, or is a more concerted intervention, will depend on how much their national interest is affected, and on an assessment of risk and potential gain in responding in some form.

The Bandwagon Effect and Luck

In the midst of this web of influences and the gravitational pull of the strongest actors, the bandwagon effect serves to bring together the agendas of the many and varied actors and cement a somewhat assimilated agenda regarding which conflicts are worthy of attention and response, and which are not. The media in particular is susceptible to the bandwagon effect, with media corporations constantly eying their competition to make sure they are at the leading edge of (or at least keeping up with) what may be perceived as important news trends, and are not scooped. NGOs and academics are also likely to be concerned with trends in their respective fields and with the direction in which the competition is heading. As the actor that does the most talking, the media also plays a strong role in facilitating the bandwagon effect. Its tendency to focus intently on one or two conflicts, and to move in a cohesive pack, leaves little room for independent thought about which conflicts demand attention and response, both within the media agenda itself and among the individuals and institutions that are on the receiving end of the media's output. In general, there is a far-reaching sense within and among groups of actors that 'if everyone is talking about it, then it must be important'.

Finally, whether a conflict is noticed or not may have something to do with plain luck. Actors may be in the right place at the right time, or circumstances may coincidentally link actors with events or with other actors. The conflict in Rwanda is a case in point. The fact that Western reporters just happened to be heading back home after covering South Africa's first post-apartheid elections at the time meant that they could cover Rwanda's conflict on their way home. This coincidence was largely responsible for the relatively high level of attention the conflict received. It may well otherwise have been ignored, just as similar large-scale massacres in Burundi had been one year before. The response to conflict in Somalia in the early 1990s was also partly an issue of timing. It represented an attempt to counter cries of double standards in Western choice of interventions following the Gulf War. The coincidence of the tenth anniversary of the Rwandan genocide helped boost attention to the conflict in Darfur (not least for the media and the public). With regards to US policymakers, attention to Darfur can also be partially explained by timing in connection with other foreign policy issues, namely the political need to achieve a peace deal in southern Sudan (satisfying Christian and oil lobby groups), and perhaps the need to divert attention from their problematic occupation of Iraq, in the lead-up to US presidential elections in 2004.

Conversely, conflicts and events that happen to coincide with other high-profile conflicts and events (that are better able to attract attention) are likely to remain hidden from view. Conflicts in the DRC, Sierra Leone, Angola and Ethiopia-Eritrea lost most of the little attention they were receiving as concerns over the conflict in Kosovo began to dominate attention, and as the possibility of military intervention in that region grew and became an explosive reality. It must be said, however, that a limited amount of attention in some of these conflicts was restored to counter cries of double standards after Western interventions in Kosovo and East Timor. The rebel takeover of the Central African Republic in 2003 remained off the Western agenda, not least because it happened as the invasion of Iraq was about to begin. Similarly, much of the attention to Ethiopia's intervention in Somalia in late 2006, which was viewed in some ways as being relevant to anti-Western terrorism and was thus attracting moderate levels of attention, was lost when former President Saddam Hussein was executed the day after Ethiopian troops entered Mogadishu and attention shifted to Iraq.

Concluding Remarks

The way in which conflicts rise to demand the collective attention of a broad range of actors capable of response, or remain silently below their very consciousness, is now much clearer. Factors such as national/political interest, geographic proximity and access, ability to identify, ability to sympathize, simplicity, and sensationalism, help to determine the priorities of each actor, and it is the relative strength and influence of each actor and its level of interest, together with the bandwagon effect, and sometimes plain luck, that determine whether these priorities will or will not take root and spread among other actors. Where these factors do not link a conflict with powerful and interested actors, that conflict is likely to remain 'off the radar', regardless of its scale.

The problem of stealth conflicts is systemic. Power and wealth among each of the actors capable of responding to conflict – policymakers, media, public and academia – largely determine whose perspectives will be reflected in the broader agenda-setting process and how far and deeply those perspectives will be projected. As Sidney Tarrow (2005, 61) reminds us, 'society's "common sense" buttresses the positions of elites and defends inherited inequalities.' With power and wealth concentrated in the West, it is Western perspectives and priorities that dominate the agenda-setting process. The mechanisms behind the internal dynamics of the actors, and the influences among them, make this situation unavoidable in many ways. Policymakers at the national level are put in power to look after their own people and their allies. Media corporations are essentially businesses interested in profits, and as such pursue issues they see as being relevant to their consumers, and simple and sensational are profitable styles of presentation. The general public remain largely at the mercy of the media for their information about the outside world, and generally need to have a link of some sort (identity and/or sympathy) to have a significant interest in foreign conflicts. Aid organizations can only go and help people where there are funds available, and funds generally come from the policymakers and/or follow the TV cameras. Academics studying international affairs are likely to be linked with their government, or at least with their country, in some way. Deeply ingrained nationalism held by the individuals making up each of these institutions, together with attachments with other group identities, help cement this state of affairs.

The media may see itself as a watchdog actor, ensuring that policymakers face up to important issues; the general public have the potential to rise up in large numbers and force their governments to pay attention to an issue; aid organizations may see themselves as going places and helping people where their governments are unwilling or unable; and academics may see themselves as the objective and detached observers of the world and its events. In theory, this appears to constitute an effective (albeit informal) system of checks and balances to government power in the agenda-setting process, and may work to a certain degree in relation to domestic issues. When it comes to the issue of foreign conflict, however, such a system is largely ineffective. The realities of nationalism, identity, funding mechanisms and the distribution of power, among other factors, tend to bring the agendas of all of these actors together in such a way that reflects the interests of the powerful. This comes at the expense of attention being allocated to most of the world's conflicts, including the deadliest. Those actors that are in a position to respond are unlikely to be interested, and those that are interested are usually not in a position to respond.

It cannot be forgotten that the powerful actors of the world cannot respond to every conflict. There is certainly a limit to the time, attention and resources that can be allocated in response to foreign conflicts, although it is also clear that much more can be done if the inclination is there – as the powerful actors do demonstrate from time to time. Selectivity in responding to foreign conflict is sadly inevitable, as is the phenomenon of stealth conflicts, although the world's largest and deadliest conflicts should certainly not be among them. Improving the situation is not so much a question of eliminating selectivity, but of reducing the extreme nature of responses that currently dominates: overwhelming responses to a select few (often small-scale) conflicts, and almost nonexistent responses to most other (usually much larger) conflicts; that is, making responses more proportionate to the scale and severity of the conflict.

But there are no magic bullets, and any improvement that seeks to use the internal dynamics or the web of influence among actors is vulnerable to the systemic weaknesses that come with them. There is still hope (however unlikely) that an advocacy group appalled by the silence on the conflict in the DRC, for example, could rise up and manage to attract a significant level of attention by the media, who could use concentrated emotive humanitarian-style reporting to shame other powerful actors into being more responsive to that conflict. This could be a positive turn of events, and the DRC might find a more direct and sturdier road to a state of peace as a result. The world's deadliest conflict would finally be on the receiving end of attention proportionate to its scale. On the other hand, such a move might simply bring about a brief 'carnival of charity', with institutions and individuals, feeling a need to do something, throwing attention and aid in a haphazard manner that might not reach the intended targets, and could serve instead to boost the fortunes of militant groups, and with the carnival quickly moving on when things get messy, or when the next chosen conflict is selected and manages to rise up above the rest.

This style of response might well serve to assuage the selective indignation, sympathy, and possibly the guilt, of the party that is responding, and the human capacity for self-delusion is surprisingly effective in convincing those responding that they have helped justice prevail and have saved the day, but it remains deeply flawed as a needs-based response to conflict. Moderation and balance are what is needed, and response to conflict and its aftermath is never a short-term in-and-out affair. Effective response to conflict requires a deep understanding of the situation and a willingness to think and act with a long-term perspective.

A viable solution to the problem of stealth conflicts is thus not something that can easily be achieved within the current system that connects the policymakers, media, public and academics, yet finding a way to change such a system (that is based on the needs and interests of the actors that comprise it) hardly seems realistic. But when even a cursory look reveals how grossly distorted the image of the state of conflict in the world is from the reality, surely the realization of some form of proportion between image and reality, and between scale and response, is not too much to hope for, particularly when so much information about the world is potentially available.

Finding ways to draw attention to this distortion and to the factors that have led to it, and putting more information about more conflicts in front of more people on a more regular basis may be the most realistic starting point in an effort to alleviate the problem of stealth conflicts.

Bibliography

ABC homepage (Australia), <http://www.abc.net.au/default_800.htm>, accessed 30 July 2006.

ABC News (2006), 'George Clooney Speaks about Crisis in Darfur', 30 April, <http://abcnews.go.com/ThisWeek/story?id=1907005>, accessed 2 February 2007.

Abrahamian, E. (2003), 'The US Media, Huntington and September 11', *Third World Quarterly* 24:3, 529–44.

Abramson, J.B. (1990), 'Four Criticisms of Press Ethics', in Lichtenberg (ed.).

Adelman, H. and Baxter, L.J. (2004), 'The Multinational Force for Eastern Zaire: The Conception, Planning and Termination of OP Assurance', in Adelman and Rao (eds).

Adelman, H. and Rao, G.C. (eds) (2004), *War and Peace in Zaire/Congo: Analyzing and Evaluating Intervention, 1996–1997* (Asmara: Africa World Press).

Afrol News homepage, <http://www.afrol.com>.

Afrol News (2006), 'Arms Exporters to Embargoed Congo Revealed', 17 October, <http://www.afrol.com/articles/21997>, accessed 2 February 2007.

Alagappa, M. and Inoguchi T. (eds) (1999), *International Security Management and the United Nations* (Tokyo: UNU Press).

Albright, M.K. and Kralev, N. (2001), 'Around-the-Clock News Cycle: A Double-Edged Sword', *Harvard International Journal of Press/Politics* 6:1, 105–8.

Alford, P. (2006), 'No War in Iraq, Say Japanese', *Australian*, 31 March.

Algan, E. (2003), 'Privatization of Radio and Media Hegemony in Turkey', in Artz and Kamalipour (eds).

All Africa homepage, <http://allafrica.com>.

Allen, T. (1999), 'Perceiving Contemporary Wars', in Allen and Seaton (eds).

Allen, T. and Seaton, J. (eds) (1999), *The Media of Conflict: War Reporting and Representations of Ethnic Violence* (London: Zed Books).

Althaus, S.L. and Tewksbury, D. (2002), 'Agenda Setting and the "New" News: Patterns of Issue Importance among Readers of the Paper and Online Versions of the *New York Times*', *Communication Research* 29:2, 180–207.

Amazon homepage, <http://www.amazon.com>, search conducted 1 April 2007.

AME Info (2006), 'Al Jazeera International Reveals Global Line-Up of Bureaux', 26 December, <http://www.ameinfo.com/98633.html>, accessed 26 December 2006.

Amnesty International (2005), 'Democratic Republic of Congo: Arming the East', AI Index: AFR 62/006/2005, 5 July.

—— (2007), 'Guinea, "Soldiers Were Shooting Everywhere": The Security Forces' Response to Peaceful Demands for Change', AI Index: AFR 29/003/2007, 27 June.

Anderson, B. (1983), *Imagined Communities* (London: Verso).

Annan, K. (1994), 'Peace-keeping in Situations of Civil War', *New York University Journal of International Law and Politics* 26:4, 623–31.

Appiah-Mensah, S. (2005), 'AU's Critical Assignment in Darfur', *African Security Review* 14:2, 7–21.

Armstrong, D. (2003), 'US Pays Back Nations That Supported War', *San Francisco Chronicle*, 11 May.

Arnett, P. (1998), 'State of the American Newspaper: Goodbye, World', *American Journalism Review*, November, < http://www.ajr.org/Article.asp?id=3288>.

Arnold, G. (2005), *Africa: A Modern History* (London: Atlantic Books).

Artz, L. and Kamalipour, Y.R. (eds) (2003), *The Globalization of Corporate Media Hegemony* (Albany: State University of New York Press).

Associated Press (1999a), 'NATO OKs Yugoslavia Airstrikes', 23 March.

—— (1999b), 'Sudan, Opposition Sign Peace Deal', 26 November.

—— (2008), 'UN: Sudan's North-South Peace Is Fragile', 20 February.

Australian homepage, <http://www.theaustralian.news.com.au>.

Australian World News online (2006a), <http://www.theaustralian.news.com.au/index/0,,2703,00.html>, accessed 1–19 July.

—— (2006b), <http://www.theaustralian.news.com.au/index/0,,5003763,00.html>, search conducted 24 December 2006.

Aydinli, E. and Matthews, J. (2000), 'Are the Core and Periphery Irreconcilable? The Curious World of Publishing in Contemporary International Relations', *International Studies Perspectives* 1, 289–303.

Baker, J. (1996), 'Report First, Check Later', *Harvard International Journal of Press/Politics* 1:2, 3–9.

Baker, W. and O'Neal, J.R. (2001), 'Patriotism or Opinion Leadership? The Nature and Origins of the "Rally 'Round the Flag" Effect', *Journal of Conflict Resolution* 45:5, 661–87.

Barnett, M.N. (1998), 'The Limits of Peacekeeping, Spheres of Influence, and the Future of the United Nations', in Legpold and Weiss (eds).

Bauman, Z. (2001), 'The Great War of Recognition', *Theory, Culture & Society* 18:2–3, 137–150.

BBC News (1999), 'World: Americas: Clinton's Statement: Stabilising Europe', BBC News, 25 March, <http://news.bbc.co.uk/2/hi/americas/303693.stm>, accessed 9 January 2007.

—— (2005), 'Australian Firm "Aided Killings"', 7 June, <http://news.bbc.co.uk/1/hi/world/africa/4613581.stm>, accessed 10 June 2005.

—— (2007), 'UN Boss Starts Africa Tour in DRC', 27 January, <http://news.bbc.co.uk/2/hi/africa/6304043.stm>, accessed 27 January 2007.

BBC Scotland (2001), 'Dyke: BBC Is "Hideously White"', 6 January, <http://news.bbc.co.uk/1/hi/scotland/1104305.stm>, accessed 2 July 2006.

BBC World Service (2004a), Art Beat, 21 October.

—— (2004b), Focus on Africa, 8 November.

—— (2004c), In Praise of God, 26 December.

—— (2005a), News Hour, 20 April.

—— (2005b), Focus on Africa, 19 May 2005.

—— (2005c), News Hour, 12 July.

—— (2005d), World News, 29 November.

—— (2005e), Talking Point, 11 December.

—— (2006), News Hour, 30 April.

Bellah, R.N. (1992), *The Broken Covenant: American Civil Religion in Time of Trial* (Chicago: University of Chicago Press).

Bennett, L.W. (1990), 'Toward a Theory of Press-State Relations in the United States', *Journal of Communication* 40:2, 103–25.

Bennett, L.W., Lawrence, R.G. and Livingston, S. (2007), *When the Press Fails: Political Power and the News Media from Iraq to Katrina* (Chicago: University of Chicago Press).

Bennhold, K. (2005), 'Doctors' Group Refuses More Donations: Charity Sets off Storm with Tsunami Aid Halt', *International Herald Tribune*, 6 January.

Berkeley, B. (2001), *The Graves Are Not Yet Full: Race, Tribe and Power in the Heart of Africa* (New York: Basic Books).

Billig, M. (1995), *Banal Nationalism* (London: Sage Publications).

Bishop, R. (2001), 'News Media, Heal Thyselves: Sourcing Patterns in News Stories', *Journal of Communication Inquiry* 25:1, 22–37.

Blank, S. et al. (2001), *Responding to Low-Intensity Conflict Challenges* (Honolulu: University Press of the Pacific).

Board of Studies NSW (2004), 'Modern History Stage 6: Syllabus', <http://www.boardofstudies.nsw.edu.au/syllabus_hsc/pdf_doc/mod_history_stg6_syl.pdf>, accessed 28 March 2008.

Bob, C. (2005), *The Marketing of Rebellion: Insurgents, Media and International Activism* (Cambridge: Cambridge University Press).

Boettcher, W.A. III (2004), 'Military Intervention Decisions Regarding Humanitarian Crises', *The Journal of Conflict Resolution* 48:3, 331–55.

Bookstein, A. (2003), 'Beyond the Headlines: An Agenda for Action to Protect Civilians in Neglected Conflicts', Oxfam.

Brookings Institution homepage, list of regional and country studies, <http://www.brook.edu/data/brookings_taxonomy.xml?taxonomy=Politics,%20Global>, accessed 20 December 2006.

—— About homepage, <http://www.brookings.edu/about.aspx>, accessed 14 April 2008.

Brooten, L. (2005), 'The Feminization of Democracy under Siege: The Media, "the Lady" of Burma, and US Foreign Policy', *NWSA Journal* 17:3, 134–56.

Brown, M.E. (ed.) (1996), *The International Dimensions of Internal Conflict* (Cambridge: The MIT Press).

Buchanan-Smith, M. and Randel, J. (2002), 'Financing International Humanitarian Action: A Review of Key Trends', *HPG Briefing*, No. 4, November.

Calas, F. and Salignon, P. (2004), 'Afghanistan: From 'Militant Monks' to Crusaders', in Weissman (ed.).

Campbell, G. (2004), *Blood Diamonds* (Boulder: Westview Press).

CARE (2002), 'Innovations: CARE USA 2002 Annual Report', <http://www.care.org/newsroom/publications/annualreports/2002/2002annualreport.pdf>, accessed 24 December 2006.

Carnegie Commission on Preventing Deadly Conflict (1997), 'Preventing Deadly Conflict: Final Report 1997', <http://www.ccpdc.org/pubs/rept97/toc.htm>, accessed 8 March 2007.

Carnegie Endowment homepage, <http://www.carnegieendowment.org>, accessed 4 April 2007.

Chan, S. (2003), 'Power, Satisfaction and Popularity: A Poisson Analysis of UN Security Council Vetoes', *Cooperation and Conflict* 38:4, 339–59.

Chanley, V.A. (1999), 'US Public Views of International Involvement from 1964 to 1993: Time-Series Analyses of General and Militant Internationalism', *Journal of Conflict Resolution* 43:1,23–44.

Chesterman, C. (ed.) (2001), *Civilians in War* (Boulder: Lynne Rienner).

Chomsky, D. (1999), 'The Mechanisms of Management Control at the New York Times', *Media, Society & Culture* 21:5, 579–99.

Chomsky, N. (1999), *The New Military Humanism: Lessons from Kosovo* (Monroe, ME: Common Courage Press).

Cilliers, J. (1999), 'Private Security in War-Torn African States', in Cilliers and Mason (eds).

—— (2000), 'Resource Wars – A New Type of Insurgency', in Cilliers and Dietrich (eds).

Cilliers, J. and Dietrich C. (eds) (2000), *Angola's War Economy: The Role of Oil and Diamonds* (Pretoria: Institute for Security Studies).

Cilliers, J. and Mason, P. (eds) (1999), *Peace, Profit or Plunder? The Privatisation of Security in War-Torn African Societies* (Pretoria: Institute for Security Studies).

Clapham, C. (1998), *African Guerrillas* (Oxford: James Currey).

Clark, J.F. (2001), 'Realism, Neo-Realism and Africa's International Relations in the Post-Cold War Era', in Dunn and Shaw (eds).

—— (ed.) (2002), *The African Stakes of the Congo War* (New York: Palgrave Macmillan).

Clarke, W.S. (1998), 'Waiting for "The Big One": Confronting Complex Humanitarian Emergencies and State Collapse in Central Africa', in Manwaring and Fishel (eds).

CNN, homepage, <http://edition.cnn.com>.

—— (1998), '1998 Year in Review: Top 10 World Stories', <http://cnn.com/SPECIALS/1998/year.review/worldnews/index.html>, accessed 2 January 2007.

—— (2004), 'Bush, Annan Call for End to Sudan Fighting', 7 April, <http://www.cnn.com/2004/ALLPOLITICS/04/07/bush.un.sudan/index.html>, accessed 26 December 2006.

Cockburn, A. and St. Clair, J. (2000), 'CNN and Psyops', Counterpunch, 26 March, <http://www.counterpunch.org/cnnpsyops.html>, accessed 15 August 2002.

Coghlan, B. et al. (2006), 'Mortality in the Democratic Republic of Congo: A Nationwide Survey', *Lancet* 367:9504, 44–51.

Cohen, B. (1963), *The Press and Foreign Policy* (Princeton: Princeton University Press).

Cohen, S. (2001), *States of Denial: Knowing about Atrocities and Suffering* (Cambridge: Polity Press).

Coker, C. (2001), *Humane Warfare* (London: Routledge).

Cooley, A. and Ron, J. (2002), 'The NGO Scramble: Organizational Insecurity and the Political Economy of Transnational Action', *International Security* 27:1, 5–39.

Cortright, D. and Lopez, G.A. (2000), *The Sanctions Decade: Assessing UN Strategies in the 1990s* (Boulder: Lynne Rienner).

Coultan, M. (2006), 'US Lobby Stonewalls Illegal Arms Curb', *Sydney Morning Herald*, 24 June.

Crocker, C.A. and Hampson, F.O. with Aall, P. (eds) (1996), *Managing Global Chaos: Sources of and Responses to International Conflict* (Washington D.C.: United States Institute of Peace Press).

Dadge, D. (2004), *Casualty of War: The Bush Administration's Assault on a Free Press* (Buffalo: Prometheus Books).

Daily Telegraph (2006), 'Don't Become Anti-American: Murdoch's Call to Australia', 15 November.

Dallaire, R. (2003), *Shake Hands with the Devil: The Failure of Humanity in Rwanda* (London: Arrow Books).

Daniel, D.C. and Hayes, B.C. with Oudraat, C.J. (1999), *Coercive Inducement and the Containment of International Crises* (Washington D.C.: United States Institute of Peace Press).

Darcy, J. and Hofmann, C. (2003), 'According to Need? Needs Assessment and Decision-Making in the Humanitarian Sector', *Humanitarian Policy Group Report*, No. 15.

Davis, A. (2003), 'Whither Mass Media and Power? Evidence for a Critical Elite Theory Alternative', *Media, Culture & Society* 25:5, 669–90.

De Beer, A.S. (2000), 'New Mirror in South Africa? International News Flow and News Selection on the Afrikaans Daily, Beeld', in Malek and Kavoori (eds).

De Beer, H. and Gamba, V. (2000), 'The Arms Dilemma: Resources for Arms or Arms for Resources?', in Cilliers and Dietrich (eds).

De Burgh, H. (ed.) (2005), *Making Journalists* (Oxon: Routledge).

Department of Foreign Affairs and Trade (Australia) (2002), 'Australia Implements Bilateral Smart Sanctions against Government of Zimbabwe', Media Release, FA146, 13 October.

—— (2003), 'Advancing the National Interest: Australia's Foreign and Trade Policy White Paper'.

Devine, P.G. (1995), 'Prejudice and Out-Group Perception', in Tesser (ed.).

Die Welt, <http://www.welt.de/archiv>, search conducted 5 January 2007.

Dunn, K.C. (2001), 'MadLib #32: The (Blank) African State: Rethinking the Sovereign State in International Relations Theory', in Dunn and Shaw (eds).

Dunn, K.C. and Shaw, T.M (2001), *Africa's Challenge to International Relations Theory* (Houndmills: Palgrave).

Economist (2007), 'Peacekeeping: Call the Blue Helmets', January 6–12.

Eitelberg, M.J. and Little, R.D. (1995), 'Influential Elites and the American Military after the Cold War', in Snider and Carlton-Carew (eds).

Engel, U. and Olsen, G.R. (2005), *Africa and the North: Between Globalization and Marginalization* (London: Routledge).

Entman, R. (1991), 'Framing US Coverage of International News: Contrasts in Narratives of the KAL and Iran Air Incidents', *Journal of Communication* 41:4, 6–27.

—— (2000), 'Declarations of Independence: The Growth of Media Power after the Cold War', in Nacos, Shapiro and Isernia (eds).

Eriksson, J. (1999), 'Observers or Advocates? On the Political Role of Security Analysts', *Cooperation and Conflict* 34:3, 311–30.

Eriksson, M., Wallensteen, P. and Sollenberg, M. (2003), 'Armed Conflict, 1989–2002', *Journal of Peace Research* 40:5, 593–607.

Ero, C. (1995), 'ECOWAS and the Subregional Peacekeeping in Liberia', *The Journal of Humanitarian Assistance*, <http://www.jha.ac/articles/a005.htm>, accessed 12 August 2001.

European Union, Common Foreign and Security Policy homepage, <http://ec.europa.eu/comm/external_relations/cfsp/sanctions/measures.htm>.

Evans, G. and Newnham, J. (1998), *The Penguin Dictionary of International Relations* (London: Penguin Books).

Eveland W.P. Jr., Marton, K. and Seo, M. (2004), 'Moving Beyond "Just the Facts": The Influence of Online News on the Content and Structure of Public Affairs Knowledge', *Communication Research* 31:1, 82–108.

FAIR (Fairness and Accuracy in Reporting), Interlocking Directorates, <http://www.fair.org/index.php?page=2870>, accessed 27 February 2007.

FAIR (1991), '"Slaughter" Is Something Other Countries Do', *Extra!*, May/June, <http://www.fair.org/extra/best-of-extra/slaughter-not-us.html>, accessed 5 July 2000.

Federation of American Scientists homepage, < http://www.fas.org>.

Feizkhah, E. (2004), 'Brothers in Arms', *TIME Magazine*, 7 October.

Felix, B. (2006), 'PanAfrica: Tough Questions for Former Heads of State', *Inter Press Service*, 23 April.

Festinger, L. (1957), *A Theory of Cognitive Dissonance* (Stanford: Stanford University Press).

Forgotten Humanitarian Crises (2002), Conference Paper, Conference on the Role of the Media, Decision-Makers and Humanitarian Agencies, Copenhagen, 23 October.

Fox News, homepage, <http://www.foxnews.com>.

—— (2006), 'Top 10 International News Stories for 2006', 30 December, <http://www.foxnews.com/story/0,2933,238037,00.html?sPage=fnc.specialsections/_2006review>, accessed 2 January 2007.

Friends of the Congo homepage, <http://www.friendsofthecongo.org>.

Gallup (2006), Gallup Poll Social Series: World Affairs, 2006, <http://brain.gallup.com/documents/questionnaire.aspx?STUDY=P0602006>, accessed 14 March 2007.

Genocide Intervention Network homepage, <http://www.genocideintervention.net>.

George, A.L. (1993), *Bridging the Gap: Theory and Practice in Foreign Policy* (Washington D.C.: United States Institute of Peace Press).

Ghandour, A. (2004), 'The Modern Missionaries of Islam', in Weissman (ed.).

Gibbs, D.N. (2001), 'Social Science as Propaganda? International Relations and the Question of Political Bias', *International Studies Perspectives* 2:4, 416–37.

Gilbert, M. (2001), *History of the Twentieth Century* (London: HarperCollins).

Giradet, E.R. (1996), 'Reporting Humanitarianism: Are the New Electronic Media Making a Difference?', in Rotberg and Weiss (eds).

Global Policy Forum homepage, <http://www.globalpolicy.org/security/membship/veto/vetosubj.htm>, accessed 16 March 2008.

Global Witness (2007), 'Hot Chocolate: How Cocoa Fuelled the Conflict in Côte D'Ivoire', <http://www.globalwitness.org/media_library_detail.php/552/en/hot_chocolate_how_cocoa_fuelled_the_conflict_in_co>, accessed 24 December 2007.

GMI (Global Market Insite) survey (2004), 14 June, <http://www.gmi-mr.com/gmipoll/docs/wave1/Q15-22.pdf>, accessed 4 December 2006.

Gnamo, A.H. (2004), 'The Role of the Interahamwe in the Regional Conflict: The Origins of Unrest in Kivu, Zaire', in Adelman and Rao (eds).

Goldberg, J. (2005), 'Breaking Ranks: What Turned Brent Snowcroft against the Bush Administration?', Letter from Washington, *The New Yorker*, 31 October.

Goodhand, J. (2006), *Aiding Peace? The Role of NGOs in Armed Conflict* (Boulder: Lynne Rienner).

Google Zeitgeist (2001), homepage, <http://www.google.com/press/zeitgeist2001.html>, accessed 3 March 2007.

Gordon, D.F., Miller, D.G. Jr. and Wolpe, H. (1998), *The United States and Africa: A Post-Cold War Perspective* (New York: W. W. Norton).

Gow, J., Paterson, R. and Preston, A. (eds) (1996), *Bosnia by Television* (London: British Film Institute).

Gowing, N. (1996), 'Real-time TV Coverage from War: Does It Make or Break Government Policy?', in Gow, Paterson and Preston (eds).

Graber, A. (ed.) (1994), *Media Power in Politics* (Washington D.C.: Congressional Quarterly Inc.).

Gray, C. (2007), *War, Peace, and International Relations: An Introduction to Strategic History* (London: Routledge).

Grignon, F. (2003), 'There Will Be No Excuses for Not Knowing', *Observer*, 25 May.

Haass, R. (1999), *Intervention: The Use of American Military Force in the Post-Cold War World*, Revised Edition (Washington D.C.: The Brookings Institution).

—— (2002), 'Think Tanks and US Foreign Policy: A Policymaker's Perspective', *The Role of Think Tanks in US Foreign Policy, US Foreign Policy Agenda* 7:3, 5–8.

Hallin, D. (1986), *The "Uncensored War": The Media and Vietnam* (New York: Oxford University Press).

Hamilton, J.M. and Jenner, E. (2002), 'Redefining Foreign Correspondence', The Joan Shorenstein Center on the Press, Politics and Public Policy, Working Paper Series, 2003–2.

Hampson, F.O. (1996), 'Why Orphaned Peace Settlements Are More Prone to Failure', in Crocker and Hampson (eds).

Hampson, F.O. and Malone, D. (eds) (2002), *From Reaction to Conflict Prevention: Opportunities for the UN System* (Boulder: Lynne Rienner).

Haney, P.J. and Vanderbush, W. (1999), 'The Role of Ethnic Interest Groups in US Foreign Policy: The Case of the Cuban American National Foundation', *International Studies Quarterly*, 43, 341–61.

Hanson, V.D. (2003), *Why the West Has Won* (London: Faber and Faber).

Harbom, L. and Wallensteen, P. (2005), 'Armed Conflict and Its International Dimensions, 1946–2004', *Journal of Peace Research* 42:5, 623–35.

—— (2007), 'Armed Conflict, 1989–2006', *Journal of Peace Research* 44:5, 623–34.

Harden, B. (1990), *Africa: Dispatches from a Fragile Continent* (New York: W. W. Norton & Company).

Harris, B. (2004), 'Aussie Counts 3.8m Dead in Congo', *The Australian*, 9 December.

Harriss, J. (ed.) (1995), *The Politics of Humanitarian Intervention* (London: Pinter).

Harvard University International Studies Program homepage, <http://bcsia.ksg.harvard.edu/?program=ISP>, accessed 17 January 2007.

Harvard University Libraries, Hollis Catalogue, <http://holliscatalogue.harvard.edu>, search conducted 30 March 2007.

Hawkins, V. (2002), 'The Other Side of the CNN Factor: Media and Conflict', *Journalism Studies* 3:2, 225–40.

—— (2004), *The Silence of the UN Security Council: Conflict and Peace Enforcement in the 1990s* (Firenze: European Press Academic Publishing).

Henrikson, A.K. (2002), 'Distance and Foreign Policy: A Political Geography Approach', *International Political Science Review* 23:4, 437–66.

Herbst, J. (2000), 'African Peacekeepers and State Failure', in Rotberg (ed.).

Herman, E.S. and Chomsky, N. (1994), *Manufacturing Consent: The Political Economy of the Mass Media* (London: Vintage).

Herring, E. and Robinson, P. (2003), 'Forum on Chomsky', *Review of International Studies* 29:4, 551–2.

Hill, K.Q. (1998), 'The Policy Agendas of the President and the Mass Public: A Research Validation and Extension', *American Journal of Political Science* 42:4, 1328–34.

Hobsbawm, E. (1997), *On History* (New York: The New Press).

Hochschild, A. (1999), *King Leopold's Ghost: A Story of Greed, Terror, and Heroism in Colonial Africa* (New York: Mariner Books).

Hoddie, M. and Hartzell, C. (2003), 'Civil War Settlements and the Implementation of Military Power-Sharing Arrangements', *Journal of Peace Research* 40:3, 303–20.

Holm, H. (2002), 'Failing Failed States: Who Forgets the Forgotten?', *Security Dialogue*, 33:4, 457–71.

Honwana, A. (2001), 'Children of War: Understanding War and War Cleansing in Mozambique and Angola', in Chesterman (ed.).

Huliaras, A. (2004), '(Non)policies and (Mis)perceptions: The United States, France and the Crisis in Zaire', in Adelman and Rao (eds).

Human Rights Watch (2000), 'World Report 2000: Events of 1999', <http://www.hrw.org/wr2k/Front.htm#TopOfPage>, accessed 24 January 2006.

—— (2002), 'World Report 2002: Events of 2001', <http://www.hrw.org/wr2k2/intro.html>, accessed 24 January 2006.

—— (2003), 'World Report 2003: Events of 2002', <http://www.hrw.org/wr2k3/introduction.html>, accessed 24 January 2006.

—— (2004), 'World Report 2004: Events of 2003', <http://hrw.org/wr2k4>, accessed 24 January 2006.

—— (2005), 'World Report 2005: Events of 2004', <http://hrw.org/wr2k5>, accessed 24 January 2006.

'Human Security Brief 2006' (2006), <http://www.hsrgroup.org/images/stories/HSBrief2006/contents/finalversion.pdf>, accessed 23 February 2007.

'Human Security Report 2005' (2005), <http://www.humansecurityreport.org>, accessed 29 October 2006.

Humanitarian Law Project/International Educational Development and Parliamentary Human Rights Group (2000), 'Armed Conflict in the World Today: A Country by Country Review', <http://www.hri.ca/doccentre/docs/cpr/armedconflict2000.shtml>, accessed 2 February 2002.

Humanitarian Studies Unit (ed.) (2001), *Reflections on Humanitarian Action: Principles, Ethics and Contradictions* (London: Pluto Press).

Huntington, S.P. (1996), *The Clash of Civilizations and the Remaking of World Order* (New York: Simon and Schuster).

ICG (International Crisis Group) (1999), 'Africa's Seven Nation War', *ICG Democratic Republic of Congo Report*, no. 4, 21 May.

—— (2006), 'Securing Congo's Elections: Lessons from the Kinshasa Showdown', *International Crisis Group Policy Briefing*, Africa Briefing N°42, Nairobi/Brussels, 2 October.

ICISS (International Commission on Intervention and State Sovereignty) (2001), *The Responsibility to Protect: Research, Bibliography, Background*, (Ottowa: International Development Research Centre).

ICRC (International Committee of the Red Cross) (2006), '2007 ICRC Appeals', Rex 06/786.

IISS (International Institute for Strategic Studies), Armed Conflict Database homepage, <http://www.iiss.org/publications/armed-conflict-database>.

—— Staff/Expertise homepage, <http://www.iiss.org/staffexpertise/list-experts-by-subject>, accessed 4 April 2007.

Indo-Asian News Service (2008), 'Journalism More than "Rough Draft of History" ', 8 March.

Ingebritsen, C. (2002), 'Norm Entrepreneurs: Scandinavia's Role in World Politics', *Cooperation and Conflict* 37:1, 11–23.

International Herald Tribune homepage, <http://www.iht.com/cgi-bin/search.cgi>, search conducted 4 January 2007.

IRC (International Rescue Committee) (2000), 'Mortality in Eastern DRC: Results from Five Mortality Surveys', <http://www.theirc.org/resources/mortality.pdf>, accessed 31 March 2008.

—— (2001), 'Mortality in eastern Democratic Republic of Congo: Results from Eleven Mortality Surveys' <http://www.theirc.org/media/www/mortality_study_eastern_dr_congo_februaryapril_2001.html>, accessed 31 March 2008.

—— (2003), 'Mortality in the Democratic Republic of Congo: Results from a Nationwide Survey', <http://www.theirc.org/resources/drc_mortality_iii_exec.pdf>, accessed 31 March 2008.

—— (2004), 'Mortality in the Democratic Republic of Congo: Results from a Nationwide Survey' <http://www.theirc.org/resources/DRC_MortalitySurvey2004_RB_8Dec04.pdf>, accessed, 31 March 2008.

—— (2008), 'Mortality in the Democratic Republic of Congo: An Ongoing Crisis', <http://www.theirc.org/resources/2007/2006-7_congomortalitysurvey.pdf>, accessed 31 March 2008.

IRIN (Integrated Regional Information Networks) Global Report (2006), 'More Money for CERF, but Challenges Remain', 21 December, <http://www.irinnews.org/S_report.asp?ReportID=56811&SelectRegion=Global>, accessed 2 February 2007.

Isernia, P. (2000), 'Where Angels Fear to Tread: Italian Public Opinion and Foreign Policy', in Nacos, Shapiro and Isernia (eds).

Isernia, P., Juhasz, Z. and Rattinger, H. (2002), 'Foreign Policy and the Rational Public in Comparative Perspective', *Journal of Conflict Resolution* 46:2, 201–24.

Iyengar, S. and Kinder, D.R. (1987), *News That Matters: Television and American Opinion* (Chicago: The University of Chicago Press).

Jakobsen, P.V. (2000), 'Focus on the CNN Effect Misses the Point: The Real Media Impact on Conflict Management Is Invisible and Indirect', *Journal of Peace Research* 37:2, 131–43.

Jenni, K.E. and Loewenstein, G. (1997), 'Explaining the "Identifiable Victim Effect"', *Journal of Risk and Uncertainty*, 14, 235–57.

Jones, B.D. and Cater, C.K. (2001), 'From Chaos to Coherence? Toward a Regime for Protecting Civilians in War', in Chesterman (ed.).

Jurkowitz, M. (2006), 'Now in Its Adolescence, the Internet Evolves into a Supplementary News Source', Pew Research Center Publications, 1 August, <http://pewresearch.org/pubs/42/now-in-its-adolescence-the-internet-evolves-into-a-supplementary-news-source>, accessed 1 March 2007.

Kaldor, M (2007), *New & Old Wars*, Second Edition (Stanford: Stanford University Press).

Keen, D. (1999), '"Who's It Between?" "Ethnic War" and Rational Violence', in Allen and Seaton (eds).

Kegley, C.W. Jr. and Wittkopf, E.R. (1999), *World Politics: Trends and Transformation*, Seventh Edition (Boston: Bedford/St. Martin's).

King, C.I. (2001), 'Pat Robertson and His Business Buddies', *Washington Post*, 10 November.

Kleistra, Y. and Mayer, I. (2001), 'Stability and Flux in Foreign Affairs: Modelling Policy and Organisational Change', *Cooperation and Conflict* 34:4, 381–414.

Knightley, P. (2003a), 'History of Bunkum? Iraq: The Notorious War', *British Journalism Review* 14:2, 7–14.

—— (2003b), *The First Casualty: The War Correspondent as Hero, Propagandist and Myth-Maker from the Crimea to Iraq* (London: André Deutsch).

Kralev, N. (2005), 'Rice Targets 6 "Outposts of Tyranny"', *The Washington Times*, 19 January.

Kramer, M. (2001), *Ivory Towers on Sand: the Failure of Middle Eastern Studies in America* (Washington D.C.: Washington Institute for Near East Policy).

Krasno, J. (2003), 'Colleges and Universities Fail to Meet Demands for Teaching International Relations', *UN Chronicle*, June-August.

Kristof, N. (2004), 'Dare We Call It Genocide?', *New York Times*, 16 June.

—— (2007), 'Darfur and Congo', On the Ground (blog), 20 June, <http://kristof.blogs.nytimes.com/2007/06/20/darfur-and-congo/?scp=4&sq=congo>, accessed 9 January 2008.

Kull, S. (1995–96), 'What the Public Knows That Washington Doesn't', *Foreign Policy*, 101, winter, 102–15.

La Balme, N. (2000), 'Constraint, Catalyst, or Political Tool: The French Public and Foreign Policy', in Nacos, Shapiro and Isernia (eds).

Lacina, B. and Gleditsch, N. (2005), 'Monitoring Trends in Global Combat: A New Dataset of Battle Deaths', *European Journal of Population* 21:2–3, 145–66.

Lacina, B., Gleditsch, N. and Russett, B. (2006), 'The Declining Risk of Death in Battle', *International Studies Quarterly*, 50, 673–80.

Laffey, M. (2003), 'Discerning the Patterns of World Order: Noam Chomsky and International Theory after the Cold War', *Review of International Studies* 29:4, 587–604.

Laremont, R.R. (ed.) (2002), *The Causes of War and the Consequences of Peacekeeping in Africa* (Portsmouth: Heinnemann).

Lavergne, M. and Weissman, F. (2004), 'Sudan: Who Benefits from Humanitarian Aid?', in Weissman (ed.).

Le Carré, J. and Stearns, J. (2006), 'Getting Congo's Wealth to Its People', *The Boston Globe*, 22 December.

Le Monde homepage, <http://www.lemonde.fr>.

Le Pape, M. (2004), 'Democratic Republic of Congo: Victims of No Importance', in Weissman (ed.).

Le Soir homepage, < http://www.lesoir.be/>.

Leitenberg, M. (2006), 'Deaths in Wars and Conflicts in the 20th Century', Occasional Paper No. 29, Cornell University, Peace Studies Program.

Lepgold, J. (2000), 'Scholars and Statesmen: Framework for a Productive Dialogue', in Nincic and Lepgold (eds).

Lepgold, J. and Nincic, M. (2001), *Beyond the Ivory Tower: International Relations Theory and the Issue of Policy Relevance* (New York: Columbia University Press).

Lepgold, J. and Weiss, T.G. (eds) (1998), *Collective Conflict Management and Changing World Politics* (Albany: State University of New York Press).

Lichtenberg, J. (ed.) (1990), *Democracy and the Mass Media* (Cambridge: University of Cambridge).

Lieberfeld, D. (2002), 'Evaluating the Contributions of Track-Two Diplomacy to Conflict Termination in South Africa, 1984–90', *Journal of Peace Research* 39:3, 355–72.

Lind, J. and Sturman, K. (eds) (2002), *Scarcity and Surfeit: The Ecology of Africa's Conflicts*, (Pretoria: African Centre for Technology Studies and Institute for Security Studies).

Lischer, S.K. (2003), 'Collateral Damage: Humanitarian Assistance as a Cause of Conflict', *International Security* 28:1, 79–109.

Livingston, S. (1995), 'Suffering in Silence: Media Coverage of War and Famine in the Sudan', in Rotberg and Weiss (eds).

—— (1997), 'Clarifying the CNN Effect: An Examination of Media Effects According to Type of Military Intervention', Harvard Research Paper R–18, Joan Shorenstein Barone Center on the Press, Politics and Public Policy, Harvard University.

Livingston, S. and Eachus, T. (1995), 'Humanitarian Crisis and US Foreign Policy: Somalia and the CNN Effect Reconsidered', *Political Communication* 12, 413–29.

Lozano, J. et al. (2000), 'International News in the Latin American Press', in Malek and Kavoori (eds).

Luck, E.C. (2001), 'The Enforcement of Humanitarian Norms and the Politics of Ambivalence', in Chesterman (ed.).

Macht, J. (2001), 'New Medium, Old Rules: The On-Line Editor Comes of Age', *Harvard International Journal of Press/Politics* 6:1, 128–31.

Mack, A. and Khan, A. (2000), 'The Efficacy of UN Sanctions', *Security Dialogue* 31:3, 279–92.

MacKinlay, J. (2000), 'Defining Warlords', in Woodhouse and Ramsbotham (eds).

MacIver, D. (ed.) (2004), *Political Issues in the World Today* (Manchester: Manchester University Press).

Magyar, K.P. (2001), 'Low Intensity Conflicts: The African Context', in Blank et al.

Mail & Guardian homepage, <http://www.mg.co.za>, search of both print and online archives, conducted 5 January 2007.

Malan, M. (1998), '"Peace Enforcement": The Real Peace Support Challenge in Africa', *African Security Review* 7:5, 11–25.

—— (2002), 'The Post-9/11 Security Agenda and Peacekeeping in Africa', *African Security Review* 11:3, 54–66.

Malaquias, A. (2001), 'Reformulating International Relations Theory: African Insights and Challenges', in Dunn and Shaw (eds).

Malek, A. and Kavoori, A.P. (eds) (2000), *The Global Dynamic of News: Studies in International News Coverage and News Agenda* (Stanford: Ablex Publishing Corporation).

Manwaring, M.G. and Fishel, J.T. (eds) (1998), *Toward Responsibility in the New World Disorder: Challenges and Lessons of Peace Operations* (London: Frank Cass).

Marks, M.P. (2002), 'The "We" Problem in Teaching International Studies', *International Studies Perspectives*, 3, 25–41.

Marvin, C. and Ingle, D.W. (1996), 'Blood Sacrifice and the Nation: Revisiting Civil Religion', *Journal of the American Academy of Religion*, LXIV:4, 767–80.

Massey, S. (1998), 'Operation Assurance: The Greatest Intervention That Never Happened.' *The Journal of Humanitarian Assistance*, 15 February, <http://www.jha.ac/articles/a036.htm>, accessed 5 August 2001.

McCombs, M.E. (2004), *Setting the Agenda: The Mass Media and Public Opinion* (Cambridge: Polity Press).

McCombs, M.E. and Shaw, D.L. (1972), 'The Agenda-Setting Function of the Mass Media', *Public Opinion Quarterly*, 36, 176–85.

McElroy, R.W. (1992), *Morality and American Foreign Policy: The Role of Ethics in International Affairs* (Princeton: Princeton University Press).

McLaughlin, G. (2002), *The War Correspondent* (London: Pluto Press).

McNair, B. (2005), 'What is Journalism?', in de Burgh (ed.).

Mearsheimer, J. and Walt, S. (2006), 'The Israel Lobby', *London Review of Books* 28:6, 23 March, <http://www.lrb.co.uk/v28/n06/mear01_.html>, accessed 15 February 2007.

Mellinger, G. (2003), 'Counting Color: Ambivalence and Contradiction in the American Society of Newspaper Editors' Discourse of Diversity', *Journal of Communication Inquiry* 27:2, 129–51.

Mennecke, M. (2007), 'What's in a Name? Reflections on Using, Not Using and Overusing the "G-Word"', *Genocide Studies and Prevention* 2:1, 57–72.

Meredith, M. (2005), *The State of Africa: A History of Fifty Years of Independence* (Johannesburg: Jonathan Ball Publishers).

Mermin, J. (1997), 'Television News and American Intervention in Somalia: The Myth of a Media-Driven Foreign Policy', *Political Science Quarterly* 112:3, 385–404.

—— (1999), *Debating War and Peace: Media Coverage of US Intervention in the Post-Vietnam Era* (Princeton: Princeton University Press).

Messiant, C. (2004), 'Angola: Woe to the Vanquished', in Weissman (ed.).

Minear, L., Scott, C. and Weiss, T.G. (1994), *The News Media, Civil War, and Humanitarian Action* (Boulder: Lynne Rienner).

Ministry of Foreign Affairs of Japan homepage, <http://www.mofa.go.jp/region/index.html>, accessed 9 January 2007.

Mintz, A. (2004), 'Foreign Policy Decision Making in Familiar and Unfamiliar Settings: An Experimental Study of High-Ranking Military Officers', *Journal of Conflict Resolution* 48:1, 91–104.

Moeller, S.D. (1999), *Compassion Fatigue: How the Media Sell Disease, Famine, War and Death* (New York: Routledge).

Moisy, C. (1996), 'The Foreign News Flow in the Information Age', Discussion Paper D-23, The Joan Shorenstein Center on the Press, Politics and Public Policy, Harvard University, November.

MONUC (United Nations Mission in the Democratic Republic of Congo) homepage, <http://www.monuc.org>.

Morgenthau, H. (1973), *Politics among Nations: The Struggle for Peace and Power*, (New York: Knopf).

Morris, S. (2004), 'Clinton's Calamities', *Australian*, 19 July.

Morrison, A. and Blair, S.A. (1999), 'Transnational Networks of Peacekeepers', in Alagappa and Inoguchi (eds).

MSF (Médecins Sans Frontières) (2004), 'MSF International Financial Report', 31 December.

Muchai, A. (2002), 'Arms Proliferation and the Congo War', in Clark (ed.).

Murphy, C.N. (2001), 'Forward: Africa at the Center of International Relations', in Dunn and Shaw (eds).

Mutz, D.C. and Soss, J. (1997), 'Reading Public Opinion: The Influence of News Coverage on Perceptions of Public Sentiment', *Public Opinion Quarterly* 61:3, 431–51.

Nacos, B.L., Shapiro, R.Y. and Isernia, P. (eds) (2000), *Decisionmaking in a Glasshouse: Mass Media, Public Opinion and American and European Foreign Policy in the 21ˢᵗ Century* (Lanham: Rowman and Littlefield).

National Defense Council Foundation (2002), 'World Conflict List 2002', <http://www.ndcf.org/Conflict_List/World2002/2002Conflictlist.htm>, accessed 9 February 2007.

—— (2003), 'World Conflict List 2003', <http://ndcf.homeip.net/ndcf/Conflict_List/conflict.html>, accessed 27 October 2005.

National Research Council (2001), *Forced Migration and Mortality* (Washington D.C.: National Academy Press).

Neuman, W.R., Just, M.R. and Crigler, A.N. (1992), *Common Knowledge: News and the Construction of Political Meaning* (Chicago: The University of Chicago Press).

New Earth Media (2006), *How Governments Work: The Inside Guide to the Politics of the World* (London: Dorling Kindersley).

Newman, E. (2004), 'The "New Wars" Debate: A Historical Perspective is Needed', *Security Dialogue* 35:2, 173–89.

Newsweek (1999), 'The Face of Evil', 19 April.

New York Times homepage, <http://www.nytimes.com>.

Nincic, M. and Lepgold, J. (eds) (2000), *Being Useful: Policy Relevance and International Relations Theory* (Ann Arbor: The University of Michigan Press).

Nkiwane, T.C. (2001), 'Africa and International Relations: Regional Lessons for a Global Discourse', *International Political Science Review* 22:3, 279–90.

OCHA (Office for the Coordination of Humanitarian Affairs) Financial Tracking System homepage, < http://ocha.unog.ch/fts2>.

O'Donnell, T. (2007), 'Naming and Shaming: The Sorry Tale of Security Council Resolution 1530 (2004)', *The European Journal of International Law* 17:5, 945–68.

Oketch, J.S. and Polzer, T. (2002), 'Conflict and Coffee in Burundi', in Lind and Sturman (eds).

Olsen, G.R., Carstensen, N. and Høyen, K. (2002), 'Humanitarian Crises: What Determines the Level of Emergency Assistance?', in Forgotten Humanitarian Crises.

Oprah Winfrey Show (2006), aired on ZNBC (Zambia), 1 May.

Otunnu, O. (2004), 'Uganda as a Regional Actor in the Zairian War', in Adelman and Rao (eds).

Oxfam International (2006), 'Meeting Real Needs: A Major Change for Donors to the Democratic Republic of the Congo 2006', 13 February, <http://www.oxfam. org/en/policy/briefingnotes/bn_DRC_donor_conference_060213>, accessed 6 February 2007.

Papathanassopoulos, S. (2001), 'Media Commercialization and Journalism in Greece', *European Journal of Communication* 16:4, 505–21.

Parenti, M. (2000), *To Kill a Nation: The Attack on Yugoslavia* (London: Verso).

Parker, G. (ed.) (2005), *The Cambridge History of Warfare* (Cambridge: Cambridge University Press).

Parker, P. (ed.) (2004), *The Collins Atlas of Military History* (London: Collins).

Peace Research Abstracts Journal (2000–2003), 37–40:6.

Pew (2002a), 'Americans Favor Force in Iraq, Somalia, Sudan and…", The Pew Research Center for the People and the Press, 22 January, <http://people-press. org/reports/display.php3?PageID=185>, accessed 4 December 2006.

—— (2002b), 'What the World Thinks in 2002', Pew Global Attitudes Project, The Pew Research Center for the People & the Press, Washington, D.C.

—— (2003), 'Views of a Changing World, June 2003', Pew Global Attitudes Project, The Pew Research Center for the People & the Press, Washington, D.C.

—— (2007), 'Tuberculosis Story: Lots of Coverage, Lots of Interest, Public Wants More Coverage of Darfur', 7 June, <http://people-press.org/reports/display. php3?ReportID=336>, accessed 31 March 2008.

Pew Charitable Trusts, 'Foreign Policy and Global Attitudes', <http://www.pewtrusts. org/our_work.aspx?category=298>, accessed 18 March 2008.

Pew Research Center for the People and the Press homepage, <http://people-press. org>, accessed 14 April 2008.

Philo, G. (2002), 'Television News and Audience Understanding of War, Conflict and Disaster', *Journalism Studies* 3:2, 173–86.

PIOOM (the Interdisciplinary Research Programme on Root Causes of Human Rights Violations), <http://www.goalsforamericans.org/gallery/v/maps/atf_ world_conf_map.pdf.html>.

Ponting, C. (2001), *World History: A New Perspective* (London: Pimlico).

Post (Zambia) (2004), 26 May.

Pottier, J. (2002), *Re-Imagining Rwanda: Conflict, Survival and Disinformation in the Late Twentieth Century* (Cambridge: Cambridge University Press).

Princen, T. (1992), *Intermediaries in International Conflict* (Princeton: Princeton University Press).

PRIO (International Peace Research Institute, Oslo), Centre for the Study of Civil War homepage, <http://www.prio.no/page/CSCW_research_detail/CSCW_ programs_projects/9649/40946.html>, accessed 20 December 2006.

—— Foreign and Security Policies program homepage, <http://www.prio.no/page/ Project_detail/Research_menu_right/9244/37665.html>, accessed 17 January 2007.

—— UCDP/PRIO Armed Conflict Dataset homepage, <http://new.prio.no/CSCW-Datasets/Data-on-Armed-Conflict/UppsalaPRIO-Armed-Conflicts-Dataset/>, accessed 20 December 2006.

Project Ploughshares, Armed Conflict Report, <http://www.ploughshares.ca/build/ArmedConflicts.htm>.

Prunier, G. (2006), 'The Politics of Death in Darfur', *Current History*, 105, 691, 195–202.

Pugh, M., Cooper, N. with Goodhand, J. (2004), *War Economies in a Regional Context: Challenges of Transformation* (Boulder: Lynne Rienner).

Puttnam, D. (2003), 'News: You Want It Quick or Good?', *British Journalism Review* 14:2, 50–57.

Ramonet, I. (2004), *Wars of the 21st Century: New Threats, New Fears* (Melbourne: Ocean Press).

Redd, S.B. (2002), 'The Influence of Advisors on Foreign Policy Decision Making: An Experimental Study', *Journal of Conflict Resolution* 46:3, 335–64.

Reeves, R. (2003), 'There is a Character Missing from the Cast of Political Life: The Public Intellectual', *New Statesman*, 7 July.

Reno, W. (1999), *Warlord Politics and African States*, (Boulder: Lynn Rienner).

Reuters UK homepage, <http://uk.reuters.com>.

Reuters (2004), 'US Blocks UN Text on Massacre in Tiff Over Court', 29 November.

RFI (Radio France International) (2005), Newspaper Roundup, 28 November.

Rieff, D. (2004), 'Kosovo: the End of an Era?', in Weissman (ed.).

Roberts, A. (2001), 'Humanitarian Principles in International Politics in the 1990s', in Humanitarian Studies Unit (ed.).

Roberts, H. (2003), *The Battlefield Algeria 1988–2002: Studies in a Broken Polity*, (London: Verso).

Roberts, J.M. (2000), *The Penguin History of the Twentieth Century: The History of the World, 1901 to the Present* (London: Penguin Books).

Robins, M.B. (2003), '"Lost Boys" and the Promised Land: US Newspaper Coverage of Sudanese Refugees', *Journalism* 4:1, 29–49.

Robinson, P. (2000), 'The Policy-Media Interaction Model: Measuring Media Power during Humanitarian Crisis', *Journal of Peace Research* 37:5, 613–33.

—— (2001), 'Theorizing the Influence of Media on World Politics: Models of Media Influence on Foreign Policy', *European Journal of Communication* 16:4, 523–44.

—— (2002), *The CNN Effect: The Myth of News, Foreign Policy and Intervention* (London: Routledge).

Rogers, E.M. and Dearing, J.W. (1994), 'Agenda-Setting Research: Where Has It Been, Where Is It Going?', in Graber (ed.).

Rogers, E.S. (1996), 'Economic Sanctions and Internal Conflict', in Brown (ed.).

Rønning, H. (2005), 'African Journalism and the Struggle for Democratic Media', in de Burgh (ed.).

Rorty, R. (1994), 'The Unpatriotic Academy: We Need Our National Identity', *New York Times*, 13 February.

Rotberg, R.I. (ed.) (2000), *Peacekeeping and Peace Enforcement in Africa* (Washington D.C.: Brookings/World Peace Foundation).

Rotberg, R.I. and Weiss, T.G. (eds) (1996), *From Massacres to Genocide: the Media, Public Policy, and Humanitarian Crises* (Massachusetts: The World Peace Foundation).

Rothchild, D. (1997), *Managing Ethnic Conflict in Africa: Pressures and Incentives for Cooperation* (Washington D.C.: Brookings Institution Press).

Rowell, A., Marriott, J. and Stockman, L. (2005), *The Next Gulf: London, Washington and Oil Conflict in Nigeria* (London: Constable & Robinson).

Savarese, R. (2000), '"Infosuasion" in European Newspapers: A Case Study on the War in Kosovo', *European Journal of Communication* 15:3, 363–81.

Save the Children (2003), 'State of the World's Mothers, 2003: Protecting Women and Children in War and Conflict' (Westport).

SBS (2004), *World Guide: The Complete Fact File on Every Country*, Twelfth Edition (South Yarra: Hardie Grant Books).

Schnabel, A. and Thakur, R. (eds) (2000), *Kosovo and the Challenge of Humanitarian Intervention, Selective Indignation, Collective Action, and International Citizenship* (New York: United Nations University Press).

Schoenbach, K. (2007), '"The Own in the Foreign": Reliable Surprise – An Important Function of the Media?', *Media, Culture & Society* 29:2, 344–53.

Seib, P. (2003–2004), 'The News Media and the "Clash of Civilizations"', *Parameters*, winter, 71–85.

Shapiro, R.Y. and Jacobs, L.R. (2000), 'Who Leads and Who Follows? US Presidents, Public Opinion, and Foreign Policy', in Nacos, Shapiro and Isernia (eds).

Shaw, C. (2003), 'TV News: Why More is Less', *British Journalism Review* 14:2, 58–64.

Shaw, M. (1996), *Civil Society and Media in Global Crises: Representing Distant Violence* (New York: Pinter).

Sheridan, G. (2004), 'Silence is Deafening on Our Foreign Policy', *Sunday Telegraph*, 3 October.

Shiraev, E. (2000), 'Toward a Comparative Analysis of the Public Opinion-Foreign Policy Connection', in Nacos, Shapiro and Isernia (eds).

SIPRI (Stockholm International Peace Research Institute) (1998–2003), *SIPRI Yearbook: Armaments, Disarmament and International Security* (London: Oxford University Press).

Slim, H. and Visman, E. (1995), 'Evacuation, Intervention and Retaliation: United Nations Humanitarian Operations in Somalia, 1991–1993', in Harriss (ed.).

Small Arms Survey 2005: Weapons at War (2005), Graduate Institute of International Studies, Geneva, <http://www.smallarmssurvey.org>, accessed 5 January 2007.

Smillie, I. and Minear, L. (2004), *The Charity of Nations: Humanitarian Action in a Calculating World* (Bloomfield: Kumarian Press).

Smith, G. (2007), 'A Politician's Private Life', BBC Editors' Blog, 10 January, <http://www.bbc.co.uk/blogs/theeditors/2007/01/reporting_ruth_kellys_decision.html>, accessed 5 March 2007.

Smith, M.L.R. (2003), 'Guerrillas in the Mist: Reassessing Strategy and Low Intensity Warfare', *Review of International Studies*, 29, 19–37.

Smith, T. (2005), Foreign Attachments: The Power of Ethnic Groups in the Making of American Foreign Policy (Cambridge: Harvard University Press).

Smith, T.W. (2000), 'Teaching Politics Abroad: The Internationalization of a Profession?', *PS: Political Science & Politics* 33:1, 65–73.

Snider, D.M. and Carlton-Carew, M.A. (eds) (1995), *US Civil-Military Relations: In Crisis or Transition?* (Washington D.C.: The Center for Strategic & International Studies).

Snow, D. (2004), 'Class Cuts Leave Spies Speechless', *Sydney Morning Herald*, 20–21 November.

Snow, D.M. (1997), *Distant Thunder: Patterns of Conflict in the Developing World*, Second Edition (New York: M.E. Sharpe).

Sonwalkar, P. (2002), '"Murdochization" of the Indian Press: From By-line to Bottom-line', *Media, Society & Culture* 24:6, 821–34.

Soroka, S.N. (2002), 'Issue Attributes and Agenda-Setting by Media, the Public, and Policymakers in Canada', *International Journal of Public Opinion Research* 14:3, 264–85.

—— (2003), 'Media, Public Opinion, and Foreign Policy', *Harvard International Journal of Press/Politics* 8:1, 27–48.

Sosale, S. (2003), 'Envisioning a New World Order through Journalism: Lessons from Recent History', *Journalism* 4:3, 377–92.

Spanier, J. and Wendzel, R.L. (1996), *Games Nations Play*, Ninth Edition (Washington D.C.: Congressional Quarterly Inc).

Stacks, J.F. (2003/04), 'Hard Times for Hard News: A Clinical Look at US Foreign Coverage', *World Policy Journal* XX:4, winter.

Stares, P.B. (ed.) (1998), *The New Security Agenda: A Global Survey* (Tokyo: Japan Centre for International Exchange).

Stearns, P.N. (2005), *Global Outrage: The Impact of World Opinion on Contemporary History* (Oxford: Oneworld Publications).

Stewart, C. (2006), 'Road to the Point of No Return', *Weekend Australian*, 24–25 December.

Stratfor, <http://www.stratfor.com>, search conducted 5 January 2008.

Straubhaar, J. and La Pastina, A. (2003), 'Television and Hegemony in Brazil', in Artz and Kamalipour (eds).

Straus, S. (2005), 'Darfur and the Genocide Debate', *Foreign Affairs* 84:1, 123–33.

Strobel, W.P. (1996), *Late-Breaking Foreign Policy: The News Media's Influence on Peace Operations* (Washington D.C.: United States Institute of Peace Press).

Sydney Morning Herald (2006), 'Look What Happened While We Weren't Watching', 4–5 November.

Tai, Z. (2000), 'Media of the World and World of the Media: A Cross-National Study of the Rankings of the "Top 10 World Events" from 1988 to 1998', *Gazette* 62:5, 331–53.

Tai, Z. and Chang, T. (2002), 'The Global News and the Pictures in their Heads: A Comparative Analysis of Audience Interest, Editor Perceptions and Newspaper Coverage', *Gazette* 64:3, 251–65.

Talbot, S. and Chanda, N. (eds) (2002), *The Age of Terror: America and the World After September 11* (New York: Basic Books).

Tarrow, S. (2005), *The New Transnational Activism* (Cambridge: Cambridge University Press).

Taylor, P.M. (2000), 'Introduction' (special issue on the media and the Kosovo conflict), *European Journal of Communication* 15:3, 293–8.

TBN (Trinity Broadcasting Network) (2005), 'Remembering Them Veteran's Day Special', <http://www.tbn.org/index.php/2/4/p/572.html>, accessed 27 March 2008.

Terry, F. (2002), *Condemned to Repeat? The Paradox of Humanitarian Action* (Ithaca: Cornell University Press).

—— (2004), 'The Humanitarian Impulse: Imperatives Versus Consequences', in Adelman and Rao (eds).

Tesser, A. (ed.), *Advanced Social Psychology* (New York: McGraw-Hill).

UN Document (2000), 'Report of the Panel on United Nations Peacekeeping Operations', Document A/55/305-S/2000/809.

UN Document (2004), 'Report of the High-Level Panel on Threats, Challenges, and Change, A More Secure World, Our Shared Responsibility', Document 1/59/656.

UN homepage, <http://www.un.org>, accessed 4 July 2006.

UN News Service (1999), '"Humanitarian Favouritism" Threatens the World's Most Needy: UNICEF', 22 December.

—— (2003), '40 Million Africans on Brink of Starvation, Security Council Told', 7 April.

—— (2007), 'Côte d'Ivoire: Country Has 'Historic Chance' to Resolve Differences, Says Outgoing UN Envoy', 9 February.

UN Peace and Security homepage, <http://un.org/peace>, accessed 30 July 2006.

UN Press Briefing (1999), 'Press Conference by Democratic Republic of Congo', 7 January, <http://www.un.org/News/briefings/docs/1999/19990107.congo.brf.html>, accessed 22 January 2005.

UN Press Release (1996), SG/SM/5901, 28 February.

UN Security Council (2002), Report of the Panel of Experts on the Illegal Exploitation of Natural Resources and Other Forms of Wealth of the Democratic Republic of the Congo, S/2002/1146.

UNMIK (United Nations Mission in Kosovo) homepage, <http://www.un.org/kosovo>, accessed 5 September 1999.

US Department of State homepage, <http://www.state.gov>, accessed 15 December 2006.

Van Parijs, P. (2000), 'The Ground Floor of the World: On the Socio-economic Consequences of Linguistic Globalization', *International Political Science Review* 21:2, 217–33.

Verwimp, P. and Vanheusden, E. (2004), 'The Foreign Policy of Belgium during the Zaire/Congo Crisis: March 1996–March 1997', in Adelman and Rao (eds).

Voice of America (2006), 'Brain Drain, Brain Gain', *African Journal*, 12 May.

Wallace, T.C. (1998), 'Why Minimum Force Won't Work: Doctrine and Deterrence in Bosnia and Beyond', *Global Governance* 4:2, 235–56.

Walt, S.M. (1998), 'International Relations: One World, Many Theories', *Foreign Policy*, spring, 29–46.

Wanta, W. and Hu, Y.W. (1993), 'The Agenda-Setting Effects of International News Coverage: An Examination of Differing News Frames', *International Journal of Public Opinion Research*, 5, 250–64.

Wardell Armstrong (2003), 'Scoping Study on the Artisanal Mining of Coltan in the Kahuzi Biéga National Park', <http://www.casmsite.org/Documents/Coltan_Report_Apr03.pdf>, accessed 24 December 2007.

Washington Post homepage, <http://www.washingtonpost.com>.

Watson Institute (2006), 'Strengthening Targeted Sanctions through Fair and Clear Procedures', Targeted Sanctions Project White Paper, Brown University.

Webcat, <http://webcat.nii.ac.jp>, accessed May 2003.

Weekend Australian (2004), '60 Years on, D-Day Timeline', 60th Anniversary Tribute of D-Day, 6 June.

—— (2005), 'No News is Bad News at the ABC', 23–24 April.

—— (2006), 'Congo Deadliest', January 7–8, p. 11.

Weiss, T.G. (1999), 'Sanctions as a Foreign Policy Tool: Weighing Humanitarian Impulses', *Journal of Peace Research* 36:5, 499–509.

—— (2000), 'The Politics of Humanitarian Ideas', *Security Dialogue* 31:1, 11–23.

—— (2001), 'Researching Humanitarian Intervention: Some Lessons', *Journal of Peace Research*, 38:4, 419–28.

Weiss, T.G. and Collins, C. (2000), *Humanitarian Challenges & Intervention*, Second Edition (Boulder: Westview Press).

Weissman, F. (ed.) (2004), *In the Shadow of 'Just Wars': Violence, Politics and Humanitarian Action* (Ithaca: Cornell University Press).

Wilson E.J. III (2000), 'How Social Science Can Help Policymakers: The Relevance of Theory', in Nincic and Lepgold (eds).

Wolff, S. (2007), *Ethnic Conflict* (Oxford: Oxford University Press).

Wolfsfeld, G. (2001), 'The News Media and the Second Intifada: Some Initial Lessons', *Harvard International Journal of Press and Politics* 6:4, 113–118.

Woodhouse, T. and Ramsbotham, O. (eds) (2000), *Peacekeeping and Conflict Resolution*, (London: Frank Cass).

World Almanac and Book of Facts 2004 (2004), (New York: Almanac Books).

World Public Opinion (2006), 'World Public Says Iraq War Has Increased Global Terrorist Threat', 3 December, <http://www.worldpublicopinion.org/pipa/articles/home_page/172.php?nid=&id=&pnt=172&lb=hmpg1>, accessed 4 December 2006.

Wu, H.D. (2003), 'Homogeneity around the World? Comparing the Systemic Determinants of International News Flow between Developed and Developing Countries', *Gazette*, 65:1, 9–24.

Yomiuri (Japanese edition) (1999), 24 December.

Young, C. (2002), 'Contextualising Congo Conflicts: Order and Disorder in Postcolonial Africa', in Clark (ed.).

Youngson, P. (2001), 'Coercive Containment: The New Crisis Management', *International Relations* 15:5, 37–52.

Zahn, S. (2006), 'TBN Rolls Out Red, White, and Blue Carpet July 4th Weekend', TBN homepage, <http://www.tbn.org/index.php/7.html?nid=132>, accessed 27 March 2008.

Zaller, J. and Chui, D. (1996), 'Government's Little Helper: US Press Coverage of Foreign Policy Crises, 1945–1991', *Political Communication*, 13, 385–405.

ZNBC (Zambia) (2005), Main News, 9 January.

Index